Young and Female

Praise for this book

'*Young and Female* beautifully weaves together the narratives and voices, stories and studies of rural women from several countries around the world, offering a compelling anthology that addresses one of the fundamental changes reshaping the agricultural landscape of the contemporary world: the transformation of a rural woman into a farmer. This farmer is no longer merely a helper, but a farmer in her own right. The book illuminates her uniqueness through robust research and a multifaceted exploration, resulting in an engaging read. Each chapter offers unique and thought-provoking insights into how women are toiling in the absence of adequate training and land ownership rights, while also showcasing how these individuals are using the limited opportunities available to creatively redefine their lives and the futures of generations to come.'

Kuntala Lahiri-Dutt, AO, Professor, Resource, Environment & Development Department, Crawford School of Public Policy, The Australian National University, Australia

'*Young and Female* offers indispensable insights into the often-overlooked experiences of young women in agriculture, shedding light on their aspirations and the challenges they face in becoming farmers. This book brings fresh and much-needed perspectives to agrarian scholarship, gender and development, and youth studies. It masterfully weaves empirical data from four countries, placing the findings in thought-provoking comparison and dialogue. Through its critical analysis, it provides essential insights for addressing gender and generational inequities in the agricultural sector—offering a vision for rural futures that are more diverse, equitable, and sustainable.'

Lisa Bossenbroek researcher in rural sociology, iES Landau, Institute for Environmental Sciences, University of Kaiserslautern-Landau (RPTU) Germany

'*Young and Female* pays tribute to the vital, often overlooked roles that young women play in cultivating food, caring for land and community, and shaping the future of agriculture. The powerful collective of stories in this book reminds us: Women's work feeds the world.'

Trina Moyles, author of Women Who Dig: Farming, Feminism, and the Fight to Feed the World (University of Regina Press, 2018)

Young and Female

International perspectives
on the future of farming

Edited by
Sharada Srinivasan, Lu Pan, and Aprilia Ambarwati

Practical
ACTION
PUBLISHING

Practical Action Publishing Ltd
25 Albert Street, Rugby,
Warwickshire, CV21 2SD, UK
www.practicalactionpublishing.com

A catalogue record for this book is available from the British Library.

A catalogue record for this book has been requested from the Library of Congress.

ISBN 978-1-78853-434-5 Paperback
ISBN 978-1-78853-436-9 Electronic book

Citation: Srinivasan, S., Lu, P., and Ambarwati, A. (2025) *Young and Female: International perspectives on the future of farming,* Rugby, UK: Practical Action Publishing http://doi.org/10.3362/9781788534369

Since 1974, Practical Action Publishing has published and disseminated books and information in support of international development work throughout the world.

Practical Action Publishing is a trading name of Practical Action Publishing Ltd (Company Reg. No. 1159018), the wholly owned publishing company of Practical Action. Practical Action Publishing trades only in support of its parent charity objectives and any profits are covenanted back to Practical Action (Charity Reg. No. 247257, Group VAT Registration No. 880 9924 76).

Cover design by Katarzyna Markowska, Practical Action Publishing
Typeset by vPrompt eServices, India

Contents

Acknowledgements

This book would not have been possible without the young farmers who shared their stories and time, and funding from the Social Sciences and Humanities Research Council (SSHRC) (Insight 435-2016-0307) for the research.

Funding support for this book to be published open access has been provided by the Canada Research Chair in Gender, Justice and Development, the International Institute of Social Studies at the Erasmus University Rotterdam, and the College of Humanities and Development Studies at China Agricultural University, Beijing.

We are also grateful to Alicia Filipowich for her editorial support on several drafts of each chapter.

About the contributors

A. Haroon Akram-Lodhi is Professor in the Department of International Development Studies at Trent University, Canada. His research interests include: agrarian political economy, feminist development economics, peasant economics, political ecology and sustainable rural livelihoods, and food systems analysis. https://www.trentu.ca/ids/faculty-research/dr-haroon-akram-lodhi

Aprilia Ambarwati is a researcher at the AKATIGA Center for Social Analysis in Bandung, Indonesia. Her research interests include rural youth in agriculture, rural youth employment, and the dynamics of village governance. https://www.researchgate.net/profile/Aprilia-Ambarwati

Alexa Avelar received her MA in Sociology from the University of Guelph in 2019 and conducted her graduate research on young women farmers in Canada. She is currently attending Dalhousie University in Canada for her PhD in Sociology & Social Anthropology. https://www.researchgate.net/profile/Alexa-Avelar

Hannah Jess Bihun has an MA in Geography from the University of Manitoba, Canada.

Charina Chazali is Director of AKATIGA Center for Social Analysis in Bandung, Indonesia. She received her master's degree at the International Institute of Social Studies (The Hague, Netherlands) in the field of Social Policy for Development. https://www.akatiga.org/language/en/portofolio/charina-chazali/

Annette Aurélie Desmarais was Canada Research Chair in Human Rights, Social Justice and Food Sovereignty at the University of Manitoba, Canada, from 2013-2023. She has authored and co-edited five books centered on food sovereignty and is now Professor Emerita. Prior to obtaining a doctorate in Geography, Annette was a small-scale cattle and grain farmer in Canada for a decade. www.landfoodsovereignty.ca

Roy Huijsmans is Associate Professor at the International Institute of Social Studies in The Hague, Netherlands. His research concentrates on young people's role and position in development and change, through a focus on work, school, migration and mobilities, aspirations, and music and dance. In his research, he employs qualitative and ethnographic methods. https://www.eur.nl/en/people/roy-huijsmans

Nicola Inglefield is a University of Guelph alumnus, a former farmer who was involved in the data collection for the research in Ontario.

Travis Jansen works in a leadership role within the Ontario swine industry. He is a University of Guelph alumnus and a farmer who was involved in the data collection and writing for the research in Ontario.

Changqi Li is affiliated with China Agricultural University.

Yanqing Li is affiliated with Shanghai International Studies University, China.

Yilin Li is affiliated with China Agricultural University.

Dong Liang is affiliated with Shandong University, China.

Qirui Lin is affiliated with Beijing University of Aeronautics and Astronautics, China.

Lu Pan is Professor at the China Agricultural University. Her research interests encompass left-behind populations, rural education, and the sociology of agricultural and agrarian change in China. She is actively involved in action research in rural China to promote social support and social awareness for left-behind populations. https://www.researchgate.net/profile/Lu-Pan-17

Clara Mi Young Park is the Senior Gender Officer and Gender Team Leader in the Rural Transformation and Gender Equality Division of FAO Headquarters. Clara has worked on gender equality and human rights with civil society organizations and with the FAO in several regions including Asia Pacific, Near East and North Africa, and most recently in sub-Saharan Africa. Clara holds a PhD in Development Studies with a focus on feminist political ecology from the International Institute of Social Studies in The Hague. She has authored numerous articles in peer-reviewed academic journals and book chapters. https://www.researchgate.net/profile/Clara-Park-2

Sudha Narayanan is Senior Research Fellow at the International Food Policy Research Institute (IFPRI) based in New Delhi, India. Her research interests include agricultural economics, development economics, new institutional economics, and applied econometrics. https://www.ifpri.org/profile/sudha-narayanan

Isono Sadoko is former director of AKATIGA Center for Social Analysis in Bandung, Indonesia.

Sharada Srinivasan is Associate Professor of Development Studies at the University of Guelph in Canada. Her research and teaching are located within the broad field of gender, development, and social justice. She has explored gender discrimination, violence, generational dynamics, well-being, and empowerment through research on sex ratio imbalance, daughter discrimination, and related gendered practices, domestic violence, and youth and farming. She held the Canada Research Chair in Gender, Justice and Development (2013–2023), was the inaugural Director of the Canada India Research Centre for Learning and Engagement (CIRCLE) (2020–2023), and co-facilitates the People's Archive of Rural Ontario (PARO). https://sharada. uoguelph.ca

Ben White is Emeritus Professor of Rural Sociology at the International Institute of Social Studies, The Hague, Netherlands. He has been involved in research on agrarian change and the anthropology and history of childhood and youth since the early 1970s, mainly in Indonesia. He is author of *Agriculture and the Generation Problem* (2020). https://www.researchgate.net/ profile/Ben-White-2

Hanny Wijaya has an MA in Anthropology from Gadjah Mada University, Indonesia. She is affiliated with Sekar (Serikat Kerja Agraria) in Yogyakarta, Indonesia.

Huifang Wu is affiliated with China Agricultural University with research interests that include agrarian sociology, gender studies, development inter-ventions, rural transformation, and rural left-behind populations. http:// cohd.cau.edu.cn/art/2018/12/17/art_30046_118.html.

CHAPTER 1

Young women farmers as subjects of research and policy

Sharada Srinivasan, Lu Pan, and Aprilia Ambarwati

This book about rural young women's experiences in their pathways into farming and the particular challenges that they face at the intersection of gender and generational hierarchies is based on detailed field research in Canada, China, India, and Indonesia.

Why 'young women farmers'? Around the world, women make crucial contributions to agriculture and agrifood systems more broadly, as discussed in detail by Clara Mi Young Park in Chapter 10. Yet women farmers continue to face many constraints in access to agrarian resources and services, and recognition as farmers in their own right (see for instance, Razavi 2003, 2009; FAO 2023). The *UN Decade of Family Farming 2019–2028* includes in its seven-pillar Global Action Plan two 'transversal' pillars: 'support youth and ensure the generational sustainability of family farming' (Pillar 2), and 'promote gender equity in family farming and the leadership role of rural women' (Pillar 3). Putting the two – gender and generational – pillars together, it is clear that if visions of generationally and environmentally sustainable, smallholder-based, agricultural futures are to be realized, the problems that young women face in establishing themselves as farmers must be given more serious attention. To date, there is little scholarly or policy work that focuses on young women farmers, let alone privileging their voices.[1] Our book integrates gender and generation to privilege young women farmers' experiences and the processes or pathways that they must negotiate to become and to be recognized as farmers in their own right.

In this introductory chapter, we first outline some key points from the fields of gender and generation studies as applied to agrarian contexts. We then explain our approach and draw out some of the main themes that our study has identified in young women farmers' experiences.

The remainder of the book is divided into four sections, each devoted to one of the four countries. Each country section has two chapters. An overview chapter sets out the agricultural context, policies, and social norms within which young women enter or continue to farm, and what we know about the situation of young women farmers in each country. This is followed by a chapter consisting of four to six extended case studies of individual young women farmers, selected for variety and contrast in their trajectories and experiences, from field sites in each country. These individual case studies provide a rich description of young women farmers' lived realities as they relate to their entry into and experiences with farming. The concluding section of each country case study chapter reflects on the diversity and similarities among young women farmers' experiences, and the implications for action to support the aspirations of young women (would be) farmers more broadly.

In the final chapter, Clara Mi Young Park, a Senior Gender Officer with the Food and Agriculture Organization of the United Nations (FAO), reflects upon our study based on her experiences as a feminist, academic researcher, and 'femocrat' (Park 2020).

Gender, generation, and farming

Following Ester Boserup's landmark study (1970) a huge body of literature on gender in agrarian contexts has been influential in shaping policy discourse among national governments and international/multilateral development agencies, non-governmental organizations, and private foundations. This is exemplified by FAO's two major reports, *Women in agriculture: Closing the gender gap for development* (2011) and *The status of women in agrifood systems* (2023; see further in Chapter 10). Recent years have also seen growing concerns in policy circles about ageing farm populations and the mass exodus of youth from the countryside, apparently disinterested in farming and attracted by non-farm urban jobs. Much literature on rural youth has concerned itself with youth who leave the countryside rather than focusing on young farmers or on those who return later to take up farming, although some research and policy studies have paid attention to rural exodus and to young people's constraints in building farming livelihoods (for example, Bossenbroek et al. 2015; Berckmoes and White 2016; IFAD 2019; HLPE 2021; Sumberg 2021). But, as with gender concerns, this has so far rarely been translated into meaningful action (Japan offers an exception, see McGreevy et al. 2018).

The literature on women in agriculture tends to ignore generational and class aspects within the category 'women'. Similarly, studies and policies of youth in agriculture are often both class and gender blind. We argue that the intersection of gender, generation, and class leads to specific experiences, opportunities, and challenges for young women farmers who are thus a distinct category for both analysis and practice.[2] While recognizing that youth is a social relational category, we defined our target group in the study as those between 18 and 45 years. Not all, therefore, were chronologically 'young' when interviewed; this requires some explanation. Becoming a farmer (or trying to) is not an 'event', but often a long, drawn-out process. It is not limited to the period of 'youth' as defined in official regulations or statistics,[3] and is intertwined with events such as education, long-term and cyclical migration for non-farm employment, and marriage as well as sudden and catastrophic events such as personal loss, floods, forced displacement, and rehabilitation – all of which can be gendered experiences.

Our study focuses on Asia's three most populated countries – China, India, and Indonesia – which together account for more than half of the world's 500 million smallholder farms, nearly all of them less than 2.0 hectares (5 acres). These countries are home to the majority of the world's youth population and rural population, where small-scale agriculture is still the single largest source of employment and livelihoods, and where these dimensions of rural life have so far been largely neglected in research and policy. There are also important differences across the three Asian countries in terms of agriculture–industry sectoral relationships. For instance, China has undergone structural transformation whereas some write of India's 'stunted' transformation (Vijayabaskar et al. 2018; Giller et al. 2021) and of Indonesia's 'truncated' agrarian transition (Li 2011, 2017). By way of contrast, Canada, with its agrarian context of industrialized, large-scale, export-driven, capital-intensive farming that employs only a small fraction of the labour force, allows us to see both similarities and differences in young women's often difficult pathways into farming and the livelihoods and lives that result from those pathways. Despite the different agrarian socio-economic, gender, and demographic contexts, there are remarkable similarities in the experiences of young women farmers and their challenges.

Studies on gender in agrarian contexts have unequivocally established women's unique and specific contributions to smallholder farming, but have also demonstrated that women's farm work is often shaped by their domestic and unpaid care roles. Issues highlighted in the literature include women's unequal access to resources (such as land, labour, equipment and technology, and finance), training, markets, and decision-making; the gender and generational division of labour; the impacts of macro-level economic as well as climate changes on women; gendered power dynamics and discriminatory social institutions; and related problems in women's recognition as farmers in their own right.

One of the stickiest issues that feminist scholarship and gender advocacy have been concerned with is that of women's land rights, reflecting the reality that recognition of women's roles and contributions in agriculture has not translated globally into access to, control over, and/or ownership of land. Granted, in many countries, there is a recognition that women in agriculture require effective land rights. Nonetheless, discriminatory inheritance and legal arrangements remain far too common. Even when appropriate gender-responsive inheritance and legal arrangements are in place, their implementation and enforcement remain haphazard at best, and non-existent at worst, with gender issues remaining routinely ignored in the real lives of farming communities, where patriarchal structures, customs, and attitudes prevail. In patrilineal societies, including large parts of India and parts of Indonesia, women depend for access to land on their brothers' lifelong goodwill and support, even as the dowry they receive at marriage is erroneously justified as a substitute for land inheritance (Agarwal 1994; Sachs 1996; Deere and León de Leal 2001; Schwarz 2004; Jacobs 2010).

Beyond gender and effective land rights, there is a rich literature on gender dynamics and agricultural productivity, which cumulatively highlight that compared to men farmers, women farmers have different assets and wealth, that they often plant different crop mixes, and that as a result, women farmers make different input choices (Deere et al. 2014; Doss 2018). Women farmers' access to markets are not the same as that of men farmers, which in turn has implications for incomes, consumption and nutrition, and food security, all of which are gender differentiated (Razavi 2009). Agricultural extension services too are gendered. Women in farming are disproportionately impacted by shocks; they bear the brunt of the climate and biodiversity crises and the Covid-19 pandemic had gender-differentiated impacts. Yet even this rich literature fails to distinguish generational and class-based differences within women farmers when comparing them to men.

Women's abilities to participate in the rural economy and in their communities as well as to cope with and adapt to climate change and crises, are often mediated by patriarchal social institutions. Men's roles in structuring women's lives are predicated upon unequal power relations and often the use of force.

Gender relations and behavioural norms interact and create dynamics that strongly shape the livelihood activities considered appropriate for young women and men, the distribution of responsibilities for work and care, land access, the allocation of decision-making, and autonomy over earnings. Gender norms also come into play in decisions over whether and how to support the education or enterprises of daughters and sons, sisters and brothers, and female and male partners as well as migration decisions (Chant and Jones 2005; Elias et al. 2018). In addition to shaping all aspects of livelihood building, from aspirations and access to education and productive resources to opportunities for mobility, these norms play a central role in setting out what it means to be a 'good woman' (Elias et al. 2018; Sumberg 2021).

Relatively recent and less prolific than gender studies, the academic field of youth studies has developed rapidly since the 1990s, with its own concepts, frameworks, and journals but so far has had a markedly urban bias (exceptions include Robson et al. 2007; Cuervo and Wyn 2012). Research in agrarian contexts – particularly over the intergenerational transfer of land and other resources – was for a long time largely restricted to sub-Saharan Africa and Europe (White 2020; Chapter 4). It has highlighted intergenerational tensions in land transfers across the generations, while policy has devoted attention to challenges and strategies to retain youth in agriculture (FAO 2013; FAO-CTA-IFAD 2014).

While there has been a growing interest in youth and farming in recent years, bringing together insights from agrarian studies and youth studies, there is still a tendency to pay limited, if any, attention to young women in agriculture. The category of 'youth' is often presented in a gender-neutral way, which at first sight may suggest an equal attention to male and female youth, but in reality, it masks an implicit assumption that 'young farmers' are young male farmers. Just as the gender-neutral term 'farmer' often evokes the image of a male farmer, the gender-neutral terms 'youth' and 'young farmers' tend to evoke male youth and young male farmers.

Some feminist scholarship, notably in the global south, has focused on the intersection of generational and gender hierarchies and in signalling women's different needs and roles through the entirety of their life cycle. They highlight for instance, that girls are at a greater disadvantage in familial resource allocations and divisions of labour, health care access, and employment opportunities, making a case for treating young girls as a distinct category in development rather than being lumped as women and girls (Croll 2007). The cyclical nature of patriarchal power means that in many contexts, young women must wait until they become older to wield influence within households and families (Kandiyoti 1988), a pattern often found in women's organizations. Agarwal et al. (2020) note that despite the equal rights to joint family property enshrined in the 2005 Hindu Succession Amendment Act in India, daughters are less likely to inherit agricultural land when compared to widows. 'A narrow focus on differences between men and women often masks more important differences between women, including those arising from where they are in the life cycle' (Quisumbing et al. 2014: 14).

While comprehensive age-specific data are hard to obtain, recent evidence from multi-country surveys suggests that 50 per cent of rural youth aged 15–17, 37 per cent of those aged 18–24, and 32 per cent of those aged 25–34 work in agriculture in Asia, Africa, and Latin America, with Africa having the highest share – 55 per cent of those aged 15–24 (Dolislager et al. 2021). At the same time, the number of women working in agriculture, fisheries, and forestry as farmers or as waged workers has, at 37 per cent, remained relatively stable as a share of those working in agriculture, forestry, and fishing since 2010, and 36 per cent of all the world's working women are employed in agriculture and agrifood systems (FAO 2023; see Chapter 10). These are likely underestimates, given the tendency for women's work (in farming) to be underreported.

If young women are to find pathways to farming and succeed as farmers, policies need to support their different roles and be attentive to their specific needs and challenges. This requires that we recognize young women farmers in their own right, count them properly to make them visible, and privilege their voices and perspectives in research and policy.

Our study: approach and methods

This book is part of a larger project, *Becoming a young farmer: Young people's pathways into farming* (Srinivasan 2024). Our study went against much current scholarship about young people's exodus from farming and instead focused on young people's pathways *into* farming by analysing the experiences of young women and men who are (or would like to be) farmers.

The agrarian and broader social contexts within which young women farmers are embedded reveal similarities and differences not only across the four countries but also within countries. Almost everywhere, agriculture and economic policies increasingly work against small family farms and disrupt rural livelihoods in the quest for economies of scale. In addition to the differences in farming systems the four countries are noted for their relatively different levels of gender equality and varying degrees of patriarchal constraints.

Combining core concepts from the interdisciplinary fields of agrarian studies, youth and generation studies, and gender and development has helped us to understand the gendered intergenerational tensions that we see almost everywhere in rural communities. In particular, young people (women) face problems in access to farmland and other agriculture-related opportunities and resources in societies where gerontocracy, patriarchy, agrarian inequality, and corporate penetration of the agrifood sector, in varying degrees, are the order of the day. Gendered power imbalances affecting young people's access to land, labour, credit, and knowledge also shape 'heteronormative processes of capital accumulation, shaped by racism and sexism', as Leslie reminds us in a study of queer farming in the United States (Leslie 2019: 928). We recognize that heteronormativity, and challenges to it, are important dimensions to bring us beyond simple, dichotomous 'male-female' perceptions of gender in 'relational agriculture'. Seeing agriculture through a 'queer lens' has produced a substantial and important body of studies in the US[4] but we are not aware of such studies in the four countries of our study. We hope that future research will address this gap.

Our country research teams undertook field research in two sites in each country (three in Indonesia) for a total of nine sites, chosen to reflect some of each country's agricultural and economic diversity. The research privileged young farmers' own perspectives on and experiences with farming, the challenges, and the ways they deal with them as well as the impact that their practices have on farming. In-depth interviews inspired by life histories were conducted with 150 (young) women farmers, as shown in Tables 1.1 and 1.2. We also interviewed chronologically older women farmers as they recollected their younger days and experiences of becoming farmers. Each country team consisted mainly of local researchers who used their existing contacts and relationships, with both farmers and (youth) farming organizations. We agreed upon a set of criteria in identifying and selecting young farmers, while applying criteria such as 'continuers' and 'newcomers', and 'new' and 'established' farmers to the extent that the local context warranted.[5]

To better capture these processes, we opted for a life-history approach in which women farmers between the ages of 18 and 45 were invited to tell us about their life histories and trajectories into farming, from their childhood onward. As can be seen in Table 1.2, the average age at which our 150 young women farmer respondents began farming independently was 22 in China, 23 in India and Indonesia, and 26 in Canada; but beginning to farm independently is not the end of the process of 'becoming a farmer'. Limiting our coverage to those aged under 25 (the most common, and the United Nations' standard, upper age limit of 'youth') would have meant missing important stages of the process in many cases.

Women farmers in our study across the four countries had access to land in some form (as owner, family member, potential successor, renter or share tenant, working on communal land, in contract farming, or community shared/supported farming, or as wage workers), although in many cases this access is dependent on fathers, brothers or husbands (for instance in India and Flores, Indonesia). They mostly rely on their own labour and that of family members, although we have also included some women who depend mainly on hired labour. Most are actively involved in farm management.

The interviews focused on the agrarian context; the process of becoming young farmers (socialization, aspirations, access to resources, challenges along the way); innovation (practices vis-à-vis conventional farming, adopting new technologies and new ways of doing things); and young farmers and policy setting (agrarian policies affecting young farmers, their involvement in farmer organizations, their influence on policies to support them). Country research teams were free to address further country-specific issues and questions. In China, for example, country-specific questions included: women's accessibility to land through individual land transfer or sub-contract from the collective, and land readjustment for married women in their native village and husbands' village. In Indonesia, country-specific questions included gendered mechanisms over access to customary land (Flores) and village-owned land (Java site) as well as the role of birth order and sibling relationships in land division and inheritance.

Tables 1.1 and 1.2 summarize some of the important characteristics of our sample of 150 respondent farmers. Their average age at the time of the study was 34 years, with the youngest being 17 years (Indonesia) and the oldest 45 years (Canada and India). On average, the respondent farmers had begun farming when they were 15 years old and were 24 years old when they began farming independently. Most farmers in our study grew up in smallholder families.

For most of our respondents, farming is a full-time activity as well as the primary source of income. The exception is Indonesia, where farming was the primary source of income for only 27 per cent of respondents. Across the study sites, the women involved in full-time farming spent, on average, more time on farm work than men. Most respondents were continuer farmers; they were born and grew up on a farm. The Canadian sample is an exception with continuer and newcomer farmers.

Across all countries, it is hard to find disaggregated data on land ownership by gender and age (one exception being Indonesia's Demographic and Health Survey [IDHS] 2012; see Chapter 8). In practice, women are more likely to have access to, but not ownership of, land. In our study, young women farmers were less likely to own or inherit land compared to young male farmers (Tables 1.1 and 1.2). The overall situation is probably starker as our study targeted young women who succeeded in (or were on their way to) becoming farmers and did not focus on the many women who may have tried and failed.

Table 1.1 Characteristics of (young) women farmer respondents across the four study countries

	Canada	China	India	Indonesia
Number of farmers surveyed	43	33	25	49
Age started farming	19	13	15	12
Age farming independently	26	22	23	23
Minimum age	20	27	21	17
Mean age	33	36	36	31
Maximum age	45	44	45	43
% Under 35	63%	48%	40%	82%
% Married	63%	100%	92%	90%
% With >12 years education	95%	0%	12%	2%
% Working full-time	84%	97%	100%	49%
% Full-time, primary income - farming	72%	91%	84%	27%
% Full-time, primary income - animal farmer	23%	0%	4%	0%
% Full-time, primary income - plant farmer	47%	91%	76%	27%
% Full-time, primary income - farmer, not specified	2%	0%	4%	0%
% Full-time, primary income - not farming	12%	6%	16%	22%
% Farmers owning land	72%	70%	72%	84%
Average acres owned	357.92	4.03	7.79	1.19
% Farmers that have inherited land	2%	15%	64%	61%
Average acres inherited	160.00	1.27	5.02	0.66
% Farmers likely to inherit land	47%	30%	20%	20%
Average acres likely to be inherited	718.00	0.59	0.85	0.13
% Farmers renting in land	58%	12%	4%	14%
Average acres rented in	573.00	0.97	0.22	0.08
% Farmers sharing land	28%	3%	32%	14%
Average acres shared	866.83	0.22	3.25	0.10
% With access to community land	0%	21%	4%	8%
Average acres of community land		1.85	0.06	0.07

Note: Two respondents from Manitoba did not fill out the questionnaire

Table 1.2 Characteristics of (young) women farmer respondents across field sites in the study

	Canada			China			India			Indonesia			
	Ontario	Manitoba	Canada	Sichuan	Hebei	China	Tamil Nadu	Madhya Pradesh	India	Kulonprogo	Kebumen	West Manggarai	Indonesia
Number of farmers surveyed	27	16	43	13	20	33	16	9	25	6	11	32	49
Age started farming	19	19	19	10	15	13	17	11	15	17	11	11	12
Age farming independently	26	27	26	20	23	22	25	22	23	27	24	22	23
Minimum age	26	20	20	30	27	27	29	21	21	30	25	17	17
Mean age	34	33	33	38	34	36	38	33	36	36	33	30	31
Maximum age	42	45	45	44	42	44	45	45	45	43	43	40	43
% Under 35	56%	75%	63%	31%	60%	48%	31%	56%	40%	50%	82%	88%	82%
% Married	63%	63%	63%	100%	100%	100%	100%	78%	92%	100%	100%	84%	90%
% With >12 years education	96%	94%	95%	0%	0%	0%	13%	11%	12%	17%	0%	0%	2%
% Working full-time	85%	81%	84%	92%	100%	97%	100%	100%	100%	67%	73%	38%	49%
% Full-time, primary income farming	74%	69%	72%	77%	100%	91%	100%	56%	84%	50%	27%	22%	27%

(Continued)

Table 1.2 Continued

| | Canada | | | China | | | India | | | Indonesia | | | |
	Ontario	Manitoba	Canada	Sichuan	Hebei	China	Tamil Nadu	Madhya Pradesh	India	Kulonprogo	Kebumen	West Manggarai	Indonesia
% Full-time, primary income - animal farmer	30%	13%	23%	0%	0%	0%	6%	0%	4%	0%	0%	0%	0%
% Full-time, primary income - plant farmer	41%	56%	47%	77%	100%	91%	88%	56%	76%	50%	27%	22%	27%
% Full-time, primary income - farmer, not specified	4%	0%	2%	0%	0%	0%	6%	0%	4%	0%	0%	0%	0%
% Full-time, primary income - not farming	11%	13%	12%	15%	0%	6%	0%	44%	16%	17%	45%	16%	22%
% Farmers owning land	67%	81%	72%	46%	85%	70%	56%	100%	72%	100%	73%	84%	84%
Average acres owned	285.64	458.00	357.92	2.85	4.84	4.03	2.44	13.13	7.79	1.80	0.35	1.37	1.19
% Farmers that have inherited land	0%	6%	2%	38%	0%	15%	44%	100%	64%	100%	45%	59%	61%

(Continued)

Table 1.2 Continued

	Canada			China			India			Indonesia			
	Ontario	Manitoba	Canada	Sichuan	Hebei	China	Tamil Nadu	Madhya Pradesh	India	Kulonprogo	Kebumen	West Manggarai	Indonesia
Average acres inherited		160.00	160.00	3.23		1.27	2.86	6.69	5.02	0.22	0.18	0.90	0.66
% Farmers likely to inherit land	41%	56%	47%	0%	50%	30%	19%	22%	20%	0%	36%	19%	20%
Average acres likely to be inherited	97.00	1416.63	718.00		0.98	0.59	1.67	0.49	0.85		0.08	0.16	0.13
% Farmers renting in land	48%	75%	58%	31%	0%	12%	6%	0%	4%	17%	55%	0%	14%
Average acres rented in	125.46	1057.83	573.00	2.47	0.00	0.97	1.00	0.00	0.22	0.04	0.36	0.00	0.08
% Farmers sharing land	19%	44%	28%	8%	0%	3%	6%	78%	32%	17%	18%	13%	14%
Average acres shared	69.20	1436.57	866.83	0.57		0.22	7.00	2.83	3.25	0.02	0.01	0.14	0.10
% With access to community land	0%	0%	0%	0%	35%	21%	6%	0%	4%	17%	0%	9%	8%
Average acres of community land					3.05	1.85	0.50		0.06	0.12		0.09	0.07

Note: Two respondents from Manitoba did not fill out the questionnaire

Becoming a young and female farmer: themes emerging from the study

Identifying as a farmer

> 'What does it mean to be a farmer?' I asked the women, and they
> responded in more than ten different languages. Some women
> laughed, some of them wept. And others weren't sure where to
> begin because no one had bothered to ask them the question before
> (Moyles 2019: XXVI).

As Narayanan and Srinivasan (Chapter 6) point out, 'the question (and
identity) of young women farmers is enmeshed in the larger question of
recognition of women farmers'. This is true across our study's four countries.
The inability to conceptualize or recognize young women farmers as such is
immediately manifest in the lack of statistics. In many cases, young women
farmers are invisible in statistics or agro-economic studies, being subsumed
under the 'farm household' umbrella. In Canada, the Census of Agriculture
forms have changed their definition of 'farm operator' various times, allowing
only one operator of a family farm until 1991 when up to three operators could
be listed and women's names appeared to increase in the farming population;
the sex of each operator has only been recorded since 1996. Indonesian
statistics give the age and gender only for the so-called 'farm heads' (Chapter 8).
While statistics do not always ignore them, the numbers of women farmers
are certainly underreported because male farm heads often fail to report
women's contributions in their household to on-farm activities. They are also
excluded from the recognition and support as farmers in their own right, in
formal and informal institutions as well as in society. Too often young women
farmers' views, perceptions, and activities are hidden or misrepresented by
male household heads in surveys that are used to collect raw data.

Although all of us, men and women alike, go through a period called
'youth', in many world languages, 'female youth' as a social category and
identity is non-existent, with women moving from being girls to adult women
marked by marriage, childbearing and rearing, and other reproductive responsibilities. Except in Canada, most respondents had less than 12 years of
education. The necessity and availability of work in the informal sector often
means young women are withdrawn from school early on. Social norms about
the value of women's education, girls and young women's role in care work,
and the expectation to marry relatively early also contribute to generally lower
educational attainments among rural women.

In the Chinese context, there is a term for 'female youth' in the countryside
(*nian qing nv xing*). When rural adolescents finish middle school and flock
to the city as migrant workers, they constitute a special category of young
migrants. Among them, industrial capital in south-east China prefers female
youth. When they marry and return to their home village for childbearing,
female youth are mainly deemed to be caregivers. In films, news reports, and
other social media, the images of rural female youth are usually more related

with manufacturing in towns and cities than with farmland. In Hindi and Tamil, the two dominant languages in the study sites in India, while there are terms for male youth (Hindi: *yuva*; Tamil: *ilainan*) and female youth (Hindi: *yuvati*; Tamil: *ilam penn*), it is 'male youth' that is commonly used and known; no distinct category for female youth exists in the popular imagination. In Indonesia, the Minister of Agriculture's 2013 Guidelines on Agricultural Youth Generation Development does not mention young women farmers. In general, the term *pemuda* (young male) is used to refer to young people of both genders. Likewise, the Indonesian Youth Law only uses *pemuda* without mentioning *pemudi* (young female).

Most young women farmers in Manitoba and Ontario identified themselves as farmers out of their own volition when we put a call out for study participants. However, one woman from Manitoba, who was interviewed along with her husband, did not define herself as a farmer, despite her involvement in the farm tasks and decisions:

> 'I consider myself married to a farmer and ... that I live on a farm. So, I do farming tasks but as far as my passions and my dreams, [they] aren't in farming. So, just like I have to do laundry sometimes, I'm not a launderer'.

Although most women did identify themselves as farmers in Manitoba, this case is indicative of the struggles that many face to overcome the embedded view of women as helpers or labourers on the farm rather than as farmers themselves. In contrast, being a sixth-generation farmer is something that Hannah (Chapter 3) is very proud of.

In China, 'farmer' is a loosely defined vocation, such that rural people identify themselves as farmers insofar as they work on the land, whether part-time or full-time, large scale or small. Young women farmers do not query their identity as 'farmer'. What often puzzles them is how to get rid of the burden of farming or be a farmer with greater autonomy vis-à-vis the market. Historically women have been seen as subsidiary labour in Chinese agriculture. Their increasing involvement in farming along with rural–urban migration in the last few decades, or the 'feminization of agriculture', is debated as an obstacle to agriculture development. Young women farmers who take up farming by themselves are seen as being the 'housekeeper' of a family farm, not the entrepreneur or the subject of development. Yan (Chapter 5) is an exception to this, describing the cooperatives that she helped establish as her career. An exceptionally successful farmer and after many years of hard work, Yan is now at the centre of attention and support from government and agricultural elite circles in the country, a rarity among rural women.

In the case of the two India field sites, neither the young women farmers we interviewed nor their community, family members, and other farmers associated farming with a woman's identity, even though most respondents had been farming independently for a considerable period of time (the average age when they began farming independently is 23 years). But as the respondents talked about their farming activities with researchers, many came to realize that these indeed made them a farmer. In Indonesia, most of the women respondents carry out farming activities in almost all stages of farming. However, sometimes they referred to themselves as 'helping my husband' (for those who are married) or 'helping my parents' (for single women farmers). This is contrary to the reality of young women farmers who effectively manage their farms, such as 33-year-old Jamin (Chapter 9), who defines herself as a farmer and insists that she is not just helping her husband.

Cultivating a variety of crops and raising livestock, these (young) women farmers are passionate and display intimate knowledge about farming, handling labour, and marketing – whether it be about: Community Shared Agriculture and dairy farming in Canada; raising indigenous cattle and forming Dalit women farmers' groups in Tamil Nadu; setting up cooperatives to organize and support other smallholders in China; or maintaining labour exchange in several stages of farming in Indonesia.

Young women farmers often juggle farming with other roles related to household work and child rearing as part of their care responsibilities. What this means for young women farmers' identities is brought out most sharply by women's references to their farm or land as their child and attending to them like they would to their children. The Chinese case studies illustrate the wider pattern of feminization of farm work wherein the traditional gender division of labour that relegates women to the reproductive sphere also extends to the production sphere of family farming. Women work long hours, undertake all farming activities, and their work is indispensable to family farming; yet, it is often undervalued, sometimes by the women themselves.

A large part of the reason why young women farmers across different contexts are not identified as farmers has to do with the stickiness of gender expectations and gender roles assigned to and expected of women and men, with farmers perceived as male within local farming communities, among women, governments, and the wider public. There is also the widespread perception, including among women farm workers, that men's work is more important. This is reflected in discriminatory wages, which in turn lead to the reduced value of women's work (for instance, Kundu and Das 2019). Along with this are gender norms that maintain care work (childbearing and rearing, elderly care and other care work) as central to women's identity and responsibilities.

Similar to women's care work that is described as never ending, Kaitlyn, a Canadian young woman farmer, reflected, 'I think that there are lots of times that my list never ends, and my boyfriend's does'. Chinese young women farmers such as Li who are 'left behind' anticipate spending their lifetime farming for themselves and for the benefit of children (especially their sons) and grandchildren. At the same time, family responsibilities may crowd out certain lucrative options within farming as illustrated by a young woman farmer in Madhya Pradesh, with two small children. She said that she would have loved to diversify into dairy but that cattle 'needed timely care – feeding and providing drinking water'. With her childcare responsibilities, acquiring and maintaining cattle was out of the question. In these circumstances, women tend to self-identify as caregivers rather than farmers.

Young women farmers' struggle to be recognized as farmers is thus inextricably linked to upending the gender division of labour and value assigned to (reproductive) work that frames it as (predominantly) women's work. Despite this, and the extensive literature on women's triple burden, the farmers showcased in this book did not delve too much into how they balance their care responsibilities and farming activities, and how such balancing shapes their self-identity. This does not imply that this is not a priority to our respondents. Rather, their care burden is a given; young women farmers are farmers despite their care burden, and researchers and respondents kept the spotlight on their farming roles.[6] Their identity is that of being a farmer, a woman, and a young adult.

Farming aspirations and non-farm livelihood options

A Canadian new entrant young woman farmer noted, 'I think the main reason why [farming] hadn't occurred to me prior to that was because it is never pitched as a career option … especially for women'. Chinese young woman farmer Yao was not interested in farming growing up or after marriage. If she had the chance 'to study computers, I might not be farming at present'. She prefers to engage in housework than farming even though she can manage the entire greenhouse operation by herself, and she is not interested in improving her farming skills. Yao farms to give her children a carefree childhood and to allow them to pursue their freedom in the future. Yao's example suggests that many young smallholder farmers do not choose to farm; rather they engage in it precisely because they have no choice.

The Indonesian case studies (Chapter 9) demonstrate that many young women (and men) often leave rural areas for education and/or to engage in non-farm work before returning to farming. While there may be specific reasons for their return, a common thread is the fact that they can engage in farming as it is relatively easy to take up compared to other jobs. Across China, India, and Indonesia, farming is often a default livelihood option when everything else fails. Chinese young woman farmer Wu, a very successful farmer, landed in cucumber cultivation as a last resort after she and her husband lost their city jobs and found themselves with 'no special skills to earn money'.

By way of contrast, for most of the Canadian young women newcomer, continuing, or returning farmers who we interviewed, farming was not the last resort but something that they chose to enter into or came back to – they had strong aspirations to farm. For many who grew up on a farm, the decision to farm was by no means automatic or easy. They all spoke about childhood memories of growing up on a farm, working or helping parents on the farm yet, as young women, they were often reluctant to take on a farmer identity. Kaitlyn was an exception. She worked alongside her dad from an early age, recognized farming as an important part of her identity, and this shaped her aspirations. 'High school was when I really started to realize that I was a little bit different from most of my friends'. Others were more reluctant to embrace a farmer's identity during their youth. For example, Naomi spoke about how she and her siblings hid their farming identity during their high school years. Upon completion of schooling, she entered farming reluctantly, with her father's collaboration and support. She then discovered other young people who were also farming: 'It seemed to be at the same time when there was a growing community of farmers that I hadn't known about before, and was like "this is cool, there are other young people doing this, sort of a movement starting"'. It was only in this context that her aspiration to farm emerged, and her identity as a young woman farmer coalesced.

Growing up in a farming context, whether on one's own family farm or that of others, enables some young women to develop farming aspirations and a farming identity. Yet, for many others this is not the case, making the process of becoming a farmer a long, drawn-out, and non-linear process (Huijsmans et al., 2021). Aspirations account for only part of the story. It is equally important to look at the circumstances that emerge in relation to key life events such as marriage and how these have been generative of becoming a young farmer. It is illustrative to look at Yaya's experience (Indonesia). It was after her marriage and under the guidance of her father-in-law that her farming identity emerged and her farming aspirations were realized.

Learning to farm

Women and men are socialized differently into farming in line with gender norms around care, farm work, ownership, and decision-making. Whereas men from landowning families are encouraged and socialized from a young age to take charge and grow up knowing that one day they will inherit the farm and be decision makers, women are mostly socialized to be caregivers first, to help with farm activities, and are not likely to be actively groomed as farm inheritors, even in the absence of a male heir (Cassidy 2019).

There are several aspects in the socialization and identity-formation process, often informal, that respondents referred to as building their farming skills, knowledge, and identity. Most respondents who grew up on a farm were socialized into farming through observation, helping out in or undertaking various activities. One young woman farmer in Sehore, in Madhya Pradesh, said, 'we watch and learn. I did what my grandmother did'. Grace, an Indonesian farmer, put it, 'I didn't need any training; you just have to watch others and do as they do'. An example of an informal apprenticeship is Indonesian farmer Yaya, who spent several years learning rice farming from her father-in-law as well as from working with a neighbour for wages.

Few of the young women farmers in the Chinese, Indian, and Indonesian study sites had attended agricultural schools or colleges. This is different in Canada, where formal education played a big role in becoming a farmer. The Canadian context is marked by formal internships (with and without pay), while Chinese local governments offer many training opportunities. Chinese young woman farmer Li credits agriculture extension training in her gradually becoming 'capable of farming'. She said, 'Farming is like cooking. A new wife may think her cooking is not good. But when she has cooked a lot, she becomes a good housewife'.

For Canadian young women farmers who attended university, even studying in a programme not related to farming enabled them to think critically, especially about food systems, community engagement, and sustainable agriculture, as well as to develop ideas about how to farm and skills needed in relation to organization, financial management, and building rapport. But for all of them, like young women farmers from other countries, informal learning, learning by doing, and socialization were key in developing farming abilities. As Martha, a Canadian young woman farmer, put it:

> Everyone we've ever worked for, or with, has taught us quite a bit. And things don't happen in isolation. You don't just learn about cattle when you're working on a cattle ranch, [at the same time] you learn how to run the baler and how to fix fences.

Martha's and Jenny's experiences are uncommon; buying existing successful organic farms allowed them access not only to fully functioning farms, but also to an existing network of consumers. Most important in both cases are the retiring farmers who mentored them, sharing their knowledge and skills in what can be described as a mutually rewarding relationship (also Korzenszky 2019).

In the Canadian context, aside from formal education and training, young women farmers also utilize modern information technologies to find resources, build community, and to learn, something that has been particularly useful for some women when they are more housebound due to the demands of raising a family.

Many young women engage in non-farm activities before turning to farming. Typically, this entails migration. In the Chinese context, young women farmers' migration experiences differ in the two research sites depending on their proximity to urban areas. Due to the *hukou* system, it is difficult for entire families to migrate. While a large number of women and men are able to migrate before and after marriage (indeed it was difficult to find women and men below the age of 40 years in villages near cities such as Beijing), many married women stay behind to look after their ageing parents-in-law, children or sometimes their own poor health, and, as in Li's case, undertake farming.

For many young women farmers, migration is not an aspiration but a necessity; agriculture is risky, and incomes and profits are limited. A young woman farmer in Madhya Pradesh noted, 'I would rather stay here among my family and friends and eat home cooked meals. Almost everyone in the village would say the same thing. The only reason we migrate is because we need to feed our family'. Kamla's case (Chapter 7) illustrates how stopping migration and turning to full-time farming after the birth of a child is but one pattern among many.

In the Flores research site in Indonesia, most young women farmers had no migration experience prior to farming, due to the relatively remote geographical conditions and the tendency to marry at a young age. However, in the Java sites, with better access and good transportation, many had migrated to big cities and worked in various jobs, including as housemaids, shop assistants or working in food stalls/restaurants, before returning to the village and to farming. Like young men, women's return to farming can be due to a filial obligation. Tasniah, one of the Indonesian young women farmers, returned from factory work in Bandung to help her parents. 'I felt sorry for my parents if I would refuse their request, especially as I'm the oldest child'.

Across the study sites, marriage featured importantly in young women's entry into and learning about farming. Most farmers in our sample are married. For some young women, this meant that their husbands moved into their natal homes as was true for Chinese women farmers Li and Yan, due to their uxorilocal marriages. In the Tamil Nadu field site, while marriages are virilocal, village endogamy is common practice, unlike in Madhya Pradesh or other parts in north/western India; this has an important bearing on women's relatively greater autonomy and decision-making.

Many Canadian farmer respondents mentioned that they decided to farm when they met their partner or upon marriage. Canadian farmer Martha explained: '[My partner] could probably have started this [farming] on his own, I don't think I would have been able to access the social capital in the same way had I been a single woman'. Yaya, a newcomer Indonesian farmer, learned the ins and outs of rice farming only upon her marriage. Many respondents, even those from farming families in India and Indonesia, echo Yaya's words: 'If I hadn't married Jarwo, I probably wouldn't have become a farmer'. Chinese farmer Yao's education was discontinued in her youth and she was sent off for factory work. She married and became a mother before she entered farming, learning cucumber cultivation from her husband.

Barriers to farming

In Canada, India, and Indonesia, where private land ownership is the norm, huge inequalities mark young women's access, ownership, and control of land, even though there are no formal barriers. In China, under the Household Responsibility System, legally all members of a rural collective have the right to contract collective farmland. However, women lose their access to farmland when they marry beyond the village, and their ability to contract land in their husbands' village is conditional. Similarly, renting or leasing in land leaves young women farmers perpetually insecure when it comes to land access, besides depriving them of access to capital, loans, fertilizers, and government schemes, as evident in the Indian and Indonesian contexts.

Difficulties in accessing land can intersect with challenges in accessing resources. Thus, a vicious cycle works to limit farmers' success, particularly for small, young, new, and women farmers. This is captured in a Manitoba conventional young woman farmer's experience. She talked about how she struggled to access financing for land, despite the advantage of coming from an established family farm:

> I think it doesn't matter what the dollar price of land is, it's getting established, building enough equity. When I first started, I kept wanting to buy land and I just didn't have enough equity. You rent land and you can't borrow enough money to put enough inputs in the ground to grow your crop. It was a constant battle to come up with the revenue to be able to plant the crop and get established and then build equity so that you could buy land. I would say in my experience that's the biggest barrier of getting in is just getting established without having someone in the industry. I had a couple of people that took a leap of faith and provided me with crop input credit with a handshake. In today's environment, that's really rare.

An oft repeated reality check was that income from farming alone is insufficient to secure a livelihood. Respondents had different strategies to augment income sources. While migration was not an active strategy, it is not uncommon for small/marginal farmers to migrate or have family members who migrate. In our interviews, where climate change was broached, it was in relation to immediate stresses such as drought, water shortages, or soil conditions. Given the immediate struggles that aspiring young farmers face, end of century concerns such as rising temperatures exist, but perhaps more in the background. While for small/marginal farmers relying fully on farming is simply too risky, we do not know whether this will lead to (male) migration intensification.

Next to financial barriers, as the country chapters highlight, a major barrier in the lack of translation of formal land rights into realizable rights is related to patriarchal social norms around farming, inheritance, and the lack of social acceptance of women as farmers. As a result, intra-familial transfers and land inheritance do not occur automatically. Thereby, young women farmers access land and other resources in a variety of ways that can both subvert patriarchal norms and underscore both inter- and intra-generational dynamics.

Becoming a successful (young) woman farmer

Across all study contexts, young women farmers view a successful farmer as one who owns land, has easy access to capital, machinery, and water, makes a profit from farming, is passionate about farming, and does not rely on off-farm work and income to supplement farm income. Some of our respondents clearly identified themselves as successful. For example, Martha (Chapter 3) considers herself a successful farmer. Along with her partner, they have developed a farming model that is replicable, which is very important to her. Kaitlyn (Chapter 3) identifies as a successful farmer as she 'finds joy in farming' and 'is not bankrupt'. Like Kaitlyn, respondents from the Tamil Nadu study site noted that to be successful, young women farmers needed support, especially from their family. Having familial ties to a farm and building up their own social capital amongst farming peers were key strategies that helped young women farmers in Manitoba. One young farmer, who recently lost her mother, talked about how her parents' encouragement helped to shape her future: 'No, a lot of other people, girls that I know, their parents did not encourage them to farm even if they were interested in it …. My mom and dad always encouraged me and helped me'.

In China, Yan credits some accidental events, her personal efforts, and a marriage of freedom and equality, among other factors, for her success. Among the Chinese cases, some young women farmers are quite successful from a local perspective, even though they themselves are more ambivalent about their success. Although they are entrepreneurial farmers, their motivation for farm operations is not profit but the well-being of their children.

Successful young women farmers across the different settings use different techniques and practices in farming, have varying access to training, and adopt different methods to learn about farming. Being a continuer farmer does not rule out innovation. For example, one of the Canadian continuer farmers we interviewed is an organic farmer. In China, some continuer farmers implemented new farming techniques. While farmers such as Jenny in Ontario, who runs an organic farm with her partner, intentionally use labour-intensive technology and thus tend to rely more on their own hands. Most young women farmers use technology as suited to the farming activity and its viability, provided they can access such technology. In China, in the initial stages of their vegetable business, Yan and her husband used to carry vegetables on their back to the town market. In five years, they had made enough money to buy a motor vehicle, which allowed Yan to sell vegetables by herself in the city. Li bought a mini tiller to plough hilly land that saved her rearing farm cattle. In Indonesia, unusual for a woman, Noya regularly ploughs the land herself using a water buffalo.

Some respondents have been exceptionally successful as farmers by being entrepreneurial and taking risks where others have not. Chinese farmer Wu expanded her cucumber sheds from 1 to 10, making her a successful entrepreneur. Yan, who never migrated to the city, became a successful pioneer commercial vegetable farmer: 'I started the vegetable industry in our village'. With a lot of hard work and support from her husband, she launched a cooperative and registered her own vegetable brand. The local government has promoted her cooperative as a model to encourage other rural people to undertake farming. While Indonesian farmer Yaya cultivates low-value rice as 'she has not dared to plant chillies, the costs and risks are too high', Partini took the risk and grows chillies along with rice. Returns are high, although not regular, and the greater labour inputs leave her no time for non-farm activities. Here is how Jenny, a newcomer farmer in Ontario, went about generating finances for their farm: 'Because we had a whole bunch of clients, we actually did some crowdfunding because they already knew that we wanted to farm and so we did that. And that was part of our down payment. So, we just kind of begged, borrowed, stole to make it.'

For most small landholders or farmers with no land, a recurring theme across the four countries is the near impossibility of securing a livelihood solely from farming; farm income is augmented through additional employment, mostly in the non-farm sector. Nearly half the young women farmers in the Canada sample rely on off-farm work to supplement their income. In China, many households chose the 'half work and half till' strategy, in which men migrate to towns or cities for work while women remain at home to farm. For women like Li who are left behind, land is a critical source of food and money. While migration disrupts family life for millions, it also makes available land for farming for those who remain. Thus, Wu and Yan contracted many vegetable sheds and more land to grow their operations to become successful full-time farmers. Yao and her husband manage a small vegetable greenhouse, which currently maintains the family and allows them to be free of financial burden. As her children age, Yao plans to take on a non-farm job to support a better future for them.

In Indonesia, while Yaya's rice cultivation takes care of her family's own needs, the returns are low, unlike in horticulture. Yaya and her husband Jarwo are both engaged in other farm and non-farm work. Partini, who is engaged full-time in growing rice and chillies while her husband undertakes construction work and tends their goats, estimates that their non-farm income provides about 60 per cent of total income, and farming 40 per cent. The non-farm income, being more regular, is used for day-to-day expenses.

Young women farmers also face substantial difficulty in negotiating male (public) spaces such as the market. Relative to older women, younger women face more obstacles travelling out of villages, especially in India. In our study, we found that when women went to the market, they were accompanied by their male spouses or other male family members. In general, when itinerant traders are the main produce buyers, they set the prices. A young woman farmer in Madhya Pradesh emphasized that the more educated a woman farmer, the less likely she is to be cheated.

The problem of farm management can be acute for young women farmers who are single or widowed, as the case studies from Tamil Nadu and Madhya Pradesh in particular highlight. Procuring inputs, hiring labour, and selling outputs – each represents a formidable challenge. Not all are able to accomplish these without a hired male farm manager or male relative. Many initiatives such as the self-help groups in India as well as training in China have aided young women farmers in their attempts to navigate male-dominated spaces.

Young women farmers looking forward

Generally, the young women farmers who we interviewed in Canada expressed optimism about the future. When asked where they think they would be in the near future, most hoped that they would still be on the farm, continuing their present work. The importance of family plays into the ways that young women farmers think about their futures. Most Canadian respondents indicated that they would like to see their children farm in the future, although some recognized that this is not the career path for everyone and would accept their children's decision not to farm.

In contrast, for (young) women farmers in China, India, and Indonesia, attitudes to farming futures are ambivalent. While farming is inextricably linked to their ability to secure a good future for their children, they do not aspire for their children to become farmers. At the same time, farming features centrally as a fallback for their children as well as in the way that they imagine their own futures. As Chinese farmer Wu put it: 'I'm prepared for the worst thing that they [her sons] can't find a job and making a living in the city and return to the village. If so, the cucumber shed would be their last resort. That's why the land and the cucumbers matter so much to me. It's related to the future life of my sons'.

Reflecting on her own farming future, Wu said: 'I could not imagine what kind of life I will live without the shed … I'm accustomed to being a farmer. Maybe when I'm getting old and the life of my children are stabilized, I would keep two or three sheds and sell the extra ones'.

One young Indian woman, who holds a master's degree in computer applications but identifies as a farmer, aspires to secure an off-farm job. She illustrates the constrained agency and complex choices that many young women farmers face. She is passionate about farming but notes that farming has limited returns and would like to get a non-farm job, preferably a government job. At the same time, she is not desperate to quit farming.

In Indonesia, most respondents did not want their children to become farmers unless they become large and successful farmers. Partini envisions a somewhat brighter picture of a farming future 10 years from now, with the hope that land from her father and father-in-law will become the property of her and her husband. But when she becomes old, she thinks that someone else will farm the land as her children are not interested in farming: 'I agree with their wish not to become farmers. Farming is difficult, there's no money in it'. Contrast this with Indonesian farmer Menik, who belongs to an elite family, owns land, and is the first in her family to manage part of her land as a commercial farmer. Owning land in her own right as well as the village land received as compensation for work, she has no concerns about her continued existence as a farmer.

While there are several strategies that can directly support farming activities that young women farmers undertake as well as dismantle obstacles to achieving gender equality in farming, young women farmers have little time or interest for support when it involves a time commitment, being already overburdened with farm work and care work. Strategies will have to address how to build capacity for young women farmers in a way that lightens their burdens of work and care, rather than adding to their burden.

Bringing together the generational and gender dimensions in smallholder farming in Canada, China, India, and Indonesia, this chapter has underscored the importance of treating young women farmers as a distinct analytical and empirical category. The intersection of gender, generation, and class – among other characteristics – leads to specific experiences, opportunities, and challenges over the life cycle for young women farmers. Our study highlights the need to rethink the rural family. For young women farmers, an orthodox understanding of gender divisions of labour in which care work is assigned to women and farming is situated as predominantly the domain of men is wrong and unhelpful. Instead, young women farmers navigate the complex realities of farm work and care in ways that sustain their families and their farms.[7]

Notes

1. Moyles' passionate travel narrative, *Women who dig* (2018), shares the stories of women farmers from eight countries in Africa, Asia and the Americas. White's *Agriculture and the generation problem* (2020) explores the generational dynamics and tensions in smallholder farming communities worldwide, with a focus on the intersections of gender, generation, and class.
2. While other relevant hierarchies such as race, caste, and ethnicity operate in different rural contexts, hierarchies of gender and generation operate in all contexts, as does class, although the latter is less pronounced in our Canadian and Chinese cases compared to India and Indonesia.
3. Statistics Canada data on farm operators uses three broad age segments: 15–34, inclusive; 35–54, inclusive; and 55 and over. There is no uniform definition of youth across government departments in China. The Bureau of Statistics of China defines youth as those between the ages 15 and 34 and takes it as official criterion in demographic census. In the agricultural census, youth labourers are those below 35 years old. In the *Medium and Long-term Youth Development Plan (2016–2025)*, issued by the State Council of China, youth is defined as between 14 and 35 years old. In India, the National Youth Policy of 2014 defines youth as those belonging to the 15–29 age group (Vijayabaskar et al. 2018). Indonesian laws and regulations define youth in various ways: 16–30 years in Law No. 40 of 2009 on Youth, up to 35 years in the Ministry of Agriculture's Regulation No. 7 of 2013 on Guidelines on Agricultural Youth Generation Development, while the latest Agricultural Census (2023) has introduced a new category of 'Millennial Farmers' aged 19–39 years.
4. See, for example, the Special Issue on 'Gender and Sexuality in Agriculture' in *Society & Natural Resources* (Leslie et al. 2019: 32–38) and the many studies cited in the editors' introductory article.

5. 'Continuer' young farmers are those who take over their parents' farm and 'newcomer' young farmers are those who are not from farming backgrounds.
6. The term helper implies that women undertake chores only when instructed to do so and renders invisible their agency as farmers.
7. Recently emerging areas such as 'queer farming' studies are also helping to demonstrate this.

References

Agarwal, B. (1994) *A field of one's own: Gender and land rights in South Asia.* Cambridge: Cambridge University Press.

Agarwal, B., Anthwal, P. and Mahesh, M. (2020) *Which women own land in India? Between divergent data sets, measures and laws.* GDI Working Paper 2020-043. Manchester: The University of Manchester.

Berckmoes, L. and White, B. (2016) 'Youth, farming, and precarity in rural Burundi'. *European Journal of Development Research* 26: 190–203. https://doi.org/10.1057/ejdr.2013.53

Boserup, E. (1970) *Woman's role in economic development.* London: Allen & Unwin.

Bossenbroek, L., Van der Loeg, J.D. and Zwarteveen, M. (2015) 'Broken dreams? Youth experiences of agrarian change in Morocco's Saiss region'. *Cahiers Agricultures* 24: 342–48. https://doi.org/10.1684/agr.2015.0776

Cassidy, A. (2019) 'Female successors in Irish family farming: Four pathways to farm transfer'. *Canadian Journal of Development Studies* 40(2): 238–53. https://doi.org/10.1080/02255189.2018.1517643

Chant, S. and Jones, A.G. (2005) 'Youth, gender and livelihoods in West Africa: Perspectives from Ghana and the Gambia'. *Children's Geographies* 3(2): 185-99. https://doi.org/10.1080/14733280500161602

Croll, E. (2007) 'From the girl child to girls' rights'. *Third World Quarterly* 27(7): 1285–1297. https://doi.org/10.1080/01436590600933669

Cuervo, H. and Wyn, J. (2012) *Young people making it work: Continuity and change in rural places.* Melbourne: Melbourne University Publishing.

Deere, C.D. and León de Leal, M. (eds) (2001) *Empowering women: Land and property rights in Latin America.* Pittsburgh: Pittsburgh University Press.

Deere, C.D., Doss, C., Oduro, A. and Swaminathan, H. (2014) 'The gender asset and wealth gap'. *Development* 57: 400–09. https://doi.org/10.1057/dev.2015.10

Dolislager, M., Reardon, T., Arslan, A., Fox, L., Liverpool-Tasie, S., Sauer, C. and Tschirley, D. (2021) 'Youth and adult agrifood system employment in developing regions: Rural (peri-urban to hinterland) vs. urban'. *The Journal of Development Studies* 57(4): 571–93. https://doi.org/10.1080/00220388.2020.1808198

Doss, C. (2018) 'Women and agricultural productivity: Reframing the issues'. *Journal of International Development* 36(1): 35–50. https://doi.org/10.1111/dpr.12243

Elias, M., Mudege, N., Lopez, D.E., Najjar, D., Kandiwa, V., Luis, J., Yila, J., Tegbaru, A., Ibrahim, G., Badstue, L., Njuguna-Mungai, E. and Bentabu, A.

(2018) 'Gendered aspirations and occupations among rural youth, in agriculture and beyond: A cross-regional perspective'. *Journal of Gender, Agriculture and Food Security* 3(1): 82–107. https://doi.org/10.22004/ag.econ.293589

Food and Agriculture Organisation FAO (2011) *The state of food and agriculture 2010–11. Women in agriculture: Closing the gender gap for development.* Rome, Italy: FAO. https://www.fao.org/4/i2050e/i2050e00.htm

FAO (2013) 'African youth in agriculture, natural resources and rural development'. *Nature & Fauna* 28(1). http://www.fao.org/3/as290e/as290e.pdf

FAO (2023) *The status of women in agrifood systems.* Rome, Italy: FAO. https://doi.org/10.4060/cc5343en

FAO-CTA-IFAD (2014) *Youth and agriculture: Key challenges and concrete solutions.* Rome: Food and Agriculture Organization of the United Nations, Technical Centre for Agricultural and Rural Cooperation, and the International Fund for Agricultural Development. http://www.fao.org/3/a-i3947e.pdf

Giller, K.E, Delaune, T., Vasco Silva, J., Descheemaeker, K., van de Ven, G., Schut, A.G.T., van Wijk, M., Hammond, J., Hochman, Z., Taulya, G., Chikowo, R., Narayanan, S., Kishore, A., Bresciani, F., Teixeira, H.M., Andersson, J.A. and van Ittersum, M. (2021) 'The future of farming: Who will produce our food?' *Food Security* 13: 1073–99. https://doi.org/10.1007/s12571-021-01184-6

High Level Panel of Experts (HLPE) (2021) *Promoting youth engagement and employment in agriculture and food systems.* A report by the High-Level Panel of Experts on Food Security and Nutrition. Rome: Committee on World Food Security. https://openknowledge.fao.org/server/api/core/bitstreams/034c7cf9-9215-4304-a264-ecb0215a50d2/content

Huijsmans, R., Ambarwati, A., Chazali, C. and Vijayabaskar, M. (2021) 'Farming, gender and aspirations across young people's life course: Attempting to keep things open while becoming a farmer'. *European Journal of Development Research* 33(1): 71–88. https://doi.org/10.1057/s41287-020-00302-y

International Fund for Agricultural Development (IFAD) (2019) *Rural development report 2019: Creating opportunities for rural youth.* Rome: International Fund for Rural Development. https://www.ifad.org/documents/38714170/41190221/RDR2019_Overview_e_W.pdf/699560f2-d02e-16b8-4281-596d4c9be25a

Jacobs, S. (2010) *Gender and agrarian reforms.* London: Routledge.

Kandiyoti, D. (1988) 'Bargaining with patriarchy'. *Gender and Society* 2(3): 274–90. https://doi.org/10.1177/089124388002003004

Korzenszky, A. (2019) 'Extrafamilial farm succession: An adaptive strategy contributing to the renewal of peasantries in Austria'. *Canadian Journal of Development Studies* 40(2): 291–308. https://doi.org/10.1080/02255189.2018.1517301

Kundu, A. and Das, S. (2019) 'Gender wage gap in the agricultural labor market of India: An empirical analysis'. *Journal of Economics and Political Economy* 6(2): 122–42. https://doi.org/10.1453/jepe.v6i2.1872

Leslie, I.S. (2019) 'Queer farmland: Land access strategies for small-scale agriculture'. *Society & Natural Resources* 32(8): 928–46. https://doi.org/10.1080/08941920.2018.1561964

Li, T. (2011) 'Centering labour in the land grab debate'. *The Journal of Peasant Studies* 38(2): 281–98. https://doi.org/10.1080/03066150.2011.559009

Li, T. (2017) 'After development: Surplus population and the politics of entitlement'. *Development and Change* 48: 1247–61. https://doi.org/10.1111/dech.12344

McGreevy, S., Kobayashi, M. and Tanaka, K. (2018) 'Agrarian pathways for the next generation of Japanese farmers'. *Canadian Journal of Development Studies* 40(2): 271–90. https://doi.org/10.1080/02255189.2018.1517642

Moyles, T. (2019) *Women who dig: Farming, feminism and the fight to feed the world*. Regina, Saskatchewan: University of Regina Press.

Park, C.M.Y. (2020) 'Beyond the business case for gender: A feminist ecologist in the FAO', by R. Elmhirst and B.P. Resurrecion in Conversation with Clara Mi Young Park'. In B. Resurrecion and R. Elmhirst (eds), *Negotiating gender equity in environment and development: Voices from feminist political ecology*. London: Routledge.

Quisumbing, A.R., Meinzen-Dick, R., Raney, T.L., Croppenstedt, A., Behrman, J.A. and Peterman, A. (2014) 'Closing the knowledge gap'. In A.R. Quisumbing, T.L. Raney, J.A. Behrman, R. Meinzen-Dick, A. Croppenstedt, and A. Peterman (eds), *Gender in agriculture: Closing the knowledge gap*, pp. 3–31. Dordrecht: Springer.

Razavi, S. (2003) 'Introduction: Agrarian change, gender and land rights'. *Journal of Agrarian Change* 3(1–2): 2–32. https://doi.org/10.1111/1471-0366.00049

Razavi, S. (2009) 'Engendering the political economy of agrarian change'. *Journal of Peasant Studies* 36(1): 197–226. https://doi.org/10.1080/03066150902820412

Robson, E., Panelli, R. and Punch, S. (eds) (2007) *Global perspectives on rural childhood and youth: Young rural lives*. New York: Taylor & Francis Group.

Sachs, C. (1996) *Gendered fields: Rural women, agriculture and environment*. Boulder, CO: Westview Press.

Schwarz, U. (2004) *To farm or not to farm? Gendered paths to succession and inheritance*. Münster: LIT Verlag.

Srinivasan, S. (ed.) (2024) *Becoming a young farmer: Young people's pathways into farming in Canada, China, India and Indonesia*, Rethinking Rural series. Palgrave Macmillan. Open Access https://link.springer.com/book/10.1007/978-3-031-15233-7

Sumberg, J. (ed.) (2021) *Youth and the rural economy in Africa: Hard work and hazard*. Boston, MA: CABI.

Vijayabaskar, M., Sudha, N. and Srinivasan, S. (2018) 'Agricultural revival and reaping the youth dividend'. *Economic and Political Weekly* 53(26/27): 8–16.

White, B. (2020) *Agriculture and the generation problem*. Halifax and Rugby: Fernwood Publishing and Practical Action Publishing.

CHAPTER 2

The rise of young women farmers in Canada

Alexa Avelar, Sharada Srinivasan,
and Haroon Akram-Lodhi

Introduction

Like many other developed and developing countries, Canada is facing a generational crisis in agriculture. The rising average age of Canadian farmers, which is currently 55, indicates an apparent unwillingness or an inability for young people to enter farming (Statistics Canada 2017c). Yet this apparent crisis has one dimension that is little understood and which may have important implications – young women farmers. While the share of young farmers in the farming population in Canada is diminishing, the number of young women within this declining population is in fact growing, albeit very slowly (Statistics Canada 2016b). However, at present, little is known about the characteristics of young women farmers in Canada. This chapter describes the circumstances facing young women farmers in Canada today. The chapter begins by summarily reviewing the gender dimensions of farming's development in Canada. This is followed by looking at the demographics of young women farmers. The chapter then explores some of the specific challenges that young women farmers in Canada face as well as the broad contours of support available for this group. The last section describes the research with young women farmers in Canada that inspires this chapter and sets out the questions guiding the case studies presented in Chapter 3.

This chapter is grounded in a review of official statistics and literature that is notable for having significant gaps and often being dated. For this reason, scholarly literature has been supplemented to an extent, and only when necessary, by reputable non-peer-reviewed sources such as news media, which have covered these issues with more frequency than scholarly researchers. In addition, we have addressed gaps by reviewing studies that focus either on women farmers or on young farmers. Most of the peer-reviewed studies that we utilized use qualitative methods, relying upon small samples in specific areas of Canada. Nonetheless, some common themes have emerged across this literature that are related to the challenges that young women farmers in Canada face, and we have used these themes to structure the discussion in this chapter. In terms of official statistics, we rely on the Canadian Agricultural Census, which has reported farm operator data from as early as 1971.

One caveat is in order. In Canada, as in other countries, there is no universal age range that defines a 'young' farmer. In a way, this is appropriate since concepts such as 'youth' or 'young people', as the Introduction sets out, are 'culturally and historically constructed and can change over time and from one social context to the next' (Leavy and Smith 2010: 5), demonstrating that such concepts are relational. Thus, those over the age of 34 may still be considered 'young' to their older peers. Indeed, in some of the literature that we reviewed, the cut-off age used to define 'young' was 40 years. Statistics Canada (2017c) uses the 'Under 35' age category for 'young farmers'. Nonetheless, in the interest of keeping the literature review to a manageable size and in light of some of the literature, we will define 'young' to be between the ages of 18 and 34 (Parent 2012; Qualman et al. 2018).

Gender and agriculture in Canada

With the passage of the Canadian Homestead Act in 1872, the Dominion set the stage for the large-scale settlement of western Canada, in particular, by immigrants arriving primarily but not exclusively from Europe. In 1921, the earliest year for which data is available, a million Canadians – one-third of all employed individuals – were working in agriculture; the majority of this employment was in small-scale family farming (Statistics Canada 2017d). In the context of Canada, small-scale family farming between the 1870s and the 1950s can be defined as the production of crops and livestock on land that was family-owned, using labour supplied by family members, for the purpose of household subsistence along with production for local, regional, national, and export markets. Small-scale farming made intensive use of household labour, which was applied in conjunction, at first, with animal traction, and then later with mechanical technologies. It was only later in the period that seeds began to be purchased and agrochemicals began to be used.

Small-scale family farming was (and is) patriarchal. From 1859 onwards, women had the right to 'have, hold and enjoy all her personal property' (Forbes-Chilibeck 2005: 27) without having to inform her husband or have his approval with regard to the use or disposal of the property. However, the system of inheritance was predicated upon property transfer regimes from fathers to sons. Men distributed their property through their wills, including the estate of their widows, to their sons, and particularly their eldest son. If a man did not write a will, his property 'ultimately passed on to his eldest son' (Belshaw 2016: 347). As a result, primogeniture was a key feature of the farming household and community. In this way, father-to-son inheritance shaped farm succession to ensure that the family farm was passed on to males of subsequent generations, clearly disadvantaging and disempowering young women who lacked the *de facto* rights needed to inherit property, including the land needed to farm (Belshaw 2016). Inheritance and succession thus sustained a patrilineal culture within Canadian farming in which a perceived virtue was that the family farm would be passed on to future generations through sons.

This also shaped social views as to 'who' exactly was a farmer. The presumption was that men were farmers and women were homemakers, and this applied beyond the family into its extended kinship network and the social institutions of the community (Price 2012). As a consequence, the recognition and visibility of women on the farm and in the agricultural community and beyond was limited. Thus, patrilineal household structures perpetuated patriarchal hierarchies across generations as the history of Canadian farming became one in which men dominated 'socio-economic processes, resources, institutions and ideologies' (Leckie 1993: 214), while women became attached, while often still young, to a male economic figure, primarily her husband, but often extending to her father, brother, or son.

During the Second World War, this patriarchal and patrilineal structure was disrupted after 'over a million Canadian women took to the farms and fields' (Moyles 2018: XVII) while men were sent overseas. Indeed, the Canadian state attempted to '*feminize* farming' (Moyles 2018: XVII) by calling women farmers 'Farmerettes' and distributing posters of women engaged in farm tasks to 'encourage women to dig in and do their part to sustain the war efforts in Canada and Europe' (Moyles 2018: XVIII). However, this restructuring of farm labour did not survive the war; farming reverted to its pre-war patriarchal and patrilineal structure, and stories of the Farmerettes are rarely written (Moyles 2018).

In the decades since the 1950s, family farming in Canada has changed but it remains male-dominated and patriarchal (Statistics Canada 2017c). Although a significant proportion of family farming in Canada remains relatively small-to-medium scale, the most important development in farming in the last half-century has been the rise to prominence of large-scale, capital-intensive farming, with expensive inputs such as farm machinery, seed, chemicals, and feed for livestock (Wiebe 2017). Large-scale operations typically specialize in the production of one crop or one type of livestock in order to reap economies of scale – as more is produced, cost per unit of production falls, helping to cover the costs of expensive inputs. At the same time, Canada's agricultural subsidy programmes are based on 'payment per unit of production with high caps on the total amount of program money any single operation can receive' (Wiebe 2017: 146), which has resulted in the largest farmers getting most of the available government funding.

By increasing production levels, lowering the price per unit, and increasing market sales, the rise of large-scale farms in Canada is consistent with the state's regulatory regime (Qualman et al. 2018: 102), which focuses on increasing both the volume and value of agricultural exports by increasing on-farm efficiencies, maximizing production, and therefore enhancing profitability (Wiebe 2017: 140–43). As a result, Canadian agrifood exports rose threefold between 1989 and 2014, even as its primary stakeholders – farmers – were 'doing worse and worse' (Wiebe 2017: 143) because of the imbalance in market power between 'farmers and agribusiness corporations' (Qualman et al. 2018: 102).

At the same time, these structural changes in agriculture, from the dominance of small-scale to large-scale farms, have marginalized small- and medium-scale farms (Wiebe 2017: 144), whose mixed production model and 'ecologically (diverse) and culturally sensitive farming practices' (Wiebe 2017: 141) cannot compete with large-scale monocultural entities. As a result, most farm families operating at a small-to-medium scale are forced to rely on off-farm employment income, asset sales, depreciation, social assistance transfers, and the acquisition of debt (Wiebe 2017: 145; Qualman et al. 2018: 104). In far too many cases, market pressures and debt imperatives have forced small- and medium-scale family farmers to sell up and leave agriculture.

The agrarian question facing small- and medium-scale farming in Canada has to a limited extent disrupted some patriarchal and patrilineal norms because it has also produced a crisis of rural masculinity. Male power in Canadian farming has been based upon the *de facto* ownership of the farm and key agricultural resources within it (Shortall 1999; Heather et al. 2005: 89). Thus, central to the mechanisms of 'traditional' gender relationships in Canadian farming has been the constraints surrounding women's access to key agricultural resources (Leckie 1993), which have delegitimized women's capacity to be a farmer. As Canada's small- and medium-scale farms fail to meet market and debt imperatives, gender-based norms in access to agricultural resources have themselves been upended. This is accompanied by advocacy and policy efforts at gender equality that have laid the foundation for the increased relative visibility of women in Canadian farming and possibly for the apparent disproportionate rise in young women farmers in Canada.

Are women farmers young?

Statistics Canada defines 'Farm operator' in the 2016 Census of Agriculture as 'those persons responsible for the management decisions in operating an agricultural operation'. These can be 'owners, tenants or hired managers' who are responsible for the management decisions related to the farm, which includes 'planting, harvesting, raising animals, marketing and sales, and making capital purchases and other financial decisions' (Statistics Canada 2017b). Remarkably, it was only as recently as the 1991 Census that women could be identified as a farm operator.

In 2001, the Agricultural Census found that 98 per cent of farms were family operated, while 22.5 per cent of farms were reporting themselves to be family-operated corporations[1] (Statistics Canada 2017c). The average area per farm increased from 779 acres[2] in 2011 to 820 acres in 2016 (Statistics Canada 2017a). Between 2011 and 2016, the total number of farm operators in Canada decreased from 293,925 to 271,935, a decline of 7.5 per cent

(Statistics Canada 2016b, 2017c). However, the number of female farm operators increased. In 1991, women accounted for 25.6 per cent of farm operators, which rose to 28.7 per cent in 2016 (Statistics Canada 2016b, 2017a, c). Thus, more women are participating in agriculture as farm operators. Table 2.1 and Table 2.2 offer a more nuanced picture of the distribution of farm operators by age and gender as well as by number of farm operators.

Table 2.1 examines the total number as well as the proportion of agricultural operators by age group and gender. It shows that women between the ages of 55 and 69 have the largest absolute number of female-only agricultural operations, followed closely by women between the ages of 35 and 54. Interestingly, the largest percentage of female-only farm operators is in the 70 and older age category, followed by women under 35. The smallest portion of female-only farm operators lies in the mixed ages category of farm operators, holding only 1.6 per cent of total agricultural operations.

The average age of farm operators in Canada also increased between 2011 and 2016 from 54 to 55 years, with farmers aged 55 to 59 being the largest share of farm operators (Statistics Canada 2017c). Women represented 30.7 per cent of farm operators between the ages of 35 and 54, which is the highest percentage of female farm operators among all age categories of farm operators in the census (Statistics Canada 2017a). The number of young farmers under the age of 35 increased by 3 per cent between 2011 and 2016 (Statistics Canada 2017c, 2017a). Women accounted for 26.4 per cent of young farmers under the age of 35 (Statistics Canada 2017a); however, the number of agricultural operations with only female operators under the age of 35 is growing much faster than that of males. Between 2011 and 2016, sole male farm operators under 35 increased by 24.4 per cent, whereas sole female farm operators under 35 increased by 113.3 per cent (Statistics Canada 2017c).

Table 2.2 displays the number of farm operators per farm in 2011 and 2016, comparing males only, females only, and both, while also examining the gender of farmers on farms with a single farm operator and farms with two or more operators. The Yukon, Northwest Territories, and Nunavut are not included in these totals, and farm operators for two or more distinct farms are only counted once (Statistics Canada 2016a). The data show that while the total number of farm operators decreased over the five-year period, the number of female farm operators increased by 1.3 per cent. In particular, there are more females as single farm operators, increasing from 13.3 per cent to 16.8 per cent of all female farm operators during the period (Statistics Canada 2016a). By contrast, the number of male single farm operators has decreased slightly over the same period, falling from 52.2 per cent to 51.8 per cent of all male farm operators (Statistics Canada 2016a).

Thus, the data appear to indicate that farm operators remain principally male, while the age of farm operators is increasing and the number of farm operators is decreasing. However, within the under 35 age group, the number of farm operators is rising. Moreover, within this category, farms with only female operators are growing at almost five times the rate of that of male farm

Table 2.1 Total number of agricultural operations and proportion by age and sex of operators, Canada, 2016

Age group	Male only		Female only		Both male and female	
	Number of agricultural operations	Percentage of agricultural operations in age group*	Number of agricultural operations	Percentage of agricultural operations in age group*	Number of agricultural operations	Percentage of agricultural operations in age group*
All under 35	8,734	68.3	1,045	8.2	3,001	23.5
All between 35 and 54	37,562	62.8	4,442	7.4	17,816	29.8
All between 55 and 69	43,765	64.6	5,432	8.0	18,499	27.3
All 70 or older	17,217	71.1	2,634	10.9	4,374	18.1
Mixed ages	8,979	31.0	450	1.6	19,542	67.5

Note: * Totals may not equal 100% due to rounding
Source: Statistics Canada 2017c, Census of Agriculture.

Table 2.2 Farm operators per farm, 2011 and 2016

	Males in 2011	Males in 2016	Females in 2011	Females in 2016	Both sexes in 2011	Both sexes in 2016
Farms with one operator	111,480	100,620	10,740	13,110	122,220	113,730
Farms with two or more operators	101,775	93,345	69,925	64,860	171,700	158,205
Number of operators on all farms	213,255	193,965	80,665	77,970	293,925	271,935

Source: Statistics Canada 2016a.

operators. Unfortunately, the data are not clear about whether farms with two or more operators are exclusively male- or female-run – only that more women are found on farm operations with two or more operators. In this light, it is clear that a better understanding of the characteristics of young women farmers can offer important insights into: the future of farming in Canada; addressing continuing gender inequalities in Canada's farming communities; and understanding how the needs of young women farmers can be better supported. The Census of Agriculture, however, does not provide an accessible cross-tabulation of gender and age with other important factors, such as farm size, net market income, and debt that would give a much clearer picture of who these young women farmers are and the conditions that they face.

Young women farmers as 'new' farmers

Some young women farmers enter the agricultural industry with no previous experience. Their experiences differentiate them from other young women farmers as they do not have access to resource inheritance, farming experience, and social connections. FarmON Alliance conducted a survey in 2012 that was targeted toward farmers interested in developing sustainable and locally oriented farm businesses. It found that of 430 respondents, 73 per cent reported having no background in agriculture before exploring farming, taking farm training, or choosing farming as a career (Knibb 2012). This survey did not identify differences on the basis of gender. Another survey-based study (Laforge et al. 2018) found that among young farmers under the age of 35, women are particularly visible, and that many young women farmers do not come from a farming background. New and young farmers do not necessarily have the same skill set and social connections needed for success as those who have lived on farms their entire lives (Ngo and Brklacich 2014; CBC News: The National 2017[3]; Epp 2017).

Continuing young farmers – those from farming families – acquire farming skills through 'learning to do by doing' throughout their childhoods, teenage, and young adult years (4-H Canada 2018). Thus, young farmers acquire skills in crop and animal care as well as in business management (Errington 1998). However, it should be noted that young women and men may be taught different skills based on the gendered division of labour found on family farms. For young farmers that come from farming backgrounds and who are continuing to operate the family farm, inheritance is a key mechanism to ensure that they can continue to farm. As a result, succession – the transfer of managerial control of farm assets (Errington 1998)[4] – becomes a primary feature in planning for the future. This would appear to be an advantage for those that are continuing a family farm. However, advancements in modern agriculture have led to significant changes in farm management and succession practices; 'multi-generation farms are becoming less common' (Pouliot 2011: 2). As a result, farm succession to a family member is now different and, in many ways, a more difficult process than in decades past

(Pouliot 2011: 3), especially when many aspiring young farmers, who attend post-secondary education at the same rate as the general population, 'delay ... their planned entry into farming' (Ahearn 2016: 1).

Barriers to young women farmers

All young farmers, especially those without a farming background, face significant barriers to enter into and remain in farming. In addition to a lack of skills and social connections, access to land and capital, the rising cost of inputs, falling output prices, and, as a result, (very) low net farm incomes can all serve to deter or prevent entry into farming (Qualman et al. 2018). In the following sections, we discuss some of the key constraints that young women farmers face.

Generation, gender roles, and the gender division of labour

The institutional and legal foundations of patriarchal and patrilineal household structures and a resulting set of social norms and values that underpin so-called 'traditional' gender roles and gender divisions of labour have historical origins that we discussed earlier. What is salient here is that these social norms and values continue to hold sway. Heather et al. (2005: 88)[5] found in their study of Albertan farm women that gender roles tend to be more strictly prescribed in rural areas and that these roles are still viewed as 'natural' and unchangeable. As a result, young women living on a farm are still all too often not defined in relation to the farm as a farmer. They are also not defined in relation to their children as a mother. Rather, they continue to be defined in relation to their husbands as 'farm wives' (Sumner 2005) who lack experience in 'the business of farming', especially when they are younger (Hall and Mogyorody 2007). This helps to explain Whatmore's (1991: 90) earlier finding that farm women view unpaid care and domestic work as something for which they have principal responsibility as an 'ongoing chore'.

More than a decade later, Van de Vorst (2002) found similar occurrences within Manitoban farm families in which descriptions of farming routines historically focused only on the commercial activities that men performed (2002: 1–3), thereby ignoring women's contributions to the farm and the home, such as taking 'meals, vehicles, and workers to the field' (Van de Vorst 2002: 77). These farm women also describe how time-consuming it is to pack meals and bring them to the men, finding that they were not doing the work, but 'chasing it around' for the men (Van de Vorst 2002: 78). These farm women also took on administrative responsibilities or bookkeeping related to the farm operation's business matters, which further contribute to the commercial production process on the farm by 'freeing men from these detailed and time-consuming chores' (Van de Vorst 2002: 78–79). Van de Vorst also draws on a survey that reveals how Manitoba farm women spend 54 hours per week in family and household work (2002: 83), despite the 'mechanization of housekeeping and the availability of processed foods, manufactured clothes, and professional healthcare' (Van de Vorst 2002: 83). It is rather telling in the ways that this form of women's labour is not recognized as 'farm' labour, when these contributions keep other farm tasks on track. Farm women also seem hesitant to recognize these forms of labour as 'farm' labour, even though these tasks are necessary to maintain the farm's functionality, especially during its busiest times.

Nearly two decades later, in Avelar (2019), young women farmers in southern Ontario describe similar experiences in which they 'switch off' from certain farm tasks in order to perform domestic chores or childcare duties (2019: 65),[6] even though their male partners or other family members were just as capable of doing those tasks. The responsibility for domestic or childcare-related tasks is relinquished to women on the basis of gender roles. A number of these young women farmers did not necessarily acknowledge the ways that their gender and gender roles impact their daily lives until asked, which further suggests the normalization and acceptance of gendered behaviour within the agricultural community and among individuals themselves.

These studies suggest that across time and spaces, traditional gender roles continue to impact young women farmers. Beyond unpaid care and domestic work, Martz and Brueckner (2003) reviewed 20 years of studies to demonstrate that women are more likely to identify as taking care of the farm accounts and caring for small animals while men are viewed as 'the farmer'. While it is demonstrably the case that young farm women undertake on-farm work, with young farm women assuming principal responsibility for the performance of unpaid care and domestic work, it can be difficult to discern the types and amount of women's labour that is directly involved in farming, especially on family farms (Smith, 1986; Hall and Mogyorody 2007: 290; Chambers 2010), in part because women (and men) tend to underreport their labour involvement.

As already noted, family farming in Canada is in a period of crisis; rural women experience this in particularly gendered ways (Sumner 2005: 78). In more 'traditional' farm families, Fletcher (2013) found that some farm women may feel like they are unable to live up to the ideal of a 'farm wife' due to the increased financial pressure to generate income. To do so, when family farms are struggling financially, women's farm-based businesses may often provide vital income to support the family farm (Van de Vorst 2002). More commonly, though, 'to survive, it is the women who are most likely to look for off-farm income' (Van de Vorst 2002; Heather et al. 2005: 87; Sumner 2005), whether it be part-time or full-time employment. These women tend to be younger and because of the agrarian crisis, have become more active agents in establishing a new identity for themselves on the family farm as they adapt and change to provide income, albeit slowly (Martz and Brueckner 2003: 41; Martz 2006). When women provide the extra income needed to keep the farm functioning, the farm may become reliant on that source of income in difficult economic times. Thus, despite increased agency, notions of putting the farm first and the individual last are placed on young farm women, whose own well-being may continue to be less valued than that placed on the farm, the family, and indeed the community (Heather et al. 2005; Fletcher 2013). At the same time, when women farmers have to enter into off-farm work, this can lead to an off-farm career that only serves to further marginalize the farming identity of women (Hall and Mogyorody 2007: 290). Finally, due to the farm crisis, more rural women now often report a 'triple day' (Krug 2003; Heather et al. 2005: 91) as they divide their time between unpaid care and domestic work, farm work, and off-farm work. While most of these authors do not specifically discuss young women farmers, as set out in this collection's Introduction, it is young women in their prime who are often combining these multiple roles and responsibilities that put them in a position that is both stressful and precarious.

Gender, generation, and access to capital

Contemporary farming in Canada has high capital requirements to access land and inputs, even as net farm incomes are low. Moreover, land is expensive, often beyond the reach of those that do not benefit from a succession plan. Young farmers typically do not have access to sufficient start-up capital to undertake farming without assistance, be it from family or, far more unusually, government support programmes. If they turn to financial institutions, young farmers often struggle to gather enough collateral to qualify for loans (Pouliot 2011). Thus, the financial requirements of farming are one of the most difficult barriers for young farmers to address, and this is true whether they are from established farm backgrounds or are completely new to farming (Robinson 2003). Moreover, even if they can access capital from financial institutions, these young farmers will be left with a debt burden; for some it is probable that there is a strong risk aversion to adding more debt on top of their student debt (Agriculture and Agri-Food Canada 2010: 9).

Supply management in Canada places additional financial constraints upon young farmers. Agriculture and Agri-Food Canada found that young farmers who enter agricultural industries operating under supply-management systems, such as the dairy industry, may not be able to do so without accessing their parents' quota[7] (2010: 8). This is because farming at the scale required to take part in supply management requires large financial investments in land, livestock, machinery, and production rights (Pouliot 2011: 3), and, as we have just noted, access to capital is a particular constraint that young farmers face. Those that are not from a farming background may not be able to access the same government support programmes as existing farmers because 'they do not meet the minimum farm income test required to access this assistance' (Agriculture and Agri-Food Canada 2010: 8). This leaves new and young farmers in a difficult position as they are not able to afford to run a successful supply-management farm operation on their own. Again, while much of this literature does not specifically discuss the situation for young women farmers, it is quite likely that the barriers for this group are accentuated as they face gender biases in financial markets, especially when they are seen to be making a non-traditional career choice.

Gender, generation, and alternative agriculture

Conventional family farming and the social roles that it has historically fostered are now being challenged by the rise of alternative agriculture,[8] in which labour-processes and the ideological orientation of farmers is vastly different from that of their forebearers (Hall and Mogyorody 2007). In particular, alternative, ecological, and more sustainable farming systems may appear to offer a chance of greater equity in gendered and generational divisions of labour and decision-making (Krug 2003; Hall and Mogyorody 2007; Laforge et al. 2018: 131). Sumner (2005: 78) reports that as of 2001, one-third of 'all self-declared organic farm operators in Canada are women'. This statistic, along with the increase in the number of women farm operators under the age of 35 revealed in the Agricultural Census, implies that alternative agriculture has created space for young women with a social justice agenda and embodying an 'environmental consciousness' (Sumner 2005: 78). Leckie (1993) found that young women did not enter farming for the same reasons as young men; young women entered farming for reasons of independence and social and environmental justice. However, Hall and Mogyorody (2007) report that labour on organic farms still demonstrates gendered divisions of labour in which men tend to do most of the field work, maintenance, and machine operation work, and women are more prominent in harvesting, bookkeeping, taking care of livestock, and performing unpaid care and domestic work. Women in alternative agriculture, however, were more likely to report the equitable sharing of major farm decision-making (Hall and Mogyorody 2007: 297). While a majority of Canadian provinces are home to large-scale industrial farms (Mills 2013: 24), these patterns demonstrate an arc toward increased gender equity in farming systems of a specific type that make up a small, growing portion of Canadian farming.

In the Junior Farmers Association of Ontario's (2013) new farmer survey, its 250 respondents identified 'education and training' as one of the most difficult challenges for new farmers, of which young women form the fastest growing segment. An important way of obviating a lack of skills and social connections was to become associated with 'someone with farming experience' (Junior Farmers 2013); 87 per cent of respondents listed this as being an important source of farm skills. Here, a particular issue that young women face on entering farming without experience is the lack of older female role models and mentors from whom to learn the role and tasks of being a farmer, rather than being a farmer's wife (Weldon 2016).

Support and advocacy for young women farmers

While more young women are entering agriculture as single farm operators, there are still far fewer young women as compared to young men in Canadian farming. Many factors affect the capacity to enter farming, and these certainly affect young women's ability to gain a foothold in the agricultural sector in Canada, especially as there are still few support mechanisms available to ease the transition. Even within farmer-run agricultural organizations in local communities, young women farmers often describe feeling 'out of place' by being both the youngest people in attendance as well as the only women in the group (Avelar 2019: 110–15). This is certainly the case for new and young women (and men) farmers entering agriculture without experience or financial support, but is also increasingly the case for those new young women farmers who are continuing the family farm. There are few government policies available for young farmers, and fewer still specifically for young farming women.

Agricultural and farm policy is formulated on a macro-level scale and can often be attributed as an issue beyond farmers' control. Moreover, the everyday effects of policy changes on farmers can be difficult to trace, and it is even more difficult to 'understand the gendered dimensions of these changes' (Fletcher 2013: 1). However, as discussed earlier, it is not in dispute that in the 21st century, Canadian public policy 'promotes high-input industrial agriculture that specializes in exports' (Sumner 2005: 82; Qualman et al. 2018), and has a long-term commitment to facilitate the exit of conventional smaller-scale family farms in order to accommodate the expansion of large-scale farms. This is clearly not a policy framework that has the potential to benefit young women farmers, given the specific challenges that they face, and the particular appeal that alternative agriculture may hold for specific groups of young (new) women farmers. This can only change if the policy framework undergoes a fundamental shift.

Government support programmes that secure markets for producers' products, help farmers adjust to changing markets, and invest in innovation could all facilitate the entry of smaller-scale new and young farmers into agriculture (Agriculture and Agri-Food Canada 2010: 7). New entrant programmes exist in Ontario in order to help new and young farmers who may not have the 'financial means or opportunity to get started in the industry' (Dairy Farmers of Ontario 2017; see also Chicken Farmers of Ontario 2017). Others have argued that the Canadian Agricultural Loans Act programme 'should be available to purchase quota' in supply-managed activities (Agriculture and Agri-Food Canada 2010: 9). Mills (2013: 28) notes that in the 'Growing Forward' programmes, young prospective farmers must have a certain level of education and work experience in order to qualify for loans and grants, which hinders those who have not grown up on farms with its 'learning by doing' ethos, or those that come from low-income families and do not have the advantage of post-secondary education. Although many such policy discussions use terms such as 'new' and 'young prospective farmers', they nevertheless deploy a gender-neutral language that either suggests a strong inherent male bias inattentive to specific gender barriers or an assumption that women and men are likely to benefit equally from such measures.

Avelar (2019), who produced one of the few studies that explicitly focuses on young women farmers, found that for young women farmers in Ontario, finances were the most difficult problem in running their operation. Many of these women were not aware of financial aid programmes available to them. Some of the farmers were aware of programmes such as Farm Credit Canada's Young Farmer Loan, but felt that they were 'locked into using FCC [Farm Credit Canada]' (Avelar 2019: 95) because it is only a loan and must be paid back. Young farmers are simply borrowing money rather than being awarded a scholarship or monetary aid, which is difficult to do in the high-risk financial situation found in farming today; a start-up loan only adds to existing debt.

While much of the policy and research examining policy are often presented in gender and generation neutral language, here we extend some of the recommendations with a focus on young women farmers. As most new farmers are from non-farming backgrounds and many are young and women, policy will be most beneficial if it highlights the role of young women first-time farmers; for example, providing educational opportunities to non-farming entrants to support their transition into agriculture. Moreover, given the role of young women in particular in alternative agriculture, policies that could facilitate entry into smaller-scale farming include facilitating the rental of and thus the availability of land and equipment, which would serve to significantly lower start-up costs (Agriculture and Agri-Food Canada 2010: 14; Epp 2017). Policy that is developed to create early succession plans and innovative farming partnerships could also help with access to land and capital. Policies should also facilitate market access. With government assistance, new and young farmers would have more viable opportunities to establish stable farm enterprises capable of providing a steady livelihood (Epp 2017).

Farm women's movements and young women farmers

Throughout the latter half of the 20th century, farm women's movements acted to collectively articulate the specific interests of rural women to communities and governments (Shortall 1999; Tanner 1999). The promotion of women in farming has been a key aspect of some farm women's movements, including the short-lived Canadian Farm Women's Network (CFWN). Farm women organized the CFWN when they found that they 'had no other forum where they could express their concerns and tackle the issues they wanted addressed' (Shortall 1999: 105). It emerged as a result of the farm crisis – financial difficulties were prominent, rural social services were cut, and the promotion of export-oriented and cost-efficient farming brought other problems to the farm (Shortall 1999: 106). However, there has been a contradiction at the heart of farm women's movements. Most groups have sought to address the needs of women in conventional family farming; their actions have arguably contributed to maintaining some of the sources of their own inequality because of their efforts to sustain conventional agriculture (Shortall 1999: 111). Only some farm women's groups – such as farm women organizing within the National Farmers Union – have sought to promote the interests of women operating small-scale farms. If the goal is to advance the position of women in general, and young women in particular, it could be argued that Canada's farm women's movements are rapidly approaching a pivotal point where there is a choice to be made: to maintain the conventional family or to promote alternative forms of agriculture. Nonetheless, young women farmers are changing the way that farming takes place, changing the social roles expected of women within rural communities, and in so doing, are paving the way for the next generation.

Becoming and being a young woman farmer in Canada

The discussion thus far supports Canada's inclusion in the research that the teams conducted for 'Becoming a Young Farmer: Young People's Pathways into Farming in Four Countries' project. While the number of young women farmers is on the rise, they are not the explicit focus of much of research or policy in Canada as elsewhere. The young women farmers in Canada interviewed for this research live and work in a time and place where old ways of thinking and progressive ideas about gender collide. We interviewed 43 young women farmers, constituting 45 per cent of the Canada study sample, across two sites – the provinces of Ontario and Manitoba.

Agriculture, young (women) farmers in Manitoba and Ontario

Manitoba is directly to the west of Ontario and is centrally located in Canada. While Ontario, Quebec, and Alberta are the top three largest contributors to agriculture and agrifood manufacturing gross domestic product (GDP) in Canada, this sector is especially important to Manitoba's economy, contributing 10.3 per cent to the province's GDP (Statistics Canada 2019). While Manitoba has fewer livestock farms, the farms tend to be larger than in Ontario. As stated in Bihun and Desmarais (2024: 67), 'Manitoba has the largest pig farms and the highest percentage of dairy farms adopting robotic milking technology in the country' (Government of Manitoba Agriculture 2017). Farms grossing less than Can$250,000 fell by 15.3 per cent between 2011 and 2016, and those grossing more than $250,000 increased by 14.2 per cent over the same period (Government of Manitoba Agriculture 2017). Furthermore, in 2015, only 6.1 per cent of farms reported selling products directly to consumers (Government of Manitoba Agriculture 2017).

Ontario is Canada's most populated province and has the highest agriculture and agrifood manufacturing GDP in the country (Statistics Canada 2019). Farming is primarily concentrated in the south-western region where highly productive soils, warmer temperatures, and adequate rainfall provide excellent yielding crops. Proximity to urban centres and the American border have also led to well-established supply chains and markets for both livestock products and field crops in this region. In 2016, Ontario had the highest number of farmers in the country with slightly over 70,000 farm operators who earned an average net operating income of $47,115 (Statistics Canada 2016a; OMAFRA 2016). On average, Ontario's farms tend to be smaller than those in Canada's western provinces.

Despite their status as a large part of the Canadian farm sector, Ontario and Manitoba both face problems in attracting and retaining youth in agriculture. Just over 9 per cent of Ontario's current farmers are under the age of 35, while it is just under 11 per cent in Manitoba (Statistics Canada 2016b). Furthermore, in both provinces, more than 50 per cent of farmers are over the age of 55, suggesting that there are not enough young farmers coming through to take the place of the previous workforce. While Canada is losing farmers of all ages, from 1991 to 2016, Manitoba and Ontario lost approximately 70 per cent of farmers under 35 years old (Statistics Canada, 2017a). Skyrocketing land prices, export-driven markets, related high input costs, and indebtedness are some of the constraints pushing youth away from agriculture (Qualman et al. 2018; Bihun and Desmarais 2024: 67).

In addition to the challenge of retaining youth, Canada also has disproportionately fewer farmers that are women. In 2016, 30 per cent of Ontario farmers were women compared to 24 per cent in Manitoba against a national figure of 29 per cent (Statistics Canada 2016b). These numbers are up slightly from 1991 (29 per cent, 22 per cent, and 26 per cent respectively), but women still face challenges in entering a sector that has been historically male dominated.

Young women farmer respondents

In Manitoba, we interviewed 16 young women farmers (35 per cent of the sample). Participants were selected using a combination of purposive, volunteer, and snowball methods in order to gain a diverse sample in terms of gender, types of production, and marketing strategies. Many of the young farmers volunteered to join our study by responding to an invitation that was shared on X (formerly Twitter), Facebook, and through the Keystone Agricultural Producers, the National Farmers Union, and the Agriculture Diploma programme at the University of Manitoba as well as via a news interview. In addition to semi-structured interviews, we used a standard questionnaire with all young women interviewed to provide information on demographics and land holding (size, ownership, and access to land). In Ontario, we interviewed 27 young women farmers (55 per cent of the sample),

Table 2.3 Profile of young women farmers interviewed, Canada

	Manitoba	Ontario	Canada
Number of female farmers	*16*	*27*	*43*
Mean age	33	34	33
% Married	63%	63%	63%
% With >12 years of education	94%	96%	95%
Average age started farming	19	19	19
Average age farming independently	27	26	26
% Working full-time	81%	85%	84%
% Primary income farming	75%	85%	81%
% Primary income – general farmer	0%	9%	6%
% Primary income – animal farmer	17%	39%	32%
% Primary income – plant farmer	83%	52%	63%
% Primary income – not farming	6%	0%	3%
% Farmers owning land	81%	67%	72%
Average acres owned	458	286	358
% Farmers who have inherited land	6%	0%	2%
Average acres inherited	160	0	160
% Farmers likely to inherit land	56%	41%	47%
Average acres likely to be inherited	1,417	97	718
% Farmers renting in land	75%	48%	58%
Average acres rented in	1,058	125	573
% Farmers sharing land	44%	19%	28%
Average acres shared	1,437	69	867

mainly in southern Ontario. Most of the interviews were conducted within 100 kilometres of the city of Guelph. Three research assistants, who were themselves farmers, conducted the interviews. Many of the farmers interviewed were found through their networks.

As shown in Table 2.3, the demographic information that we collected is fairly comparable for young women farmers in Ontario and Manitoba. The majority are married, work full-time, started farming after high school, and then began to farm independently a few years after completing their post-secondary education. Differences between the groups are related to the types of farming that they engage in as well as the size of their operations. Even though our samples are not representative, these differences are reflective of the types of farming in the respondents' respective provinces. Young women farmers in Ontario are more likely to have livestock while

Manitoba farmers are more likely to be grain farmers. It also appears that young women farmers in Manitoba tend to have more access to land than those in Ontario.[9] Consistent with the agrarian context in Ontario, young women farmers in the provincial sample have had a more difficult time accessing land than those in Manitoba.

Overall, these young women farmers are well educated and knowledgeable about their farms, and many are active members of their community, taking on roles as municipal councillors or industry board members as well as regularly attending conferences and community meetings. They are hard-working and exhibit a strong drive to succeed as farmers. They also demonstrate strong determination, confidence, and resilience – all qualities that help them as farmers and as they forge paths for themselves in male-dominated spaces.

However, consistent with the discussion in the previous sections, interviews with young women farmers reveal a number of persistent challenges for women who aspire to be successful farmers. In many instances, strongly held gender biases situate men as being more competent, capable, and qualified than women in this role. These biases influence ideas about who should farm and who should not, who should own land and farm-related businesses, and who are the qualified and legitimate leaders in the community. We must keep in mind that these are only the success stories of young women farmers. It is expected that there are countless stories of those who shied away from agriculture or who were unsuccessful in becoming a farmer, in part because they were women.

Despite the challenges that women face, in analysing these young women farmers' experiences, there are signs that gender relations are also shifting. Chapter 3 presents four case studies of young women farmers in Canada who participated in our study. Their experiences allow us to understand questions such as: What is driving young women to become farmers? What challenges have they faced along the way? And, what strategies are young women using in attempts to deal with these challenges?

Notes

1. A family farm corporation operates as a normal corporation. While there are higher accounting fees associated with being incorporated, these costs are often justified for farms due to the lower income tax rate that corporations pay.
2. 1 acre equals 0.4 hectares.
3. This piece shows that more women are becoming involved, but is not specifically about young women farmers.
4. The author uses 'he or she' in reference to the next generation, although the 'Key Concepts' section specifies that the successor is male as a reflection of 'the current practice in the majority of European farm family businesses' (Errington 1998: 124).

5. For their 2005 study, Heather et al. conducted research in three health regions in Alberta, Canada to identify the effects that farm women and rural community-based nurses perceive as stemming from 'recent structural and economic changes in agricultural land health sectors'. The team used semi-structured interviews with 34 rural women: 23 were married to farmers and 16 had grown up on farms. The latter were the focus of the resulting academic paper since they were both farm women and health care workers.

6. The study includes research conducted in nine different counties in southern Ontario, Canada that looks at the intersections of age and gender as barriers to young women farmers' visibility in the agricultural community. The study uses 15 semi-structured qualitative interviews with young women farmers between the ages of 18 and 35 who qualify as single farm operators on their farms.

7. Quota is a permit that authorizes a farmer to produce a certain quantity of a farm product over a certain period of time. Farmers must acquire quotas to produce and sell commodities in supply-managed industries. The marketing board for that specific industry coordinates the distribution and management of quotas. In Canada, these industries include chicken, egg, turkey, and dairy (cows only).

8. Alternative agriculture or sustainable agriculture loosely denotes a set of farming practices and philosophy that contrasts conventional or industrial farming practices. Alternative agricultural operations are typically small-scale productions.

9. In general, land ownership is relatively high in this sample as those who were interviewed have found a way to be a successful farmer. It should be noted that this result does not mean that land costs are not a barrier for most new farmers wanting to gain entry to the sector.

References

4-H Canada (2018) 'About 4-H Canada'. https://4-h-canada.ca/about

Agriculture and Agri-Food Canada (2010) *2009 Dialogue tour on young farmers and farm transfers*. https://publicentrale-ext.agr.gc.ca/pubview-pubaffi-chage-eng.cfm?publicationid=10545B

Ahearn, M.C. (2016) 'Theme overview: Addressing the challenges of entry into farming'. *Choices* 31(4): 1–4. http://dx.doi.org/10.22004/ag.econ.246157

Avelar, A. (2019) *[In]visible: Where are young women farmers? Investigating in a Canadian context*. Master's thesis, University of Guelph. http://hdl.handle.net/10214/16071

Belshaw, J.D. (2016) *Canadian history: Post-confederation*. Victoria: BCcampus. https://opentextbc.ca/postconfederation/

Bihun, H., and Desmarais, A. (2024) '"Regenerating" agriculture: Becoming a young farmer in Manitoba, Canada'. In S. Srinivasan (ed.), *Becoming a young farmer: Young people's pathways into farming: Canada, China, India, and Indonesia*, pp. 65–91, Palgrave Macmillan. https://link.springer.com/book/10.1007/978-3-031-15233-7

CBC News: The National (2017) 'New crop of young farmers emerging'. YouTube [Video, 02:00]. CBC News: The National. https://www.youtube.com/watch?v=dpgTBS6aBJw&t=55s

Chambers, L. (2010) 'Women's labour, relationship breakdown and ownership of the family farm'. *Canadian Journal of Law and Society* 25(1): 75–95.

Chicken Farmers of Ontario (2017) 'New entrant chicken processors policy', 4 October [online]. https://www.ontariochicken.ca/Programs/New-Entrant-Chicken-Farmer-Program.aspx

Dairy Farmers of Ontario (2017) 'New entrant program'. https://new.milk.org/all-documents/new-entrant-quota-assistance-program-2/

Epp, S. (2017) 'Barriers to new and young farmers'. Presented at the *2017 Bring Food Home Conference, Ottawa, 27-28 October 2017*. https://sustainontario.com/greenhouse/resource/new%e2%80%8b-%e2%80%8band%e2%80%8b-%e2%80%8byoung%e2%80%8b-%e2%80%8bfarmers/

Errington, A. (1998) 'The intergenerational transfer of managerial control in the farm-family business: A comparative study of England, France and Canada'. *The Journal of Agricultural Education and Extension* 5(2): 123–36. https://doi.org/10.1080/13892249885300241

Fletcher, A.J. (2013) *The view from here: Agricultural policy, climate change, and the future of farm women in Saskatchewan*. PhD thesis, University of Regina, Canada. https://ourspace.uregina.ca/items/4249da18-26bb-4623-8d5e-26e09814006b

Forbes-Chilibeck, E. (2005) 'Have you heard the one about the farmer's daughter? Gender bias in the intergenerational transfer of farm land on the Canadian prairies'. *Canadian Woman Studies* 24(4): 26–35.

Government of Manitoba Agriculture (2017) 'Manitoba: Agricultural profile, 2016 census' [online archived]. https://web.archive.org/web/20170718230100/https://www.gov.mb.ca/agriculture/market-prices-and-statistics/yearbook-and-state-of-agriculture/pubs/census-of-agriculture-mb-profile.pdf

Government of Ontario, Ontario Ministry of Food, Agriculture, and Rural Affairs (OMAFRA) (2016) 'Average net operating income per farm, Ontario, 1991–2016' [online]. https://data.ontario.ca/dataset/average-net-operating-income-by-farm-and-township

Hall, A., and Mogyorody, V. (2007) 'Organic farming, gender, and the labor process'. *Rural Sociology* 72(2): 289–316. https://doi.org/10.1526/003601107781170035

Heather, B., Skillen, L., Young, J., and Vladicka, T. (2005) 'Women's gendered identities and the restructuring of rural Alberta'. *Sociologia Ruralis* 45(1–2): 86–97. https://doi.org/10.1111/j.1467-9523.2005.00292.x

Junior Farmers Association of Ontario (2013) *Data summary of 2013 new farmer survey*. http://slideplayer.com/slide/11686578/

Knibb, H. (2012) *Learning to become a farmer: Findings from a FarmON Alliance survey of new farmers in Ontario*. Food Secure Canada. https://canadacommons.ca/artifacts/2087715/learning-to-become-a-farmer/2843013/

Krug, K. (2003) 'Farm women and local alternatives to globalized agriculture'. *Canadian Woman Studies* 23(1): 129–34.

Laforge, J., Fenton, A., Lavalée-Picard, V., and McLachlan, S. (2018) 'New farmers and food policies in Canada'. *Canadian Food Studies* 5(3): 128–52. https://doi.org/10.15353/cfs-rcea.v5i3.288

Leavy, J. and Smith, S. (2010) *Future farmers: Youth aspirations, expectations and life choices*. Discussion Paper 013, Future Agricultures Consortium. https://www.ids.ac.uk/download.php?file=files/dmfile/FAC_Discussion_Paper_013FutureFarmers.pdf

Leckie, G. (1993) 'Female farmers in Canada and the gender relations of a restructuring agricultural system'. *The Canadian Geographer* 37(3): 212–30. https://doi.org/10.1111/j.1541-0064.1993.tb00298.x

Martz, D.J.F. (2006) *Canadian farm women and their families: Restructuring, work and decision making*. PhD thesis, University of Saskatchewan, Canada. http://hdl.handle.net/10388/etd-04252006-231636

Martz, D.J.F., and Brueckner, I.S. (2003) *The Canadian farm family at work: Exploring gender and generation*. Centre For Rural Studies and Enrichment; National Farmers Union. https://www.grain.org/article/entries/3704-the-canadian

Mills, E.N. (2013) *The political economy of young prospective farmers' access to farmland: Insights from industrialised agriculture in Canada*. Major Research Paper, International Institute of Social Studies, Erasmus University Rotterdam. http://hdl.handle.net/2105/15215

Moyles, T. (2018) *Women who dig: Farming, feminism, and the fight to feed the world*. Regina: University of Regina Press.

Ngo, M., and Brklacich, M. (2014) 'New farmers' efforts to create a sense of place in rural communities: Insights from southern Ontario, Canada'. *Agriculture and Human Values* 31(1): 53–67. https://doi.org/10.1007/s10460-013-9447-5

Parent, D. (2012) 'Social isolation among young farmers in Quebec, Canada'. Presented at the *10th European Symposium of the International Systems Farming Association, Aarhus, Denmark, July 1–4*. http://ifsa.boku.ac.at/cms/fileadmin/Proceeding2012/IFSA2012WS3.2Parent.pdf

Pouliot, S. (2011) *The beginning farmers' problem in Canada*. SPAA Network Working paper #2011-9. Québec: SPAA Network. https://ageconsearch.umn.edu/bitstream/118019/2/Beginning%20farmers%20-%20Pouliot%20Nov%202011.pdf

Price, L. (2012) 'The emergence of rural support organisations in the UK and Canada: Providing support for patrilineal family farming'. *Sociologia Ruralis* 52(33): 353–76. https://doi.org/10.1111/j.1467-9523.2012.00568.x

Qualman, D., Akram-Lodhi, H., Desmarais, A., and Srinivasan, S. (2018) 'Forever young? The crisis of generational renewal on Canada's farms'. *Canadian Food Studies* 5(3): 100–27. https://doi.org/10.15353/cfs-rcea.v5i3.284

Robinson, D. (2003) 'Prepared for success: A look at the next generation of Alberta farmers'. Presented at the *14th International Farm Management Association Congress, Perth, Australia, 10–15 August 2003*. https://www.ifma.network/content/large/documents/2014/07/Robinson.pdf

Shortall, S. (1999) *Women and farming: Property and power*. London: Macmillan.

Smith, P. (1986) '"Not enough hours, our accountant tells me": Trends in children's, women's and men's involvement in Canadian agriculture'. *Canadian Journal of Agricultural Economics/Revue Canadienne d'agroeconomie* 33: 161–95. https://onlinelibrary.wiley.com/doi/10.1111/j.1744-7976.1985.tb03255.x

Statistics Canada (2016a) 'Farm operators classified by number of operators per farm and sex'. Table 32-10-0441-01. https://www150.statcan.gc.ca/t1/tbl1/en/tv.action?pid=3210044101

Statistics Canada (2016b) 'Number of farm operators by sex, age and paid non-farm work, historical data'. Table 32-10-0169-01. https://www150.statcan.gc.ca/t1/tbl1/en/tv.action?pid=3210016901

Statistics Canada (2017a) '2016 census of agriculture'. The Daily. http://www. statcan.gc.ca/daily-quotidien/170510/dq170510a-eng.htm

Statistics Canada (2017b) 'Dictionary, census of population, 2016: Farm operator'. http://www12.statcan.gc.ca/census-recensement/2016/ref/dict/pop032-eng.cfm

Statistics Canada (2017c) 'A portrait of a 21st century agricultural operation'. https://www.statcan.gc.ca/pub/95-640-x/2016001/article/14811-eng.htm

Statistics Canada (2017d) 'Canadian agriculture: Evolution and innovation. Contribution of the agricultural sector to the economy', 14 November. https://www150.statcan.gc.ca/n1/pub/11-631-x/11-631-x2017006-eng.htm

Statistics Canada (2019) 'Agriculture and agri-food economic account, 2015'. The Daily. https://www150.statcan.gc.ca/n1/daily-quotidien/190730/dq190730a-eng.htm

Sumner, J. (2005) '"Small is beautiful". The responses of women organic farmers to the crisis in agriculture'. *Canadian Woman Studies* 24(4): 78–84.

Tanner, B. (1999) *The entrepreneurial characteristics of farm women*. New York and London: Garland Publishing.

Van de Vorst, C. (2002) *Making ends meet: Farm women's work in Manitoba*. Winnipeg: University of Manitoba Press.

Weldon, T. (2016) 'More new farmers are women than men in Atlantic Canada, study shows'. *CBC News*, 6 May 2016. http://www.cbc.ca/news/canada/new-brunswick/farmers-women-atlantic-1.3571369

Whatmore, S. (1991) *Farming women: Gender, work and family enterprise*. London: Macmillan Academic and Professional Ltd.

Wiebe, N. (2017) 'Crisis in the food system. The farm crisis'. In M. Koc, J. Sumner, and A. Winson (eds), *Critical perspectives in food studies*, 2nd edn, pp. 138–53. Don Mills, ON: Oxford University Press Canada.

CHAPTER 3

Becoming visible: Stories of young women farmers in Canada

Hannah Bihun, Annette Aurélie Desmarais, Nicola Inglefield, Travis Jansen, and Sharada Srinivasan

This chapter offers glimpses into the life histories of four young women farmers in Canada – two each from Manitoba and Ontario – to shed light on the following questions: What is driving young women to become farmers? What challenges do they face in becoming and being farmers? What strategies are young women using in attempts to deal with these challenges? We conclude by reflecting on what these four case studies tell us about the social relations and conditions in which young women are farming in Canada.

Martha, a small-scale, new entrant in Manitoba

Martha is a 32-year-old mixed livestock farmer in Manitoba. She grew up in the city of Winnipeg – 'a fourth-generation Winnipegger'. Her mother was a stay-at-home mum with Martha and her three siblings, and her father was a schoolteacher. Growing up in the province's largest city, Martha didn't have much exposure to farming or agriculture in general, but she does have fond childhood memories of numerous road trips to the countryside with her family. Often, these trips were to visit her grandparents' cottage or towns in rural Manitoba to attend summer festivals or to simply enjoy the scenery of Manitoba's seemingly endless wheat fields.

Despite her urban upbringing, at the age of 25, Martha made the decision to become a farmer. Today, she farms with her partner on 1,124 acres of land where they practice holistic management of cattle, sheep, hogs, poultry, and laying hens.[1] Martha said her decision to farm was primarily a result of meeting her partner, who, although also a new entrant to farming, did have some experience in growing food. For example, he had laying hens while growing up in an urban neighbourhood overseas, and he also worked on several farms in Canada before the couple began farming together. Although meeting her partner certainly assisted her in becoming a farmer, Martha explained that for some time, farming had been in the back of her mind as a hopeful possibility for her future.

Martha's motivation to farm was driven by many factors, including a desire to produce good food for people in an environmentally sound and socially conscious manner: 'The food is good – a big focus of trying to farm this way and repair the mineral cycle or the water cycle without using a bunch of inputs. I think if people can see it and feel good about it then we don't have to feel like ... we're not trying to sell something that we don't believe in. It feels good.'

She also wanted to be her own boss, live in close proximity to nature, and be part of the supportive environment of rural communities:

> You find there's a lot more support in a rural community. When you first start, you don't know a lot of people so building that social capital, that feels kind of daunting and difficult. But then once you have it, you realize you don't stress about the same things. You don't feel so stressed about, if my pigs need feed and I need to unload this grain and my equipment isn't working, you need to realize that you're set up to do this but you also have your neighbours.

Prior to farming, Martha attended graduate school and conducted international research on issues related to natural resources. Although not directly related to farming, the education and experience that she received at university gave her some important skills in terms of thinking critically, being organized, managing a timeline, problem solving, and perhaps most importantly, building rapport with people. However, she emphasized that her university education did not provide her with many of the practical skills that she needed to farm successfully. As a young, new entrant, Martha learned about farming through grazing management school and social media, but most importantly, she learned through other people in the farm community: 'Everyone we've ever worked for, or with, has taught us quite a bit. And it doesn't happen, things don't happen in isolation. You don't just learn about cattle when you're working on a cattle ranch, [at the same time] you learn how to run the baler and how to fix fences.'

One such important influence is an older farmer with whom Martha and her partner have developed a relationship, first by renting and then subsequently purchasing some of his land. This is a farmer who practises many of the same farm strategies and holds some of the same philosophical principles as Martha herself. Since he is reaching retirement age and is without a successor, they are in the process of developing a succession plan so that Martha and her partner will slowly acquire his farm at a price that works for both parties. This relationship has benefited Martha tremendously as it has enabled her to acquire some of the knowledge that is usually missing in new entrants, but that a young farmer who comes from a farming family would have normally accessed by virtue of day-to-day living and working on the land or through interactions with parents and grandparents. The relationship with this older farmer has also provided the young couple with access to more machinery than they would otherwise have been able to afford. Importantly, the arrangement is mutually beneficial in that the older farmer is able to pass on his life's work to two young farmers who are prepared to take over and continue the farm for many years.

Farming is a complex profession that requires many skills and a lot of knowledge. Martha explained that it would be very difficult for only one person to have all of the skills needed to keep a farm running, but by working together with her partner, she has found a system that highlights each of their strengths and breaks up the work to make it possible. While they share in the daily tasks in terms of animal husbandry, Martha takes care of most of the business side of the farm. She does the marketing, accounting, and keeps track of the inventory going out, while her partner manages the on-farm inventory including the hay and fencing supplies, for example. He has also taken classes to learn to weld so that they can fix machinery and do basic repairs on the farm.

Together they are able to run the farm without much outside help. Overall, Martha and her partner have had limited access to government services and resources mainly because the established criteria and conditions for accessing these are not set up to serve a small-scale farm like theirs. Instead, they rely on the wisdom of the older or more experienced farmers that they have met along the way to help with problem solving and to keep learning and growing as young farmers. Over time she has fostered many positive connections in her farm community, but she admits that as a new entrant to farming, it has not been easy to build the necessary social and financial capital to have a successful farm operation and lifestyle.

Martha and her partner have kept their farm small for ideological and practical reasons:

> If we deplete the resource, we can't just go buy more land. We can't afford it. So, we have to make sure that we're doing something that is low input, but that can be sustained over the long term ... We care about it too. We have philosophical reasons for wanting to do it this way. But being incredibly practical, we have to farm this way. We can't afford equipment, we can't afford inputs, we have to farm this way.

Operating on a small scale and using few inputs is a business model that has enabled Martha to enter agriculture without any previous ties to a farm in Manitoba, an increasingly difficult task given the significant financial investment required to start a farm. However, keeping it small does come with its drawbacks, especially as a new entrant with limited access to capital: 'Access to financing is probably one of the biggest – is that the biggest? Yeah right now our biggest challenge is access to financing because what we're doing is not really considered viable, even though our tax returns say otherwise. So, financing is a big one.'

Martha produces eggs and poultry that are regulated under supply management in Manitoba. This adds to the financial burdens that she already faces as a young new entrant to farming because there are a number of regulations imposed on farmers producing these products, which can lead to incurring additional costs. In general, the regulations prioritize larger-scale operations and do not sufficiently consider the unique requirements of small-scale operations that are producing for local and direct marketing: 'We support supply management as a national protection ... but it's not set up appropriately for new entrants who are also having tenure issues and/or financing issues to get in. Other than that, I would say also that for anyone who is direct marketing, a lot of the regulations are set up for big industry so they're not really scale appropriate.'

She and her partner market all of their farm products directly to consumers, a choice that she says has helped them to keep the farm running, even with limited access to financing.

Martha also struggles with the gender inequalities that persist in rural farm communities. She believes that it would have been quite difficult for her to begin farming without a male partner by her side: '[My partner] could probably have started this on his own, I don't think I would have been able to access the social capital in the same way had I been a single woman.'

From her experience, the rural social structure can be quite isolating, especially for women farmers who are trying to work and live in a male-dominated field. Direct marketing and getting involved in farm organizations has helped her to combat this isolation; however, it's still difficult being one of the few women in her group of farming peers:

> Despite what people think or want to think, it is not easy for women in a rural context, even in Canada ... I don't think the challenges are the same [for men and women] and even in a household, I don't think they're the same. I think isolation is hard. For me, as a woman, I would say I may be more isolated. Well, it's hard, I do the direct-marketing so maybe I'm less isolated, but I am more [isolated] than [my partner is] from our farming peers because they're mostly men.

Additionally, Martha spoke about the challenges all farmers and rural communities face as policy and policymakers often do not have their best interests in mind. She is not idly waiting for things to change; she was elected into the national leadership of a national farm organization and has worked to make meaningful changes for farmers in Manitoba. Although she was initially reluctant to join a national organization, she has found that it provided much welcomed support that helped combat the social isolation that she often feels as a young woman farmer. It also provided her with a platform to advocate for positive change in the farm community at large. Because she has experienced first-hand the inequalities in the current agricultural system from the perspective of a small-scale farmer, Martha has worked directly and enthusiastically on supply management reform to create more scale-appropriate regulations for Manitoba farmers.

When asked if she considers herself to be a successful farmer, Martha said she believes that she and her partner have developed a model that is successful, replicable, and importantly, it has allowed them to make a living without having to work off-farm: '[Although] our families haven't funded this, [and] we didn't have external investment, this makes money ... Our income is probably below the poverty line [but] there are lots of perks to farming and we're making it work.... I would say ... this is a replicable model.'

This replicability is important to Martha as she is very aware of the declining population of young farmers in Manitoba and the overall need for more young and new farmers for the future of agriculture in the country. By choosing to exclusively direct market her products, the couple's farm is a stable operation as it is much less vulnerable to market fluctuations than a farm selling through conventional markets. This provides her with a sense of stability and optimism for their future in farming.

In summary, Martha has been working at becoming a successful farmer for a decade, and she is now in a place where she is able to make a living from farming and has also become a leader for young farmers through policy development and advocacy in a national farm organization. She developed a replicable model for new entrants to farming that could help enable entry into farming for young people who are interested, but who have fewer supports than somebody who comes from a family farm. This model prioritizes the farmer–consumer relationship by using direct marketing to allow these relationships to flourish, while also providing flexibility and financial stability for their small farm. Martha and her partner are challenging the traditional view of succession by building a meaningful relationship with an older farmer to whom they are not related. This innovation has led to a new vision of succession that enables older farmers without successors to pass on their farms to young people ready and willing to farm, but who would otherwise have limited access to land and machinery. This is an important step for the future of agriculture in Canada as more and more farmers are without successors and the number of young farmers in the country continues to plummet. Along the way, Martha certainly has faced many barriers, as most young new entrants do, but she used ingenuity, imagination, and perseverance to create a role for herself in the farm community as an advocate for change and a role model for new and aspiring young farmers of the future.

Kaitlyn, a continuing, conventional farmer in Manitoba

Kaitlyn is a 29-year-old conventional grain farmer. She grew up on a multi-generation mixed grain and livestock farm in Manitoba, where she currently farms 5,000 acres with her father and brother. Before she was even old enough to help out on the farm, she remembers her mother packing a lunch for her and sending her off to spend the day with her father on the farm. The time with her dad was her first exposure to farmwork and piqued her interest in farming at a very young age:

> Even when I was really little, before [I was] 7 years old, my mom … she would pack us a backpack, whoever was going. I'd have my little backpack, it was blue, and I had activities if I got bored – I had my little markers, I had a colouring book, I had snacks, hat, sunscreen. We were gone for the day. No matter if it was in a combine or in a semi-truck … it was the only time that I hung out with my dad because he was always so busy. It seemed cool, and I knew at a young age that, that house stuff was for the birds. Why would you be in there when you could be outside?

However, Kaitlyn did not always enjoy farmwork. Once she was a bit older, she was expected to help out on the farm; she remembered one summer when an employee quit unexpectedly and she had to step up and help her father bale hay:

> I don't recall how it went down exactly but I just remember it being like 'ok, you're going to learn how to bale!' And me thinking it was going to be the funniest thing ever and it actually being a nightmare! I still am really short so I can't reach any pedals or anything, but I remember the tractor, I remember the smell, like muscle memory pulling the gear shift back, it sounds crazy! So, it was a lot of good 12, 14-hour days, and that's just not how I pictured my summer. I kicked and screamed every day, I'd make myself so upset I'd throw up. My father still made me go out there because – we had to go.

Kaitlyn has a brother who is six years younger than her, so growing up she worked alongside her dad much more than her brother did, and consequently she benefited from this first-hand on-farm experience. This led her to recognize, at an early age, that farming was a part of who she was and this set her apart from many of her peers: 'High school was when I really started to realize that I was a little bit different from most of my friends. There were farm girls I was friends with, but they weren't as involved, I guess, they just lived on a farm … So, when high school came around, their priorities were a lot different than mine.'

After high school, Kaitlyn went to university to study pharmacy, with the intent of farming part-time; however, she quickly learned that both city life and the pharmacy programme were not for her. In the city she felt isolated, and the burden of studying while also trying to balance the expense and transition of living on her own proved to be too much. Kaitlyn returned home after her first year at university and took a summer job at the local co-op where her family farm purchased some of their agricultural inputs. While employed there, she met a number of great contacts, including a woman agronomist who inspired her to return to university and focus on agriculture:

> The first year [working at the co-op] was really nice, I met this super awesome agronomist, she was so smart. She was a bit older but was a

really good mentor. Super particular and just on top of her game. And I thought, 'oh, this kind of seems cool. Maybe I'll take some ag courses'. So, I took electives, maybe one or two electives and then I took a bunch of ag courses and courses that would transfer into agriculture. Within a week or two of school, I was like, 'Oh man, this is where I should have been all along' … You don't know people, but people are smiling at you. When they see you for a second time, they approach you.

Throughout her university degree, she worked two summers operating farm machinery for the co-op. The third summer, she knew somebody connected with Monsanto and landed a summer job as a salesperson. After graduation, she returned to the Monsanto job but when faced with the option to take that position full-time, she decided against it and instead Kaitlyn moved to Australia for the winter to work on some custom combining crews.[2] When she returned from Australia, she went back to her family farm. Today, she farms while also working as an agronomist.

As a young woman farmer, Kaitlyn has faced a lot of discrimination and has had to fight for respect from men in the industry. When asked if she believes that women face different challenges than men, she responded with an emphatic, 'yes', and reflected on various times when she has been dismissed:

> I think it's unbelievably harder. I'm 5'2", I have blonde hair, I am somewhat athletic, fit, or whatever … A lot of the times, people write me off instantly. I jump off a machine and I come to their shoulders, and instantly done; a small percentage of people have written me off forever. Some people warm up quickly once they see I know what I'm talking about. But you are constantly battling a preconceived notion of yourself, by your appearance, by what you say … Sometimes I find I have to be bossy or argumentative to get my point across to people. Probably every day you run into the concept of an old boy's club, where it's a man's world. Some people just do not want to deal with a woman, at the end of the day. And especially an outspoken one because you can't be paper floating in the wind in agriculture, you can't just be on the fence, you have to know what you think is right or wrong. When you're making your recommendations, making your own decisions, you have to know what you think.

Even at home, Kaitlyn struggles with gendered expectations as she balances all of the things she needs to get done in a day:

> Women are expected to do more things in the same amount of time, like all women are. Whether it is cleaning the house, or walking the dog, cooking is kind of a shareable thing, but the cleaning is the one that really gets us. I was just talking to my girlfriend … she hired a housecleaner and I could not believe it. She said it's the best decision she's ever made in her life … Just in the fact it freed up so much of her time. So, I think that there are lots of times that my list never ends, and my boyfriend's does.

Discrimination does not only occur because Kaitlyn is a woman; she has also faced a number of challenges as a young person attempting to establish herself as an independent farmer within her family farm corporation.[3] Being considered independently from the family farm would allow her to more readily access provincial and federal financial support offered to young farmers. Lenders such as Farm Credit Canada and Manitoba Agricultural Services Corporation (MASC) also offer low interest loans or young farmer rebates. But, as she explained, while these types of programmes claim to help young farmers, their support is quite limited as it often comes with restrictive conditions:

> Insurance, particularly MASC crop insurance, they try and claim that they support young farmers. For instance, MASC gives you a young farmer rebate, but also when you want to borrow money from them you get a reduced interest rate. I'm pretty sure I would get a little bit of a better rate on my crop insurance as well as if I was to borrow money from MASC specifically, I would get a reduced interest rate. But they cap it. Their cap gives you like 100 acres. You can't get a section [640 acres] with it! ... Crop insurance also makes it extremely difficult for young farmers to get their own insurance policy, separate from their parents' corporation. I think I spent three hours trying to prove it to the guy, and the guy knows me! I understand that they have to have regulations and policies, but at the end of the day, the majority of the business we deal with, in general, are trying to pass any blame onto someone else, capture profit ... It doesn't make any sense to me why they would make it so hard. You have to prove you have your own bins. Sometimes that isn't the case! Sometimes you own one bin in a row of your family's bins.

Government programmes are also falling short when it comes to enabling young people to begin or continue to farm. The lack of efficient support contributes to the various struggles young farmers are facing with building capital and managing cash flow, something that Kaitlyn is no stranger to: 'I haven't taken a wage from the farm in, oh, ten years maybe. So, for me it's just, I'm investing it back in, right? You've talked to a lot of people that are that way that barely take anything out of their farm, right? You give up everything, right? It's your life. It's not really a job.'

She has worked to build a reputation for herself in the farming community based on her ability, knowledge, and skills as a farmer. However, she indicated that she often feels socially isolated because many of her acquaintances are not farmers and therefore often do not understand the demanding schedule associated with farming successfully. This challenge is perhaps exacerbated by the fact that Kaitlyn does not know any other young women farmers in her rural area. She has, on occasion, met other young women farmers at conferences, but she does not regularly attend meetings or conferences of farm organizations, so these connections are limited.

Despite the struggles she has faced as a young woman farmer, Kaitlyn considers herself to be a successful farmer, who she described as someone who finds joy in farming and who is not bankrupt. However, she recognizes that for young farmers to be successful, they need to have support – and without that support she does not believe it is possible for young people to farm. Her family always made sure that they could speak openly with one another about succession planning and she will eventually acquire the family farm from her parents at a reduced rate. Although Kaitlyn has no illusions about the reality of a life in farming – one that is all at once demanding, draining, and often thankless – she loves farming, and for that reason, she feels optimistic about her future as a farmer.

Naomi, a small-scale, Community Supported Agriculture, continuing farmer in Ontario

Naomi is a young woman farmer in her late 20s who has been farming for most of her life. Naomi and her family do not come from a long line of farmers. No one in their family's recent past was involved in agriculture in any way. Naomi's father was a social worker before transitioning to full-time work on the farm and her mother has a home hairdressing business that supplements her farm work. Currently, Naomi and her three siblings (two sisters and a brother) all work part-time, in-season on the farm.

Naomi was just five years old when her parents moved from the city to purchase a 5-acre farm. After a few years on the land, when Naomi was about eight, the family began growing food for themselves and their community; a humble start, growing food for about 10 households. Since then, the farm has expanded in both acreage and production. Naomi's family is now in their 25th year on the farm. The family farm has grown to 25 acres (plus an additional 15 acres of rented land) and supplies vegetables to over 140 households during the summer growing season. In addition, the farm produces pastured meats (pork, beef, and chicken), eggs, and field crops, all of which are used on-farm or sold through a Community Supported Agriculture (CSA) programme, one farmers' market, and an on-farm store. They are considering adding wholesale clients as well. The land is farmed following the principles of organic agriculture as well as incorporating permaculture[4] practices into the land stewardship model, such as the development of swales[5] for water conservation.

In their part of south-western Ontario, the farm's complement of scale, land management practices, and products are unique. Most of the surrounding farms are large-scale, conventional farms raising dairy or beef cattle, or growing vast acreages of conventional cash crops (corn, soy, and wheat). A few other farms in the area, some of whom attend the same farmers' market, are at a similar scale but either only raise livestock or grow vegetables, not both; many of these farms do not follow organic practices.

Naomi has been actively involved in the farm business since she was 14 years old. As the farm grew and labour demands increased, Naomi and her siblings were called on more and more to help out on the farm, working part-time in the summers when they were out of school, earning an hourly wage for their work. Living on a farm close to an urban centre and going to school with city kids put Naomi and her siblings at odds with the other students at her school; it was simply not cool to be farming. So, they hid this part of their life from their friends. This tension between an urban school and rural home caused a rift between a young Naomi and the farm; especially during the high school years when she felt disconnected from her farm life. However, with high school completed, Naomi (reluctantly) began taking on a management role on the farm with great encouragement from and in close collaboration with her father. At this time, the majority of the other workers on the farm were older than her. As a young woman, she felt placed in a difficult position, being called on to have more knowledge and confidence than she felt she had at the time and found herself questioning whether she was being taken seriously by the farm's other employees.

Though Naomi did not feel completely confident at first, taking on this role and inheriting some duties from her father opened her up to a community of people – young people – who were also farming. Of this time, Naomi observed: 'It seemed to be at the same time when there was a growing community of farmers that I hadn't known about before, and was like, "this is cool, there are other young people doing this, sort of a movement starting". And it felt like a good thing to be a part of.' These newfound connections helped Naomi recognize how much she has always truly enjoyed farmwork and the inherent value in it: 'Meeting other people my age who were doing it also made it easier to realize what I was doing was good work and I enjoyed it, despite the fact that I had been pretending not to for the sake of being cool.' Within this community, Naomi can fully express her farmer identity but, to this day, she still chooses to hold back parts of her farming life from old school friends.

As a young woman farmer, Naomi feels well supported by her community. Networks such as the National Farmers Union, the Collaborative Regional Alliance for Farmer Training, and the Ecological Farmers Association of Ontario provide Naomi with a sense of community, support, and access to great swaths of agricultural and rural knowledge through relationships with peers, workshops, and farm tours: 'there's just a lot of support and people on the same page'. Although Naomi occasionally hears whispers of ageist and/or sexist ideas expressed in her community, she reports she does not experience age- or gender-related discrimination often; she thinks this might be due to her farm's proximity to a city and believes women in more rural settings may not have the same experience.

Bolstering the positive in-person community connections, there are vast virtual communities of support and knowledge exchange on social media platforms (such as Facebook) where reliable, helpful information and creative innovations are abundant and easily available. These resources play a valuable supportive role on Naomi's farm. While they are tapped into some key online resources, Naomi truly considers herself and her family to be 'not very techy'; they use very little technology in the field, avoiding the use of cell phones for example. They, of course, see the benefits of using some technology; behind the scenes, there is a farm website, a farm Facebook page, an Instagram account, and they use online database software to aid in managing their CSA programme.

After working on the farm for a full season, Naomi left to complete an undergraduate degree in International Development with a focus on rural agriculture. For Naomi, this seemed like the right and normal path to take: 'I went to university because that was just the mentality of the high school I went to and the friends that I had ... that was what you did; there wasn't another option really.' While away on an international internship (between Mexico and New Brunswick), Naomi had a revelation: 'At that point, that's when I started to realize I loved the idea of, you know, doing work in other countries but ... I kept looping back to my own rural community and that's where I could make the biggest difference and that's where I want[ed] to invest my energy.' Naomi returned, brimming with knowledge about community development, alternative energies, and sustainable agriculture as well as a strong drive to take on more responsibility on the farm and implement some of these new ideas.

With a few more seasons of experience, combined with her father's ongoing support, Naomi blossomed into her managerial role. She now manages the entire vegetable operation, fully embraces her farmer identity, and feels great pride in the farm's produce. Naomi feels immense gratitude for how things have worked out for her:

> I think I've just been really lucky with how all the pieces have fit together with the farming family, Dad being very supportive of going off to school, having that experience, finding my way on my own back to the farm, and being able to use the farm to explore what I want to do creatively ... It's not like my dad and mum have designed this system and I come in and manage the way that they want; it's always been an open discussion of how can we change things and add things and do all this ... I've been pretty privileged on that front.

Currently, every member of the family plays a role on the farm, one that speaks to their particular interests and passions. Naomi's father is the farm's only full-time, year-round employee – he stopped working off-farm about seven years ago. He manages the farm business (including all the finances), makes the major year-to-year decisions (in collaboration with the rest of the family), and takes on the farm's biggest projects as well as tending the field crops, pastures, and livestock. Naomi's mother runs her home business, while also taking care of the barn chores and the farm's administrative tasks. Naomi works part-time, in-season and shares management of the vegetable operation with her younger sister. Her other sister works for the farm two days a week, doing fieldwork one day and managing their website and social media the other. Naomi's brother, who is still in high school, does part-time work on the farm during the summer.

Naomi and her siblings secure off-farm work during the off-season and to supplement their part-time, in-season farm employment. Typically, Naomi's income is split about 50-50 between the farm and off-farm work. She explains: 'I have not found a way to secure off-season income yet. That is probably the most challenging thing for me [about farming]. I don't like having to get a second job, but it's been necessary.' Looking to the future, Naomi's goal is to take over more of the farm business and to find innovative strategies for the farm to employ her 12 months of the year, such as diversifying the farm's enterprises and income streams.

With the goal of increasing farm revenue to provide more employment to the family, one current topic of concern for Naomi's family farm is declining customer retention rates. The cause for this decline cannot be clearly attributed to any one factor; however, some CSA farmers speculate it may be due to consumer attitudes about the value of food and food prices, along with the growing availability of organic produce through mainstream grocery retailers. Naomi sees customer interactions as holding great potential for educating their community about what they do, and the farm's direct-marketing model naturally creates opportunities for these educational farmer–customer interactions. Further, though most of the farm's marketing is done in a similar fashion (that is, by word of mouth and other low-tech means), social media is playing an increasingly important role in spreading the word about the farm's offerings. While the farm has not focused very much on marketing and advertising to date, they see the need to put more energy here now.

Despite a recent decline in customer retention, Naomi's farm is well-supported and appreciated by their community, both for the food they produce and their community-building efforts. For Naomi's family, it is important to hold a space for people to connect with nature, agriculture, and the people growing their food. Having the farm store on site, hosting on-farm events, and participating in off-farm community events creates opportunities for these connections to flourish. These connections have spurred many mutually supportive relationships in Naomi's farming community: 'I really admire a lot of the farmers around us, the big dairy farmers. I think what they're doing is really incredible.' She goes on to say: 'So you know sometimes when they come to visit, I get self-conscious about how many weeds are in my field, things like that. But normally, they come to show appreciation that we're working so hard.' These strong relationship ties within rural and agricultural communities can provide great supports beyond emotional/moral support. In the case of Naomi's family farm, there are various bartering relationships with neighbours, including a trade of vegetables for a parcel of rented land and another in exchange for tractor maintenance services.

Beyond customer retention concerns, Naomi's family farm faces a myriad other challenges that strain the farm's finances. In particular, in southern Ontario, many of the last few seasons have brought atypical weather and climate patterns. For Naomi's family farm, access to water has become an ongoing challenge, having had their well run dry on more than one occasion. Despite their best efforts, the farm has experienced difficult financial struggles during these tough years, especially during the recent droughts in this area. In poor-producing years, they cannot rely on crop insurance (due to the farm's size and crop make-up) to mitigate their losses; in such seasons, finances become tight as investments made in the beginning of the year do not pay off as hoped or expected.

For Naomi's family, farm succession is still many years away. However, they have begun proactive discussions around inheritance of the farm, the farm business, and the two other properties Naomi's parents own. These early conversations indicate that assets will be split evenly between the four siblings, with each person's involvement in the farm and farm business to be determined based on individual interest and capacity.

Naomi and her partner (who does not work on the farm but aspires to) recently pooled their personal resources to purchase a small property for themselves near the family farm – a 5-acre parcel that offers Naomi a short commute to her job at the farm. Although close by, this parcel is separate from the family farm and none of the farm's production currently happens at this location.

In order to continue building and improving on her successes to date, Naomi sees areas where her knowledge (as well as that of her peers) can be strengthened. She suggested that young farmers need help in a few key areas: financing, business and financial planning mentorship, and an accommodating policy environment. Naomi sees government and non-governmental organizations each having a role in providing some of these supports and learning opportunities. In addition to formalized supports, Naomi believes that building social capital and having a strong system of support is also essential to success: 'I really think it's about not biting off more than you can chew. Just really realizing it's going to be a slow process and not trying to take on too much at the start, and tapping into your local networks, and not being afraid to ask for help or support or to borrow machinery or any of those things ... and play into your networks, build that support system before you dive right in.'

Hannah, a continuing, conventional farmer in Ontario

Hannah is 37 years old and farms in eastern Ontario. Alongside her husband and five children, they run approximately 650 acres and milk about 100 cows. Hannah was raised on a dairy, sheep, and cash crop farm in southern Ontario where she worked alongside her father, two uncles, and grandfather. Despite having four families working on the farm, Hannah was the only sibling and cousin who was passionate about farming right from the start. Hannah describes how, from an early age, she enjoyed spending her free time in the barn:

> I would have my dad wake me up at 5:00 a.m. on weekends, when I was in school, to go in the barn, even when I was too young to help. I would just sit there and hand him the towel and stuff to wipe off the cows … when I was still too short to reach the pipeline to milk the cows, I would stand on a pail and plug them in; so, I mean, I was milking cows on my own from quite a young age.

This passion for farming and commitment to the industry is evident in Hannah's life history. Throughout school she spent all her summers working on the farm which eventually led her to study Animal Sciences at the University of Guelph. It was there that she met her husband, who was also raised on a dairy farm. As Hannah pointed out, they had similar goals: 'The plan was always that the two of us were going to be on the farm full-time, eventually. That was always the plan. There was never a time where I wasn't going to be a full-time farmer, never not a time that my husband wasn't going to be a full-time farmer'.

However, becoming a full-time farmer right after university is not an easy task. To get started, Hannah took on a full-time role at a car dealership in Guelph where she had worked part-time during her studies. Beginning as an evening receptionist, she quickly worked her way up and, for a period of time, she was the company's top salesperson. Despite her success, full-time farming was still very much the plan. Within four months, she and her husband approached his parents about purchasing their quota[6] and cows and moving them to Hannah's family's farm. After carefully planning this transition and receiving approval from the bank, Hannah and her husband purchased the quota and cows at market value.

Within the next eight months, Hannah became pregnant with their first child. It was during her maternity leave that she decided she would not return to the car dealership and would stay on the farm full-time. Although this decision aligned with her long-term goals, it was tough financially as the farm could not provide her with very much income. Hannah then became pregnant with their second child and would no longer be earning the maternity pay that she had received before. Despite these challenges, things were going relatively well until a family crisis occurred. Although this was not the way that Hannah and her husband had hoped to buy into the business, the opportunity presented itself and together they took out significant loans and became partners in the family business alongside her uncle.

Now in their mid-20s, Hannah and her husband were gaining business experience that many farmers do not get until later in life. The ability to navigate these situations required tremendous self-efficacy and a positive attitude. These are competencies that Hannah acquired as a child while recovering from multiple surgeries at Sick Kids Hospital in Toronto. There, she often roomed with people who she described as being in a much worse situation than her: 'I think a lot of my positivity and my drive ... because I met those kids. So, from day one, to see what they went through and to have the positive outlook that they did, it was like, I have nothing to be upset about. Nor will I ever have anything to be upset about.'

This perspective helped Hannah to successfully manage the responsibilities that come with co-owning the family business. However, it also helped her to keep a clear head and after several months of management, she realized that this business arrangement wasn't what was best for her, her husband, or her uncle. So, just months after sorting out the previous deal, Hannah approached her uncle about buying the cows and quota and separating the business in two: 'I knew what was happening financially and I was the one who had the rapport with the bank and I knew what was coming down the pipe and I said to my husband, if we are going to make a go of this then we have to do something now. So, I looked at him and I said, "we've got to, the cows are what's making us money."'

Despite this proposal coming so shortly after the previous arrangement, her uncle was open to the idea as he and his son were more interested in cash cropping and they felt the cows were a lot of work: 'We knew we had a lot of details to iron out and everything, but he didn't like the cows. He was tired of that and he didn't want to do that anymore and he knew his son wanted to come home and didn't want to do that anymore.'

But, in business nothing is permanent and within two years, urban sprawl and competition from other farmers made dairy farming in the area difficult. It was at this time that Hannah's accountant suggested that they move to eastern Ontario, where land was relatively more affordable: 'Until he said that, it had never crossed my mind that I would not die on that farm. There was a really big source of pride for me, that I was another generation that was going to be on that farm and I mean I had just never, it just wasn't even in my thought process to move. It was just an option that I didn't even know existed'.

Family farms are the backbone of Canadian agriculture and being a sixth-generation farmer is certainly something that Hannah was very proud of. For many, leaving or selling the family farm to move is simply not an option. But, for Hannah and her husband, they had come too far with their goals and knew that moving was the best option for the success of their business. Within a year, the home farm was sold and Hannah and her family moved their operation to a farm north of Kingston, Ontario. This was a strategic decision, but the move was still very hard for the family. There is definitely a family legacy aspect to farming and when farmers leave a farm that has been owned by their family for generations, it can feel like they are losing a piece of their identity. But, after six years, Hannah and her family are finally feeling more at home:

> If we had had this interview two years ago then that wouldn't have been my answer. It has been a ... well, it has been an adjustment ... Back in our hometown, we didn't realize that we were a part of a

clique because when you're in it, you don't realize it and when your family has been there for generations then you are in. And, you are friends with everybody and everybody knows you and you get along. When you move from that into another area of farmers, it's the same thing. All of the families here have been here for generations and we were the new kids on the block.

The generations that aren't doing the work on the farm over here still own them. So, like the grandparents who are into their 70s, 80s, 90s are still owners of the farms and then there is the generation in their 50s who are farming with their children in their 20s and 30s. Neither of them has any ownership. That is the common theme over here. So, for us, being in our 30s and farming on our own and almost owning it all for 10 years on our own, we feel a little bit of resentment from those older people who you know haven't had … You know, there is a lot of pride in this business and we show cattle and that is where I think I see it a lot. Whenever we go to the local shows or fairs and we are exhibiting, and the announcement is made as to who owns the animal and it's the announcement of the grandfather's name whereas that gentleman probably has no idea what that cow looks like.

Joining a new community is challenging on its own but the fact that Hannah and her husband actually owned their business made it hard for them to connect with their peers. In farming, older generations tend to have a tough time letting go or knowing how to transition ownership and management to the next generation. Adult farmers who struggle with this can become frustrated and envious of those who have taken on ownership at an earlier age. Hannah sees this delayed transition of ownership and management as a big setback for the industry and the region as final decisions are being made by people who don't even work on the farm any more.

However, owning the farm on their own hasn't been easy. Dairy farms are very expensive and new farmers must take out significant loans to purchase them. Because these new farmers are starting out, they have very little of their own money to put into the business and most of their purchases must be made with borrowed money. When a business's assets are primarily financed through banks or other lenders rather than your own money (equity), the business is highly leveraged. Often, a highly leveraged business must use a lot of its revenue to make interest payments rather than generating profits or paying down principal. At one point, Hannah and her husband were the most highly leveraged dairy farm in Farm Credit Canada's (FCC) portfolio. This is tough for a couple who sees their peers from university driving new equipment or working in new barns as their parents continue to retain some of the farm's ownership and debt. For Hannah and her husband, having ownership at such an early age meant that they had significant mortgage payments and were forced to stretch any money they had as far as they could.

We were the highest leverage dairy farm that FCC had. It was scary on one hand but on the other it showed that they believed in us and it showed that we could do it. So, when I say that things are tight here, they are tight. When I ran the numbers with our accountant after all of our expenses, on every dollar earned, I think we had less than a penny left over.

Rather than dwell on their debt, Hannah and her husband have become excellent at managing their money and use their experiences to help others improve their financial knowledge. In particular, they enjoy helping with a 4-H programme, called Dairy Sense. 4-H is a non-profit organization aimed at helping youth reach their potential and, due to their history, a lot of their programmes in Canada are related to agriculture. Dairy Sense is a programme that teaches young dairy farmers how to use financial data to make management decisions. Supply management is a big part of finances on a dairy farm, where set prices help to protect a farmer's margins. When asked about government support, maintaining supply management[7] was a key takeaway from the interview. Hannah believes that this system is essential to maintain the success of small family farms while providing Canadian consumers with a premium quality milk product.

Apart from agricultural policy, Hannah is a vocal advocate for improving the services that are available for children with autism in Ontario. Having faced medical challenges in her youth and now raising a child with autism, Hannah is quite familiar with and passionate about getting people the services that they need. For rural areas in particular, she says the services that are available don't address the unique needs of these communities. Furthermore, services are allocated based on population density, which means that rural residents must travel further for their appointments and face longer wait times. As Hannah explains:

> As a self-employed farmer, I could apply for money for like, for special training for my son or to hire someone to look after him while I am doing what have you, but what people don't realize is that I have the ability to give him what he needs but because I am not able to be in the barn as often, we are having to hire someone to do what I could be doing but because my son needs me and we live half an hour from civilization, so to get someone to drive out here to look after him for a couple of hours, so that I can … It is just absolutely absurd. So, all of these things and programmes that the government has lined up are cookie-cutter options for people that work nine to five jobs and live in town are of zero benefit to someone on a farm in a rural part.

Mental wellness is an increasing area of focus in agriculture. Farming is a stressful occupation and it was challenging for Hannah to raise a child with special needs without having access to the services that she needed. However, Hannah was quick to highlight how these challenges often lead to some of the most rewarding experiences in her life.

> Everyone says 'oh you are so strong, like I don't know how you do it,' so I am typically the one that people come to. And so, my husband

will tell you that as well, I am the, quote, ray of sunshine, glass is always half-full, kind of person and so I do believe that. Ninety-nine per cent of the time, I do. But we all have our dark days, especially when you have a child with autism. That really can affect you. But, for me I don't necessarily internalize it … honestly, this might sound a little strange and backwards too, but our son's autism has really added some challenges and I know now looking back that I did go through about a six-month bout of depression without knowing it at the time and I probably should have done something about it. But, looking back, so on the flip side of that no one appreciates the small things in life more than the parent of a special-needs child. So, having him look me in the eye and say I love you … that takes away everything. Like who gives a crap if I owe somebody so many thousands of dollars.

This positive outlook and resilience are constant themes throughout Hannah's story. Unlike many farm transitions, she and her husband have paid market price for everything and nothing has been gifted to them. Hannah is very appreciative of the lessons and opportunities that were presented growing up on the farm but emphasized the uphill financial journey that she and her husband face. Farming is not a career for the faint of heart and Hannah has faced significant challenges in both her personal and business life. Despite these challenges, her approach to life has allowed her to and will continue to allow her to overcome the challenges that she faces as a female farmer, a young farmer, and a farming mother. Farming was always her goal and has always been her passion and she will continue to find new and better ways to keep doing what she loves.

Reflections

The experiences of Martha, Kaitlyn, Naomi, and Hannah presented in this chapter, while certainly not representative of all young women farmers in Canada, offer interesting glimpses into the lives of young women who are choosing to live in the countryside and work on the land. They shed light on young women's diverse pathways into agriculture; their motivations, interests, knowledge, skills, and aspirations; the challenges they face as well as the strategies they are adopting to overcome them. Analysing these young women's experiences also reveals great tenacity, strong drive, and commitment in deciding to enter the field of agriculture and to continue farming.

For some of the young women, traditional ways of thinking in the countryside create significant obstacles in their pathways to farming. One respondent from Ontario, who pursued agriculture as a career and hoped to take over the family farm, reported: 'In my family, you had to be a boy to be able to take over the farm.' This sentiment was echoed by others: 'their family has always said the son will take over the farm, that's why they had a son'. These anecdotes are somewhat reflected in the study's data with 50 per cent of the young male farmers expecting to inherit land while 41 per cent of the young women farmers interviewed are expecting to inherit land in Ontario; none had already inherited any land. The research in Manitoba indicated that of all of the young farmers in our study who come from a farm family, 85 per cent of males have already inherited or will inherit farmland in the future while 77 per cent of females from farming families have or will inherit farmland. However, women in both provinces, historically (and today), have had to fight to be recognized as farmers and often have not been offered equal access to farming.

These obstacles extend to women who are new to farming, where farming, especially for women is not seen as a viable career choice: 'I think the main reason why [farming] hadn't occurred to me prior to that was because it is never pitched as a career option … especially for women.' This young woman, a new entrant farmer in Manitoba, indicated that she feels she is more isolated within the farming community than her husband is because she is a woman, and most of their farming peers are men with whom she has trouble relating.

Many of the women interviewed in both provinces reported facing discrimination in their communities, where they are often not taken seriously or considered to be important, and their contributions to their farms and communities are made invisible. One Ontario respondent reported a statement made by a member of her community: 'There was a gentleman that said he had three crop failures. And what he meant was that he had three daughters.' This demeaning statement was made at a community meeting where women were present. Such ways of thinking often play out less overtly and can be especially evident in dealing with suppliers or service providers. As one Ontario respondent stated: 'If I have a guy friend visiting or my partner is with me or my dad is with me, people won't talk to me. They'll talk to them.' These same experiences were shared in Manitoba. For example, one respondent described some of her interactions with neighbouring farmers as follows: 'I've felt some weirdness just from older farmers and older folks that they sort of want to talk to my husband always, even though it's something I can answer.' However, some women reporting these experiences described them as a mere bother, something to shrug off: 'It has not been as bad as you would think. I've never really felt like it was too big of a deal,' said one Ontario respondent. A Manitoba woman farmer also treated similar interactions lightly, even finding humour in the situation: 'Well I think men get treated more seriously than women do. Like, the other day, an input dealer says, "where's the boss of the house?" Now I just play along, whatever, "he's on the [manure] pile, go find him, good luck."' Interestingly, one respondent from Ontario felt that their gender expression meant they were taken more seriously than other women: 'I would say that as a masculine-presenting woman, I get a lot of byes in places where my fellow female co-workers don't necessarily. I think I take less flack in a lot of situations because people take my opinion more seriously than somebody with a ponytail.'

In Manitoba, this is reflected in the fact that 46 per cent of the direct marketing farmers we spoke with were women, while women producing for conventional markets only accounted for 29 per cent. Similar to the sentiments expressed in Ontario, young women farmers in Manitoba indicated that they have a hard time being taken seriously and are often overlooked by other farmers or industry representatives, with the general sentiment being that it is their husbands who are the chief decision makers on the farm. Many women who grew up on a conventional or supply-managed family farm indicated that when they were growing up, they were often not given the same opportunities as their brothers for on-farm training and they felt that gender played a significant role in this dynamic. However, the direct market farmers also pointed to challenges for women farmers. As Martha indicated in the case study above, she felt that she may not have been able to establish herself as a new entrant had she tried to do it alone because she would not have been able to access the same degree of social capital among her farming peers as her husband did so readily.

Many of the young male farmers that we spoke with in Manitoba seemed to feel that the perception of women was starting to change in the farm community due to the hard work of some women farmers who have proven themselves to be equally efficient and competent. While this view may have been well intentioned, it does have a somewhat pejorative undertone in that it assumes that women must prove themselves to be equals. This is the kind of landscape that women are facing as they enter agriculture today. There has been progress for women farmers in that their numbers are rising and they are taking advantage of more opportunities on the farm and within their family farm dynamics, but there are still numerous challenges for women in their everyday interactions within their farm community that men do not face.

The stories of gender inequality and challenges for women farmers were countered by many reports from other respondents of the great support and encouragement they receive from their families. As one Ontario respondent stated: 'There's never been a barrier gender wise. That's never been an issue and I've been very lucky because I know that's not always the case.' A Manitoba respondent pointed to more gender-equal farm dynamics when she said: 'A lot of the people we know are farming with childcare and household duties split fairly. Often, it's the female who has an off-farm job to kind of support things and the husband's taking care of the work at home and then they're balancing the farm jobs.' While gender-based discrimination certainly still exists, there seems to be a shift occurring within the distribution of family responsibilities at home as well as with succession plans including more women, who are inheriting farms and running farm businesses.

Some women felt gender did not play a major role in their experience as a farmer. They did not report experiencing the forces of discrimination at all. This was especially true for members of the ecological farming community and those closer to urban centres in Ontario: 'I haven't had much experience being treated differently because I'm a woman farmer. But I think that is not very common. I think other people struggle in maybe more rural areas.' In Manitoba, 5 of the 16 women farmers indicated that they do not feel that there are different challenges for women than there are for men.

When considering the gender dimensions in farming communities, it is important to consider the type and scale of farming that young women are engaged in as these factors led to significant differences in their experiences as women farmers. Young farmers in Manitoba were asked if they thought that women face different challenges than men as farmers. About 66 per cent of young farmers producing for conventional markets said that women do face different challenges than men, while only 38 per cent of direct marketers[8] felt women had different challenges. A conventional male grain farmer said that women have a harder time being taken seriously as a farmer in some situations, while an instructor associated with a campus farm in Manitoba indicated: 'There is a dynamic that women face that young men don't face entering farming, but I also think that that's changing in the local food movement and in the organic sector.' Overall, it seems that gender inequality is a bigger challenge for women in conventional farming. As one respondent said: 'I was once the only woman in an entire room full of men at a Mennonite auction and that was pretty fun, I was getting some looks ... you just have to anticipate that you might be recognized as such in a negative light from time to time and just having internal strength in order to stand up for yourself, just continue on.'

And that is just what young women farmers in Canada are doing as they embrace farming and their numbers grow. It is worth repeating that from 2011 to 2016, there were about 9 per cent fewer men farming but only 3.5 per cent fewer women (Statistics Canada 2016). Furthermore, despite a decrease in the total number of women farmers, the number of women farming as independent operators has risen from 10,740 in 2011 to 13,110 in 2016 – a 22 per cent increase (Statistics Canada 2016). Overall, the young women farmers who participated in this research are well educated and knowledgeable about their farms, and many are active members of their community, taking on roles as municipal councillors or industry board members as well as regularly attending conferences and community meetings. They are hardworking and exhibit a strong drive to succeed as farmers. They also demonstrate strong determination, confidence, and resilience – all qualities that help them as successful farmers and as they forge paths for themselves in male-dominated spaces.

Notes

1. 1 acre equals 0.4 hectares.
2. A combine is a complex farm machine used to thresh grains. At harvest time, some farmers hire custom combining crews rather than purchasing this very expensive piece of machinery for themselves.

3. A family farm corporation is a regular corporation. While there are higher accounting fees to being incorporated, these costs are often justified for farms due to the lower income tax rate that corporations pay.
4. Permaculture is a system of agriculture that aims to integrate human activities with the natural environment to create efficient and productive naturally sustaining ecosystems.
5. Swales are shallow ditches between raised tracts of land that function as infiltration basins, designed in particular for the collection and conveyance of rainwater.
6. A quota is a permit that authorizes a farmer to produce a certain quantity of a farm product over a certain period of time. The distribution and management of quotas are coordinated by the marketing board for that specific industry. Farmers must acquire quotas to produce and sell commodities in supply-managed industries. In Canada, these industries include chicken, egg, turkey, and dairy (cows only).
7. Supply management is a national policy framework in Canada that allows a commodity's marketing board to control the supply (production) of the commodity through the use of production quotas. Farmers hold quotas that allow them to produce a certain amount of a product over a certain period of time. By controlling the distribution of quotas, the marketing boards control the supply of the commodity that helps to stabilize prices for producers.
8. For the purpose of this study we define direct marketers as those who market their products directly to consumer through models such as farm gate, farmer's markets, or community supported agriculture (CSA) that has consumers pay/invest in the farm at the beginning of the season and receive weekly shares of food throughout the growing season. For our purposes, a direct marketer may also be selling and marketing directly (in person) to local restaurants and retailers that will then sell to local consumers.

Reference

Statistics Canada (2016) 'Farm operators classified by number of operators per farm and sex'. Table 32-10-0441-01. https://www150.statcan.gc.ca/t1/tbl1/en/tv.action?pid=3210044101

CHAPTER 4

Moving to the fore: Young women farmers in China

Lu Pan and Huifang Wu

Introduction

When searching in the academic database (such as the mostly used Chinese database *China National Knowledge Infrastructure*) with the keywords 'young woman farmer', one finds almost no references, and enlarging the keyword selection to 'women farmer' still produces only a handful of results. Perhaps the reason is quite obvious. For young rural women in contemporary China, let alone young women in urban areas, the profession of 'farmer' would be a last resort in one's job hunt. When compared to the harsh and muddy conditions that one encounters working in a field, it is more convenient for young women from rural areas to work in manufacturing or the service industry in cities, which is seen as superior to farming. The Chinese imagination and vision of a professional and successful farmer is rarely connected with women – it is widely seen as a male-dominated vocation. Young women farmers as a group are invisible in China in both academic debate and in public perception. This chapter aims to increase our understanding of young women farmers in contemporary China – they do exist and have been making an important contribution to agricultural and rural development in the country since 1949. They were nicknamed the 'Iron Girls' during the collectivization period (1950s–1960s), and 'left-behind women' in the period of increased rural labour migration since the 1980s. They are the rural women who struggle with their own difficulties and challenges in farming in order to sustain their livelihoods. Although the experiences of young women farmers are unique across different time periods, there are many similarities in their life experiences that reveal how political and social norms have shaped young women farmers and their circumstances over the decades.

In this chapter, we will look retrospectively at the stories of young women farmers through the historical lens of development in China. The chapter is divided into five sections. Young women farmers grew as a social group along with the socialization construction in China after 1949. The first section documents the history and stories of rural women, especially the young women labourers who were mobilized into agricultural collectivization in the 1950s–1960s, in which they were shaped as 'iron girls' and made considerable contributions with their femininity badly overlooked. The second section moves to the 1980s–2000s when the rural commune systems ended and rural people began to have more choices in market economy beyond rural areas. Rural women faced gender inequality in their opportunities for migration due to their gender roles in caregiving. Young and middle-aged rural women became 'left-behind women' to take care of rural family and maintain agricultural production during their husbands' migration. The third section then illustrates the difficulties and challenges for young women in general in farming, including access to land, technologies, finance, and credit. As the social settings of young women farmers change with state development, the fourth section introduces current agrarian change in China and its implications for young women farmers. By reflecting on the life courses of 'young women farmers' as a social group in modern China, the concluding section introduces the case studies of young women farmers in Chapter 5.

The 'Iron Girls': young women farmers in the collectivization period (1950s to 1960s)

Rural women as the main source of agricultural labour is a phenomenon that appeared mainly after the founding of the People's Republic of China in 1949 that grew as the country modernized in the 1950s and 1960s. Before this time, patriarchal gender norms restricted rural women's participation to domestic work or household handicrafts production. In some locales, they served as auxiliary labour in some areas of agricultural production. Research into agricultural society during this period of China's history reveals that young girls would participate in livelihood activities from the age of eight or nine, doing domestic chores such as cutting grass, herding goats, and spinning. From the age of 14 or 15, girls would work as part-time labour in agriculture (Jin 2016). Nationwide, rural women's contributions to farm work were not significant in the overall agricultural production; this situation did not change until the 1950s. After the Chinese Communist Party (CCP) assumed control of the country in 1949, the national economy's recovery and growth were made the government's highest priority, and they promoted the importance of agriculture in fulfilling food security and provisioning for industry development. The CCP quickly took up the task of mobilizing women of working age to participate in agricultural production in order to respond to the massive gap in the labour force in this period. The CCP used several methods to mobilize women: ideological education, setting up women role models, and offering training in agricultural technologies, among others (Liu 2012). This mobilization was part of a larger plan that committed the state to establish and promote new rules of social control and regulation in order to construct a new nationwide social order, especially in rural areas. The CCP enacted a series of laws that dramatically improved women's social status.

This included the first Marriage Law in 1950 that abolished the tradition of arranged marriage and specified equal rights for women and men in marriage. The law endowed women with the rights to divorce and the freedom to choose their partners by themselves, which was usually arranged by parents. In terms of economic rights, the 1954 Constitution and Labour Law recognized and emphasized the rule of 'equal pay for equal work' between men and women (Hershatter 2017).

When the CCP recognized rural women as an important labour force in agriculture and the countryside more generally, young women were at the forefront during the collectivization period from the 1950s to 1960s. Agricultural collectivization was a movement to reconstruct and lead peasant agriculture to socialist collective economy. It went through different stages in China after 1949, from encouraging individual farmers to organize mutual-aid groups, and then to join cooperatives and communes. In 1958, about 98.2 per cent of farmers joined in communes which symbolized a peak time of collectivization (An 1991). In the commune system, young women were politically progressive and vigorously involved in rural infrastructure construction and agricultural production. It was young women who official propagandists glorified as 'Iron Girls' in light of their toughness as labourers. Young rural women participated in farm work – including key functions like ploughing, seeding, weeding, and harvesting – but were also important members of the labour force for construction such as building dams, roads, and irrigation systems. During the 'Great Leap Forward' (1958–62), male labourers were organized in steel production and irrigation construction, leaving the responsibility for agriculture to women. In her research in Lu village in Yunnan Province in the late collectivization period 1980–81,[1] Bossen found that women's work points[2] comprised 53 per cent of all rural labour work points, although their value was 17 per cent lower than those of the men (Bossen 2005). In Qin village of Jiangsu Province, almost all of the women aged 20 to 30 years were engaged in farm work in the late 1950s, especially deep ploughing, compact planting, manure compositing, and other activities to improve production. They were the main labour for deep ploughing and even temporarily relocated to other villages when their brigades finished their assigned work (Li 2010: 75). In Shaanxi Province during the 1950s and 1960s, all women contributed between 70 and 80 per cent of farm work and became the main force in agriculture (Hershatter 2017: 265).

Alongside the institutional transformation, rural women were able to step away from the domestic sphere and into the production sphere in their communities. While recognizing the improvements in gender relations for young women farmers after 1949, their burden in taking up full-time farm work and domestic responsibilities needs to be highlighted. Due to traditional ideals that reinforced sexual discrimination and because young rural women were often comparatively low skilled in the early days of their participation in collective labour in the 1950s, women generally received lower work points than men even though their labour hours were the same. The lower work points for women can also be connected to their domestic responsibilities – for example, they needed to return home from the fields earlier to prepare the evening meals. The CCP, as mentioned earlier, had been promoting equal pay for equal work for men and women since 1953; however, in reality, it was not fully implemented on the ground in many places. When they recalled the collectivization period many years later, it was the heavy workload that these young women farmers endured that they remembered most vividly (Hershatter 2017). Many feminist scholars focus on women farmers' bodies and obtain stories of work experiences through oral history materials. In her 2003 article, Guo examines women's memories of disease and fatigue in social production in 1954–1958. It was especially painstaking for young women farmers who were pregnant or lactating. The state largely overlooked the physical differences between women and men in its extra economic coercion activities. As some old women recalled:

> Most pregnant women had to work until parturition. Some of them even worked in the field in the morning and delivered the baby in the afternoon. In only three or five days after the delivery, women needed to farm again because all of the family members were in the field and we needed to earn work points as well. The impacts (of heavy work after childbirth) to our health were not obvious when (we were) young, however, it becomes severe when we're aging. Young women in the 1950–60s usually had a couple of kids. In order to get work points, we tried all means to overcome all the difficulties of childrearing. For young women who did not have parents-in-law to help, they even brought the kids to the field. Women in lactation sometimes rushed home in the short break of work to breastfeed their babies (Hu 2016).

The agricultural policies aimed to advocate gender equality in order to mobilize women labourers in productive activities, when in reality, they accentuated women's physical burden without deeply addressing the gender inequality in the political domain. Hu (2016) found in her research in Shaanxi Province that a few male elites dominated the economic political positions of authority in the village and these men intentionally, or unintentionally, maintained the patriarchal social order in the community during the collectivization period. Gender bias in communal labour division was common in the countryside. Male brigade[3] leaders would make labour allocation decisions. Male heads of households would be given preference for paid work opportunities outside the household or the village. When surplus communal work was available such as cattle feeder, vets, drivers, and some other non-farm works which had better payments and didn't involve work in the fields, brigade leaders would give priority to men, using the excuses of women's physical weakness or domestic work responsibilities. When the brigade needed female labourers, its leaders would force these women to engage in the same farm work as men, the former's physical limitations forgotten. In this light, some researchers argue that the subordinated features of rural women remained intact during the collectivization period; the patriarchal domination over rural women just transferred from family and clan to the state and commune (Guo 2003; Jin 2016).

Left-behind women: young women farmers upholding rural labour migration (1980s to 2000s)

The Rural Reform that started in 1978 in China symbolized the ending of agricultural collectivization and confirmed that rural households were basic and independent units of production in agriculture. The application of the household responsibility system in land tenure reform has greatly released labour in agriculture and rural women have more enthusiasm to work for their own households than during the collectivization period and can participate in agriculture based on their own capacities and demands. Family farmers were encouraged to commodify their agricultural production to involve them in the market economy. The released domestic migration policy in the 1980s generated a growing wave of rural labour migration that attracted rural youth to cities for better economic opportunities. However, the gendered rural labour migration meant that male rural migrants far outnumbered female migrants. Many censuses and investigations in the mid-1990s estimated that the male: female ratio among rural labour migrants was about 3:1 to 2:1 (Tan 1997). The gender difference was mainly due to family care constraints for married young rural women. Therefore, many young women had to stay in the countryside to attend to family while pursuing agriculture, becoming the so-called 'left-behind women'. According to a *China Economic Weekly* report in 2006 that China had a left-behind population of 87 million, of which 47 million were left-behind women, about 54 per cent. As male rural migrants are mostly concentrated between 20 and 50 years old, we can also assume that most left-behind women who were involved in agriculture were young women farmers. The abundant literature on left-behind women over the past two decades offers us a greater understanding of the lives of young women farmers.

Male migration is considered by rural households as a family strategy or part of a mix of different strategies, but scholars claim that male out-migration contributes to the increased vulnerability of the women left behind (Jacka 2012). These women frequently report feelings of loneliness, insecurity, worry, and helplessness (Ye and Wu 2008). Studies on the mental health concerns of these women show that their stress, pressure, loneliness, and fear is worse than among women whose husbands don't migrate when psychological scales are applied to both groups (Xu 2009, 2010). In some regions, poor mental health has led some left-behind women to seek comfort in religion such as Buddhism or Christianity (Wu et al. 2010; Liang et al. 2011).

Changes in marital relationship are also evident in the literature. On one hand, some women reported having a better relationship with their husbands after short spells apart due to the consequent lack of conflict (Chant 1992: 63–65; Zheng and Xie 2004; Hugo 2005). Researchers also found that migration-induced separation can lead to marital instability and family break-ups (Chant 1992: 63–65; Horton 2008). Other studies reveal the communication barriers between husbands and wives, including the different living environments of husbands and wives (Luo and Chai 2004; Li and Li 2005; Xiang 2006), increased risk of divorce (Chen 2006), and strong mental stress and sexual repression (Wang 2007). However, researchers (Zhou et al. 2002: 72) examining separated families of rural migrants assert that physical separation is not a crucial influential factor on marital relationship health, rather income and career changes are more important.

With regard to the gender relation changes generated by labour migration, scholars have disputing views. Farming and agriculture are a major domain for gender relation dynamics and the subsequent disputes. When male labourers are absent from the farm, women maintain agricultural production. An All-China Women's Federation nationwide investigation in 2006 revealed that 73.4 per cent of rural women work full-time or part-time in agricultural production (Zhen 2008). Many scholars agree that the temporary absence of rural men can sometimes facilitate greater autonomy for women, allowing them to manage their own work and take decisions on household matters (Kaspar 2005; Massey 2009). Some argue that male migration can lead to a reallocation of agricultural resources, thereby creating a valuable space for rural women in China to develop as farmers 'independently' (Li 2003). Others point out that even though the family strategy of male migration and women remaining at home is based on gender inequality and resource possession, the spatial separation of men from rural society means that women's decision-making power within the family and gender equality in the longer term would be improved (Wu 2011). It is obvious that a left-behind woman's responsibilities in all aspects of agricultural production markedly increases after her husband migrates, including purchasing means of production, ploughing, spraying chemicals, harvesting, seeding, and irrigation. For many families, assistance from parents-in-law is minimal (Ye et al. 2014). The time-consuming portion of agricultural work that the husband used to undertake is now additional responsibility for the woman as the main agricultural labourer.

Other researchers hold a contrary view that changes in women's decision-making and gender relations more generally are diminished when men are absent for long periods of time. Even though some women obtained economic independency and autonomy through their own migration experiences, women remain severely constrained by powerful gender discourses, institutions, and practices, including gendered divisions of labour and norms about women's work and men's work that disadvantage women in rural China (Jacka 2012). Chinese researchers have found that even though men have migrated, they still have an important hold, via cell phone conversations, on family decisions, especially those related to production investments (Luo et al. 2004; Zhou 2006: 84). Left-behind women are therefore still considered to be secondary decision makers even after their husbands have migrated out – men take the role of 'managers' while women are the 'producers'

(Zheng and Xie 2004: 205; Sun 2006). Jiang and Zhou (2007) suggest that wives who stay behind are under the double squeeze of production work and housework, resulting in a double dependency on men as emotional and economic support, such that these relations relegate women to a junior position to men in the countryside. Meanwhile, due to the low levels of mechanization and socialization in agriculture in some regions, the feminization of agriculture imposes an even heavier workload and physical hardship on women and impedes their involvement in other economic activities.

For some agro-economists and policymakers, agricultural production performance is the priority, not the farming practices or emotional well-being of these left-behind women. Therefore, whether women's involvement in agriculture will negatively influence agricultural production has ignited economic debates. Many economists are concerned that these women's heavy burden in caring for family members, especially children, will result in notable abandonment of farmland and further aggravate the vulnerability of agriculture (Fan and Cheng 2005). Although some empirical research backs the productivity of left-behind women (Quisumbing 1996), a general argument among Chinese economists is to accelerate young rural women's migration and their transfer to non-farming activities in order to guarantee agricultural production. In fact, there is strong multiplicity among the ages, roles, identities, family positions, and involvement in agriculture by women. Individuals develop different styles of farming, and can be classified into different types of women farmers, for example, conservative, reformative, and innovative (Bock 1994; de Rooij 1994; O'Hara 1994). In the debates on left-behind women, not only were the specificity of young women farmers and the multiplicity of all women farmers overlooked in this research, but their contributions to farming were also generally underestimated.

Difficulties and challenges for young women in farming

The bias on women's land rights

According to the Rural Land Contract Law (2018), members of rural collective economic organizations (e.g. villages) have the right to contract collective farmland. In rural communities, women and men have equal land rights. The law protects women's legal interests in land contracts and states that no organization or individual should deprive or violate women's land contract rights. Within a land contract term, which is 30 years, if a rural woman marries and does not obtain contract land near to her new residence, the woman's parents' village should not recall her land. If a woman divorces or is widowed, if they live in their parents' village, or live in a new residence but do not contract land in the new residence, their parents' village should not recall their land. The rural collective has the right to use the land, or newly cultivated land, and allocate it to newborn children or to new residents.

While these regulations promote land equality between men and women on the surface, rural women face many difficulties related to land accessibility. The land contract system indicates the rural household as the unit of land contract; however, the household head is usually male and the land rights of the household's female members are often overlooked. It is a common phenomenon that changes in a marriage often violate a rural woman's land rights. There are four forms of rights violations that rural women encounter. First, when rural women marry (within the same village or into another village), her parents' village will recall her farm land or her family will maintain it. The wife very probably cannot receive farmland in her husband's village. Although village authorities could adjust land contracts over time to meet population changes, in order to maintain land yield and productivity that coincide with longer contract periods, most village authorities follow the rule that '*zeng ren bu zeng di, jian ren bu jian di*' (do not allocate land to new population and do not recall the land when people die). When rural women marry into a new village, there is a high chance that they will not receive farmland via a land contract and will need to rely on their husband's household to gain access to land. For rural women who marry a fellow villager, the social customs and traditions do not permit the wife to claim her land rights with her own family. Second, divorced and widowed women do not get a share of their husband's farmland after their parting – it remains with the husband's household. Third, the land rights of unmarried women can also be violated. In some cases, rural collectives allocate farmland based on population trends. For households who have daughters of a marriageable age, the daughter's share is deducted from her family's allocation. However, unmarried young men retain a share of their family's farmland in the name of their future wives or children. Fourth, a rural man who lives in his wife's village cannot be allocated farmland for the couple and their children. In these four instances, the rights and interests of rural women remain impaired.

Rural women across China are often subject to land rights violations. According to a survey conducted by All-China Women's Federation and the National Bureau of Statistics in 2003, about 35 per cent of villages did not allocate farmland to women who live in the countryside but do not have a rural household registration, 14.7 per cent did not allocate farmland to women who married into the village, and only 2 per cent of the surveyed villages maintain farmland in a woman's parents' village when she has married outside the village (Wu and Zhang 2004). The social organization 农家女 (*nong jia nv*, Rural Women) surveyed migrant women aged 20–49 in Beijing in 2009. Its findings reveal that 18.8 per cent of married women did not have farmland in their parents' village; 13.5 per cent never received land in their parents' village or from their husband's village; 49.6 per cent lost their land in their parents' village after their marriage; 31.8 per cent lost their land due to a marriage crisis (Zhao 2014: 60). All-China Women's Federation's 2010 survey showed that about 21 per cent of rural women did not have land and 27.7 per cent of these women had lost their land due to marriage (Zhao 2014: 61). Such a disadvantageous position for women in terms of farmland access has passive impacts on their position in family life and in agricultural production and increases livelihood pressures on poor households.

Squeezed space in learning

There are limited channels and opportunities for rural women to learn agricultural skills and technologies. While some may benefit from instructional television programmes, books, or magazines, those who have the opportunity to study at a vocational school or with a professional organization are very limited (Qi 2019). They often have to rely on their own initiative to learn technologies. Compared to the older generation, young women farmers usually do not gain any farming experience during their childhood. For young women now in their 20s and 30s, they relocated to township or county for schooling and moved to a city for work soon after high school graduation. They are then ill-equipped when, after they marry and return to the countryside, they lack the necessary farming knowledge and skills. These young women turn to their parents or parents-in-law to teach them basic farming skills such as ploughing, sowing, and spraying pesticide.

Research reveals gender differentiation in the process of technology transfer and communication in rural China (Shang 2008; Gao 2015). First, women farmers use fewer mediums of communication than men who employ wider channels of communication technologies and are more likely to use mass media and organizational channels such as attending training courses organized by government to obtain relevant farming knowledge and information. A survey in Zhejiang Province showed that the percentage of male farmers' participation in agricultural extension services was 17.92 times that of women (He 2007). Second, women farmers read fewer books and magazines related to farming than their male counterparts. Third, women farmers obtain most of their resources and scientific knowledge within their intimate communities, especially from their parents, parents-in-law, and fellow villagers. Male farmers, on the other hand, rely more on their social networks and external resources, such as experts, friends, and fellow farmers to gain scientific knowledge. They also more actively attend agricultural exhibitions or self-financed training courses. In general, female farmers are more passive in obtaining knowledge and information about farming and do not effectively utilize external resources (Fu 2003).

Rural women's situation in obtaining skills and technologies could be partly explained by their comparatively lower level of school education. According to a survey organized by All-China Women's Federation in 2010, average number of years of school education for rural women was 5.9, lower than 7.3 for rural men and 9.8 for urban women (Shi and Liu 2014). It means many rural women don't have basic scientific knowledge to understand agrochemistry or machinery. Major barriers for rural women in learning technologies and skills are the insufficient, gender-blinded public services delivery which have blocked rural women's participation in extension services (Gao 2015).

Limited access to finance and credit

When launching a farming career, young women farmers often require credit, but current rural financial and credit systems operate with a gender bias against women. Rural Credit Cooperatives are the major channel for rural people to access financial credit and these organizations prefer to lend to male applicants and male heads of household, which impedes credit access for female members. Under these unfavourable conditions for women, rural men could receive better financial service and can obtain larger loans. In microcredit schemes in some regions, male clients are favoured over female applicants and offered larger loans (Wang et al. 2008). Research in Liaoning Province in 2011 that surveyed 126 new farmers in rural areas reveals significant gender difference in terms of access to formal credit; formal credit was offered to rural male entrepreneurs at a rate 1.6 times greater than to rural women (Huo 2014).

Regarding the limited access to formal credit, microcredit is an important source of credit for the rural population. Microcredit programmes began in China in the 1990s, and relied on international aid and donations at the outset. From the 2000s, the Chinese government gradually began promoting microcredit as a tool for poverty alleviation. The Rural Credit Cooperatives launched a microcredit programme in 2002 when they released CNY 96.7 bn (about USD 13.6 bn) to rural households, the scale of which has far surpassed that of international aid programmes (Du 2004). The development of microcredit has, to some extent, satisfied the financial demands of rural women, especially the poor, to facilitate livelihood security, employment, and income increments. Their social capital has expanded as a consequence. Research shows that microcredit has had a more significant impact for rural women than men. According to a survey in six provinces in western China (Wang et al. 2008), female-headed households can generate CNY 70 (about USD 9.8) more than male-headed households from every CNY 1,000 (about USD 140) loan. Women also have higher levels of credit than men. However, there remain issues of gender sensitivity in microcredit implementation. Rural Credit Cooperative offerings are aimed at middle-income rural households; applicants are usually male heads of households. Some government poverty alleviation programmes direct their microcredit money to poor households, but this focus does not necessarily benefit women (Du 2004). Gender sensitivity was not integrated into the design and operation of microcredit schemes, resulting in many negative impacts for rural women. Firstly, microcredit schemes confirmed women's traditional gender role and did not recognize their demands in economic activities. Second, most microcredit schemes did not take domestic power relations into account; in many cases, it was women taking the responsibility of loan repayment without any decision-making ability over the fund's actual use. Third, many rural women had to forgo a portion of their welfare and reduce their consumption needs in order to repay the loan (Wang et al. 2008).

In order to improve the effectiveness of microcredit schemes, beginning in 2008, the Ministry of Finance and the All-China Women's Federation researched and issued several policies aimed at improving the fiscal policies of microcredit schemes in order to facilitate women's employment and business ventures. All-China Women's Federation-funded research in 2012 shows that the average age of rural women who received microcredits from a women's federation was 39.5 years old and 97.9 per cent of these women used the credits in plantation, husbandry, and agro-products processing (Zhao 2014: 179). In 2016, the No. 1 document of central government, *Several opinions of the CPC Central Committee and the State Council on implementing the new concept of development and accelerating agricultural modernization to realize the goal of comprehensive well-off life*, was released. The policy highlighted the importance of safeguarding rural women's legal rights in property distribution, marriage and political participation, and guaranteeing rural women equal opportunities in accessing education, employment, financial resources, and so on. However, in reality, rural women's financial demands could barely be met. It is very common for rural women to receive smaller loans than requested in their applications (Yang and Wang 2018).

Current agrarian change in China and implications for young women farmers

Agricultural transition: shrinking space for women farmers?

Since the 1980s, household-based agricultural production, with rural women as the major labour force, has guaranteed food security at the household and national levels. The gendered labour division that 'men work and women farm' has provided the essential labour force for urbanization and industrialization. Yet women's participation in agriculture did not elevate their income or social position given that agriculture itself was perceived as an inferior vocation. Obsolete technology, low agricultural profits, and the disadvantages that women labourers encounter are very often intrinsically connected as men are the representatives of modern agricultural productivity while women represent the old agricultural labour (Boserup 2010: 42). In the 2000s, China began accelerating the country's transition towards modern agriculture with emphasis on the application of modern materials and technology, modern industrial systems and operations, and the deepening of the market economy. The development of agriculture can be summarized in three key points, which also sets up the contextual background for female farmers' engagement in farming.

First, agricultural production has increased dramatically and gross agricultural production continues to grow. Gross agricultural production was CNY 11,357.9 bn (about USD1,777 bn) in 2019, 245 times that in 1952. The major grain (maize, wheat, rice, and soybeans) output increased from 113 million tonnes in 1948 to 657.9 million tonnes in 2019 (Ministry of Agriculture and Rural Affairs 2019). The contribution rate of agricultural science and technology progress increased from 35 per cent in 1985 to 56 per cent in 2016, indicating the major role of modern technology in agricultural production (State Council of China 2016).

Second, agriculture's dominant role in the national economy has been changing. The population of rural agricultural labourers is decreasing. According to the third National Agricultural Census Bulletin in 2016, the agricultural population decreased from 424.41 million in 1996 to 314.22 million in 2016. The agricultural production value in terms of gross domestic product is also diminishing – from 31.2 per cent in 1979 to 7.97 per cent in 2016 (National Bureau of Statistics 2017a). With China's rapid industrialization, agriculture is no longer the mainstay of the national economy.

Third, entities of agricultural production and operation have been further diversified. Beyond the conventional agricultural production entities of small households, there are currently five categories of 'new' entities in China, including specialized large holders, registered family farms (as a corporate unit), agricultural cooperatives, agro-business, and agricultural socialized service organizations. These are labelled as 'new' entities to differentiate them from the traditional farming unit of small-scale rural households. According to Ministry of Agriculture statistics, by the end of 2016, with the standard of 50 mu (about 3.33 hectares), there are 3.5 million of these new agricultural entities, including 445,000 registered family farms, 1,794,000 agricultural cooperatives, 130,000 leading agro-businesses, and 1,150,000 agricultural socialized service organizations (Ministry of Agriculture and Rural Affairs 2017). Meanwhile, there are about 260,000,000 small households farming under 50 mu who account for 97 per cent of the agricultural population (Ministry of Agriculture and Rural Affairs 2017). In China's agricultural transition, the large number of small-scale farming households will coexist with the rising number of new, large-scale entities for the foreseeable future.

The modernization of agriculture in China has had far reaching impacts for rural women, one of which is the decreasing participation of women farmers in agricultural production. As a result of the massive migration of rural male labour in the 1990s and early 2000s, there was a prominent feminization of agriculture during this period. Since then, however, the proportion of women in agriculture has been decreasing. According to the 2006 National Agriculture Census, women accounted for 53.2 per cent of total employment in agriculture. In 2010, the census showed a decrease to 49.2 per cent, which was less than the proportion of rural men (National Bureau of Statistics 2008). In 2016, the percentage of women was further reduced to 47.5 per cent (National Bureau of Statistics 2017b).

Tables 4.1, 4.2, and 4.3 show the changing gender structure in the agricultural population, from which we can draw hints in order to understand the realities of young women farmers. First, the proposition and judgement of 'feminization of agriculture' is no longer valid in China in its current stage. Although there are still an enormous number of rural male migrants working

Table 4.1 Composition of the agricultural population in 2006

	Nationwide	East	Central	West	North-east
Agricultural population (10,000s)	34,874	9,522	10,206	12,355	2,791
Male (%)	46.8	44.9	45.7	48.6	49.7
Female (%)	53.2	55.1	54.3	51.4	50.3

Source: Consolidated from the second National Agricultural Census Bulletin.

Table 4.2 Gender composition of rural working population in 2010

	Rural working population	Rural working population in agriculture	Proportion (%)
Total	39,362,371	29,435,422	–
Male	21,194,743	14,966,366	50.8
Female	18,167,628	14,469,056	49.2

Source: Consolidated from the second National Agricultural Census Bulletin.

Table 4.3 Amount and composition of people in agricultural production and operation in 2016

	Nationwide	East	Central	West	North-east
Total employment (100,000s)	31,422	8,746	9,809	1,0734	2,133
Male (%)	52.5	52.4	52.6	52.1	54.3
Female (%)	47.5	47.6	47.4	47.9	45.7
Employment in large holding households (100,000s)	1,289	382	280	411	217
Male (%)	52.8	54.0	53.7	50.0	54.7
Female (%)	47.2	46.0	46.3	50.0	45.3
Employment in agrobusiness unit (100,000s)	1,092	341	265	358	128
Male (%)	59.4	59.1	60.1	56.7	66.1
Female (%)	40.6	40.9	39.9	43.3	33.9

Source: Consolidated from the third National Agricultural Census Bulletin.

off-farm, men are also entering into agriculture at a faster speed than women and once again becoming the mainstay of the agricultural population. Second, with the diversification of agricultural production modes and the rising of new entities since around 2006, we can see various patterns of women's participation in agriculture. There are women farmers in small-scale family farming, left-behind female farmers as well as female farmer entrepreneurs striving for business with their husbands. Our understanding of women farmers must be connected with agrarian transition in order to identify this group's dynamics and diversified realities.

Third, agriculture's modernization in China is luring more rural men to the countryside to enter into agriculture. Such a change to the farming population will, on the one hand, add momentum to the development of the sector but will, on the other hand, raise questions for women farmers' future employment. Just as they were often excluded from migration and off-farming opportunities, rural women could easily also be excluded from a role in the modern agricultural sector. The questions of whether China's agrarian transition will generate new patterns of gender labour division in the rural population, and whether young women can grasp opportunities in the changing agrarian structure and construct their identities as women farmers will be important research issues in the country's development. Unfortunately, among the plethora of scholarly research on agrarian transition in China and the heated discussion on modern agriculture, the role of young women farmers is completely ignored. The default entities in policy and public debate on modern agriculture are male farmers.

Rural development and rural vitalization: rural women as social foundation

Another important social transition impacting the space for young women farmers in agriculture and rural development is the national development strategy on rural vitalization. The Chinese central government issued *The opinions on the implementation of the strategy of rural vitalization* in early 2018, prioritizing rural vitalization as a fundamental development strategy in China in the following 30-year period. This strategy offers several visions for social transition towards agriculture, the countryside, and rural people; its aim is the social, economic, ecological, and spiritual well-being of the rural population. It is anticipated that by 2050, there will be a vibrant rural economy, a beautiful countryside, and a wealthy rural population in China. In pursuit of such objectives, the government considers rural women to be important agents and a driving force in the new round of rural development.

To nurture new women farmers, the Ministry of Agriculture and Rural Affairs together with the All-China Women's Federation have issued a series of policies and instituted new practices. In April 2018, the All-China Women's Federation launched the Women's Action in Rural Revitalization programme, which includes several components relating to the cultivation of women farmers. The first component targets rural female leaders, female college students, and female migrants in the countryside and offers them training in modern agriculture, e-commerce, agritourism, and handicrafts, among others, to incentivize and actively involve them in the market economy and rural development. In agriculture specifically, the programme provides trainings and demonstrations for rural women, encourages female farmers to seek employment on specialized plantations and in husbandry as well as nurture vocational women farmers by providing technical support in business operation and management. These opportunities are for both active and potential female farmers, including female migrants and college graduates with a rural background. Women's federations, for example, cooperated with the Ministry of Agriculture and Rural Affairs to organize pilot projects in 10 provinces to nurture new professional female farmers.

The second important component of the programme is alleviating poverty for rural women, aiming to improve the capacity of women in poor areas. They are encouraged to start a small business, assume multiple economic activities, or to enter the employment of large-scale commercial farms, co-ops, and corporations as wage workers. Women's federations also advocate female college students to work in village committees as a formal job to organize rural women in agricultural operation and promote their participation in public affairs.

It is to be noted that women's federations play an important role in organizing and serving rural women and female farmers in China. The institution of women's federation stems from the 1950s when it first served as a key mechanism to liberate women from feudal oppression and mobilize them for socialist construction. As official popular organizations, women's federations get fiscal transfers from the government and serve all women in China through their branches in villages, urban communities, enterprises, and son on. Under the central instruction of All-China Women's Federation and governments, women's federations at lower levels are organized and elected by women. Their main functions are to mobilize women for the state's development and safeguarding women and children's rights, especially relating to domestic affairs. Women's federations operate as quasi-official organizations to represent women in policy consultation; however, their social function to serve and cultivate women has yet to be fully realized. At the county level, it is very common that these organizations are highly marginalized in policy consultation: 'There is always a seat for women's federation in government conference but they're voiceless', are the words of some county government officials. Women's federations' institutional position reflects the general situation of gender relations in society to some extent, but also restricts their capacity to serve young women farmers. While rural women's roles in consolidating social governance and facilitating national development are recognized and highly advocated in policy, whether young rural women's own visions of development and their subjectivities in agriculture and rural industries are realized is to be explored. The discursive invisibility of and knowledge vacuum around young women farmers persists underneath the dynamic agrarian change in China. Young women farmers face enormous challenges in their pursuit of farming and well-being in a constantly transforming society, as do the Chinese scholars who analyse and record their stories during this dynamic period.

Conclusion

In spite of the scarce references directly related to young women farmers, this chapter has unfolded a picture of young women farmers between the 1950s and present day. In this period, young women farmers were either overworked agricultural labourers or suffering wives struggling to balance production and reproduction duties. Their stories were often obscured by the state's economic achievements. Young women farmers were not expected to become professional farmers nor were they seen as such, despite their contribution to agriculture's development in China. Since 2007, agriculture modernization and rural development have become national development keywords following a series of government-designed policies to cultivate new farmers in rural areas. The changing agrarian scenario has complex implications for young women farmers.

In such social dynamics, how can we understand young women farmers in our time? Or, how and why could young rural women become farmers in the current era? Is there any difference from the 1950s? Do gender relations change over time for young women farmers? Do young women farmers as a social group have unique characteristics compared to 20 years ago? Individual life should be understood by embedding into the macro history and society, and vice versa. Life stories of young women farmers would help us to understand the dynamics of this population in a transforming country like China. The following chapter will represent four cases of young women farmers from two research sites in China, reflecting this overview chapter in a more vivid way.

The first research site is called Pingxi, a township located in the mountain area with an altitude of over 1000 metres, in Sichuan Province in the south-west of China. The township is 50 km from the county seat and 70 km from the downtown Guangyuan city. In the early 1990s when market economy reform started, vegetable cultivation was initiated and farmers began to grow vegetables (such as cabbage and chilli) at a small-scale, gradually formulating a 'grain-vegetable' plantation system as a stable livelihood activity. However, due to the mountainous terrain condition, per capita land area is small and working on the land alone could not support rural families. Therefore, a large number of rural labourers have been working as migrant workers outside the town since the 1990s. There are few young farmers remaining in the village. Women and the elderly engage in grain-vegetable cultivation and devote themselves to the vegetable industry. As a result, we were just able to interview 31 young farmers under the age of 45 in three villages in this area, including 14 women farmers. Young women farmers are highly diversified and differentiated in their rural and farming activities. Most young women farmers are left-behind women who strive to maintain farmland for subsistence, while a few women farmers show stronger entrepreneurship in innovating and expanding family farming.

The second research site, Zhaizhuang village, is located in Hebei Province in the hinterland of the North China Plain. Zhaizhuang village specialized in cucumber production by smallholding rural households. Among its 267 households and 1,109 villagers, about 96 per cent of households are involved in cucumber production and only about 30 young people have migrated. Average farming scale is around four greenhouses, most smallholders with

2–3 greenhouses and several big holders with more than seven greenhouses. Comparing to the first research site and many other villages in China, the particularity of Zhaizhuang village is obvious. Without massive rural labour migration, villagers in Zhaizhuang could make moderate money from agriculture locally by virtues of their own labour, policy support, and market condition. The research team interviewed 50 young farmers in Zhaizhuang village, including 31 male farmers and 19 female farmers. Most young women farmers work together with their husbands to manage greenhouse production, while a few 'left-behind women' handle the production by themselves. Be it small scale or large, left-behind or not, young women farmers in Zhaizhuang village are more professional and have closer integration with technology and the market.

By reading these stories, readers may find similarities among the case women farmers as well as similarities between them and those in the 1950s to 1980s in earlier parts of this chapter. They still struggle with gender-biased, patriarchal social norms in the countryside when pursuing career activities on- or off-farm. Such gender and intergenerational barriers remain even though the source of authority varies from family, rural community to the state in different situations. Alongside those traditional factors, agrarian transition in China is another factor to reshape young women farmers by bringing both opportunities and challenges. Increased use of machines and technology, socialized agricultural services, and the availability of land transfer create space and conditions for young women to become farmers in a more professional way. They could access resources beyond patriarchal dominance. However, the enlarged space also means intensive competition in the market and harsh work that may force women farmers to make extraordinary efforts compared with men. Despite the challenges that women face, the general social context for young women farmers is changing, with signs of increased policy and institutional support, increasing visibility of young farmers, and gradual social recognition for the values of agriculture and countryside. At the centre of gender, generational, and transformative forces, young women farmers will continue to encounter challenges while moving to the fore of Chinese agriculture.

Notes

1. Bossen explained in her book that most records in the collectivization period were missing in the village but the records from 1980–1981 could still reflect the general situation of women's share of farm work.
2. Work point was the unit used to measure workload and payment of rural labour in the collectivization period. Rural labour's productive activities were organized by the collective and were paid based on the work points they got every day.
3. In the collectivization period, the brigade was the basic unit of organization in the rural population in production.

References

An, Z.Y. (1991) '1949–1978 nian zhongguo nongye jitihua yundong huigu' [Review of agricultural collectivization movement in China in 1949–1978]. *Qinghai shifan daxue xuebao (zhexue shehui kexue ban) [Academic Journal of Qinghai Normal University (social sciences)]* 3: 34–39. https://doi.org/10.16229/j. cnki.issn1000-5102.1991.03.007

Bock, B. (1994) 'Female farming in Umbrian agriculture'. In Maria Fonte and Leendert Van der Plas (eds), *Rural gender studies in Europe,* pp. 91–107. Assen: Van Gorcum and Comp BV.

Boserup, E. (2010 [1970]) *Woman's role in economic development.* Nanjing: Yilin Press.

Bossen, L. (2005) *Chinese women and rural development: Sixty years of change in Lu Village, Yunnan.* Nanjing: Jiangsu People's Publishing House.

Chant, S. (1992) 'Migration at the margins: Gender, poverty and population movement on the Costa Rican periphery'. In S. Chant (ed.), *Gender and migration in developing countries,* pp. 49–72. London and New York: Belhaven Press.

Chen, L. (2006) 'Nongcun Liushoufunv de jingshen yali he hunyin weiji' ['Mental stress and marital crisis of left-behind women in rural China']. *Gansu nongye [Gansu Agriculture]* 11: 85. https://doi.org/10.15979/j.cnki. cn62-1104/f.2006.11.087

China Economic Weekly (2006) 'Investigation on 50 million left-behind women's non-normal livelihood', 16 October. https://finance.sina.cn/ sa/2006-10-16/detail-ikknscsi3824371.d.htmlDe Rooij, S. (1994) 'Work of the second order'. In Maria Fonte and Leendert Van der Plas (eds), *Rural gender studies in Europe,* pp. 69–79. Assen: Van Gorcum and Comp BV.

Du, X.S. (2004) 'Zhongguo nongcun xiaoe xindai de shijian changshi' ['Practical exploration of microcredits in rural China']. *Zhongguo nongcun jingji [Chinese Rural Economy]* 8: 12–30.

Fan, L.J. and Cheng, Y. (2005) 'Liushounv: Xiandai nongcun shequ de yige xinqunti' ['Left-behind women: A new group in modern rural communities']. *Hefei xueyuan xuebao [Academic Journal of Hefei College]* 2: 9–13.

Fu, S.P. (2003) 'Nvxing zai nongye jishu chuanbo zhong de juese' ['The role of women in agricultural technology transmission']. *Xibei renkou [Northwest Population]* 2: 45–47.

Gao, H.Q. (2015) 'Nongye xiandaihua beijing xia nongcun liushou funv kexue suyang tishengtanjiu' ['Improving scientific literacy of rural left-behind women in context of agricultural modernization']. *Nongye zhanwang [Agricultural Outlook]* 11(4): 55–60.

Guo, Y.H. (2003) 'Xinling de jitihua: Shanbei jicun nongye hezuohua de nvxing jiyi' ['Collectivization of mind: Women's memories of collectivization in Ji village of Northern Shaanxi']. *Zhongguo shehui kexue [Social sciences of China]* 4: 79–92.

He, Z.M. (2007) 'Nongji tuiguang yingyong zhong nonghu canyu xingwei jiqi yingxiang yinsuyanjiu: Jiyu hangzhou huzhou liangdi diaocha de shizheng fenxi' ['Rural households' participation in agricultural technology extension and its influence factors: Based on analysis in Hangzhou and Huzhou']. MA thesis, Zhejiang University, China.

Hershatter, G. (2017) *The gender of memory: Rural women and China's collective past*. Beijing: People's Publishing House.

Horton, S. (2008) 'Consuming childhood: 'Lost' and 'ideal' childhoods as a motivation for migration'. *Anthropological Quarterly* 81(4): 925–43. https://doi.org/10.1353/anq.0.0034

Hu, Y.K. (2016) 'Renmin gongshe shiqi datian nongzuo de nvxinghua xianxiang: Jiyu dui xibu liangge cunluo de yanjiu' ['The feminization of field farming in Commune Period: Based on studies in two villages of west China']. *Funv yanjiu luncong* [*Collection of Women's Studies*] 5: 71–82.

Hugo, G. (2005) 'Indonesian international domestic workers: Contemporary developments and issues'. In S. Huang, B. Yeoh, and N. A. Rahman (eds), *Asian women as transnational domestic worker*, pp. 54–91. Singapore: Marshall Cavendish.

Huo, H.M. (2014) 'Nongcun chuangyezhe huode zhenggui xindai zhichi de yingxiang yinsu yu xingbie chayi: Jiyu shehui ziben shijiao' ['Impact factors and gender difference among rural entrepreneurs in formal credit support: From social capital perspective']. *Guizhou caijing daxue xuebao* [*Journal of Guizhou University of Finance and Economics*] 3: 87–93.

Jacka, T. (2012) 'Migration, householding and the well-being of left-behind women in rural Ningxia'. *The China Journal* 67: 1–21. https://doi.org/10.1086/665737

Jiang, M.H. and Zhou, Y. (2007) 'Nongcun liushou qizi xianxiang de shehui xingbie fenxi' ['Gender research on rural left-behind wife']. *Shehui gongzuo* [*Social Work*] 3: 48–49.

Jin, Y.H. (2016) *Zhong guo xin nongcun xingbie jiegou bianqian yanjiu: Liudong de fuquan* [*Structural transition of gender in new rural China: The floating paternity*]. Nanjing: Nanjing Normal University Press.

Kaspar, H. (2005) *'I am the household head now!': Gender aspects of out-migration for labour in Nepal*. Kathmandu: Nepal Institute of Development Studies.

Li, H.Y. (2010) *Records of rural China: Micro experiences in collectivization and reform*. Beijing: Law Press.

Li, J. (2003) 'Shilun nongcun shequ zhong liushou nvxing shenghuo fangshi de zhuanbian' ['An exploratory discussion on the change in the life style of the left-behind rural women']. *Shanxi qingnian guanli ganbu xueyuan xuebao* [*Journal of Shanxi College for Youth Administrators*] 16(2): 38–40.

Li, L.H. and Li, G.X. (2005) 'Guanzhu nongcun liushou nüxing, cujin hexie shehui goujian' ['Caring for rural left-behind women and promoting construction of harmonious society']. *Lilunjie* [*Theory Horizon*] 5: 57–58.

Liang, Y., Li, S., and Chen, W. (2011) 'Nongcun liushoufunü xinyang de chengyin, yingxiang ji jianyi' ['The reasons and effects of religious belief among left-behind women']. *Zhonguo jiti jingji* [*Chinese Collective Economy*] 22: 5–6.

Liu, J. (2012) *'Toward liberation': On agricultural labor of women in Taihang Mountain Area during the collectivization*, PhD thesis, Nankai University, China.

Luo, Y.Y., and Chai, D.H. (2004) 'Banliudong jiating zhong liushoufunü de jiating he hunyin zhuangkuang tanxi' ['Analysis on the family and marital situation of left-behind women in semi-migrant families']. *Lilun yuekan* [*Theory Monthly*] 3: 103–104.

Massey, D. (2009) *Staying behind when husbands move: Women's experiences in India and Bangladesh*. Falmer: Development Research Centre on Migration, Globalisation and Poverty, University of Sussex.

Ministry of Agriculture and Rural Affairs of the People's Republic of China (2017) 'Guoxinban juxing zhengce chuifenghui, nongyebu fubuzhang yezhenqin jieshao xinxing nongye jingying zhuti peiyu youguan qingkuang: Jiakuai peiyu xinxing nongye jingying zhuti daidong xiaononghu gongtong fazhan' ['The National Development and Reform Commission held a Policy Briefing and Vice Minister of Agriculture Ye Zhenqin Introduced the Development of New Agricultural Business Entities: Accelerating the development of new agricultural business entities to drive the common development of small farmers']. Ministry of Agriculture and Rural Affairs of the People's Republic of China, 15 December 2017. http://www.moa.gov.cn/xw/zwdt/201712/t20171219_6123309.htm

Ministry of Agriculture and Rural Affairs of the People's Republic of China (2019) 'xinzhongguo 70nian nongye nongcun jubian' ['Great changes of Chinese agriculture and countryside in 70 years']. Ministry of Agriculture and Rural Affairs of the People's Republic of China, 16 June 2021. http://www.moa.gov.cn/ztzl/70zncj/

National Bureau of Statistics (2008) 'Main Data Bulletin of the 2nd National Agricultural Census (No.2)'. https://www.stats.gov.cn/sj/tjgb/nypcgb/qgnypcgb/202302/t20230206_1902096.html

National Bureau of Statistics (2017a) 'Main Data Bulletin of the 3rd National Agricultural Census (No.1)'. https://www.stats.gov.cn/sj/tjgb/nypcgb/qgnypcgb/202302/t20230206_1902101.html

National Bureau of Statistics (2017b) 'Main Data Bulletin of the 3rd National Agricultural Census (No.5)'. https://www.stats.gov.cn/sj/tjgb/nypcgb/qgnypcgb/202302/t20230206_1902105.html

O'Hara, P. (1994) 'Out of the shadows: Women on family farms and their contribution to agriculture and rural development'. In Maria Fonte and Leendert Van der Plas (eds), *Rural Gender Studies in Europe*, pp. 50–65. Assen: Van Gorcum and Comp BV.

Qi, L.Y. (2019) 'Nongcun funv kexue suzhi fazhan xianzhuang' ['Development of scientific qualities of rural women']. *Zhongguo keji xinxi* [*China Science and Technology Information*] 1: 112–15.

Quisumbing, A.R. (1996) 'Male-female differences in agricultural productivity: Methodological issues and empirical evidence'. *World Development* 10: 1579–95. https://doi.org/10.1016/0305-750X(96)00059-9

Shang, C.R. (2008) 'Nongye keji tuiguang zhong de xingbie chayi yu tuiguang tixi de biange' ['Gender difference in agricultural technology extension and the changes of extension systems']. *Jinri Keyuan* [*Modern Science*] 18: 39–40.

Shi, K.L. and Liu, Y.S. (2014) 'Xin shiqi zhongguo funv jiaoyu yu shehuidiwei: Jiyu disanqi zhongguo funv shehui diwei diaocha shuju' ['Women's education and social status in new era: Based on the third China women's social status investigation']. *Zhongguo fuyun* [*China Women's Movement*] 5: 24–27.

State Council of China (2016) *The National Plan for Agricultural Modernization (2016–2020)* [website]. http://www.gov.cn/zhengce/content/2016-10/20/content_5122217.htm

Sun, Q. (2006) 'Nongcun liushou qizi jiating diwei de xingbie kaocha' ['On the family status of staying wives in rural areas from gender dimension']. *Shandong nüzi xueyuan xuebao [Journal of Women's Academy at Shandong]* 2: 29–33.

Tan, S. (1997) 'Nongcun laodongli liudong de xingbie chayi' [The gender difference in rural labor migration']. *Shehuixue yanjiu [Sociological Studies]* 1: 44–49. https://doi.org/10.19934/j.cnki.shxyj.1997.01.005

Wang, F. (2007) 'Liushou funü: Nongcun shangyan xinzhinu gushi' ['Left-behind women: The new story of Zhinu in rural villages']. *Zhongguo shehui daokan [China Society Periodical]* 4: 26–28.

Wang, Z., Li, X.Y., and Wu, D. (2008) 'Zhongguo nongcun minjian jinrong de shehui xingbie fenxi: Yi xibu xiaoe xindai zuzhi weili' ['Social gender analysis in informal finance of China: With example of microcredit organizations in West China']. *Shehui kexue yanjiu [Social Science Research]* 2: 124–32.

Wu, H.F. (2011) 'Liushou funv xianxiang yu nongcun shehui xingbie guanxi de bianqian' ['Analysis on gender relation changes through the phenomenon of left-behind women in rural China']. *Zhongguo nongye daxue xuebao (shehui kexue ban) [Journal of China Agricultural University (social edition)]* 3: 104–11. https://doi.org/10.13240/j.cnki.caujsse.2011.03.013

Wu, H., Ye, J., and Liu, P. (2010) 'Nongcun liushoufunv yu zongjiaoxinyang' ['The religious belief among left-behind women']. *Nongcun jingji [Rural Economy]* 1: 108–11.

Wu, Y. M., and Zhang, G.F. (2004) 'Nongcun funv tudi quanyi de liushi yu youxiao jiuji' ['The draining of land rights of rural women and effective aid']. *Shehui [Society]* 9: 4–7. https://doi.org/10.15992/j.cnki.31-1123/c.2004.09.002

Xiang, L. (2006) 'Nongcun liushounv: Yige zhide guanzhude ruoshi qunti' ['Rural left-behind women: A disadvantaged group deserves attention']. *Guangxi shehui kexue [Guangxi Social Sciences]* 1: 176–80.

Xu, C.X. (2009) 'Xibu nongcun liushou funv de shenxinjiankang ji qi yingxiang yinsu' ['The physical and psychological health of rural left-behind women and their influential factors in West China']. *Nanfang renkou [South Population]* 2: 49–56.

Xu, C.X. (2010) 'Xibu nongcun liushou funv jiating yali ji qi yingxiang yinsu fenxi' ['The family pressure of rural left-behind women and its influential factors in West China']. *Renkou yü jingji [Population and Economy]* 1: 73–78.

Yang, Q.L., and Wang, L.P. (2018) 'Nongcun funv daikuan xuqiu manzu chengdu de yingxiang yinsu yanjiu: Jiyu fujiansheng de diaocha shuju' ['Impact factors in satisfaction extents of rural women's demand of loan: Based on investigation in Fujian Province']. *Nongcun jinrong yanjiu [Rural Finance Research]* 11: 72–76. https://doi.org/10.16127/j.cnki.issn1003-1812.2018.11.015

Ye, J.Z. and Wu, H.F. (2008) *Dancing Solo: Women left behind in rural China.* Beijing: Social Science Literature Press.

Ye, J.Z., Pan, L., and He, C.Z. (2014) *Shuangchong qiangzhi: Xiangcun liushou zhong de xingbie paichi yu bupingdeng [Double cohesion: Gender exclusion and inequality in rural left-behind].* Beijing: Social Sciences Academics Press.

Zhao, L. (2014) *Nongcun funv yu nongcun tudi* [*Rural women and rural land*]. Hangzhou: Zhejiang Gongshang University Press.

Zhou, F.L. (2006) *Woguo liushou jiating yanjiu* [*Research on left-behind families in rural China*]. Beijing: China Agricultural University Press.

Zhou, W.W., Yan, X.P., and Liu, Z.Y. (2002) *Shengcun zai bianyuan – Liudong jiating* [*Living at the margin: Migrant families*]. Shijiazhuang: People's Press of Hebei Province.

Zhen, Y. (2008) *Zhongguo nongcun funv zhuangkuang diaocha* [*The survey on Chinese rural women*]. Beijing: Social Science Academics Press.

Zheng, Z., and Xie, Z. (2004) *Renkou liudong yu funü fazhan* [*Migration and rural women's development*]. Beijing: Social Sciences Press.

CHAPTER 5

The glowing ploughs: Stories of young women farmers in China

Lu Pan, Yilin Li, Changqi Li, Dong Liang, Yanqing Li, and Qirui Lin

This chapter offers life histories of four young women farmers in China – two each from Hebei Province in north China and Sichuan Province in south-west China. They are chosen as cases among many women farmers we interviewed mainly because of their enriched and condensed experiences. Their life stories concentrate the many important factors that surround young women farmers, including patriarchal family, generational and gender relations, labour migration, agricultural transition, and childcare, among others. The cases show women's farming trajectories as intertwined with various factors, which made young women farmers special and vital actors in rural China.

Yao Hui: A young woman's struggles
Yi Lin Li and Qirui Lin

Zhaizhuang village, Hebei Province

Yao is a 31-year-old vegetable farmer from Hebei Province in northern China. She is now planting a 400 m^2 cucumber greenhouse together with her husband. She grew up in a village in the same province. Her parents depended on farming and grew wheat and corn during Yao's childhood. In her early memories, her family was poor. To support the family, Yao's father was a migrant worker for many years while her mother remained on the farm to take care of her and her younger brother. When Yao was a teenager, her father returned home to continue farming while taking care of Yao's grandfather who was very ill. Her experience as a left-behind child and her mother's contributions to the family's care shaped both her values of child-rearing and how she views gender norms in her own family.

Yao was responsible for housework duties and farming from an early age, including cooking, herding sheep, and harvesting wheat. At age seven, she entered primary school and was responsible for her younger brother's care after school. She remembered him being naughty and needing to keep an eye on him at all times. When she was 11 years old, and her brother was 9, Yao started to cook for the family as her parents were really busy. She remembers the cauldron being very big, and she needed to place it properly on the stove and pour water into it. Yao also helped with farm work. She recalls a plague of bollworms. With a branch in her hand, she whipped the wheat and cotton until the worms fell into the basin she was holding. Walking through the field with her basin filled with worms, she remembers that the amount really impressed her. Though the infestation was serious, the family still had a good harvest. 'When I was young, my parents seldom used pesticide or chemicals. We used physical ways to control pests. The food we ate was very healthy. It's so different from present situation.'

Yao's formal education ended at age 16; she did not attend high school. There was a vocational senior high school where she could have studied to gain professional skills like information technology. Her father, however, thought the vocational high school was useless and the family should not spend money on her schooling. The family was poor and her father wanted her to work at a clothing factory where she could start earning a wage immediately. 'I really loved computers. When I was in middle school, our school was equipped with some desktop computers. I thought it's very smart and modern to learn computer. I was really eager to learn it. However, I could not go against my father. He thought it's useless and not worthy of spending the money.'

Her father's stubborn insistence prevailed, and Yao abandoned her dream and began wage work. Yao believes that her father regretted his decision to end her education. When Yao worked in Shandong Province, her father told her that she could return to school to study but she had already lost her perseverance and courage to return to school. 'If I had the chance to study computers, I might not be doing farming at present,' Yao sighed.

In China, most rural youth of Yao's age who finished middle school at 16 or 17 but failed to enter senior high school because of failure in school performance end up as migrant workers. Family farming on a small scale does not require very much labour nor does it generate sufficient income to support many family members. For these young people, working in the city meant earning money to support the family while widening one's visions and opportunities for the future. Nowadays rural youth who left middle school still prefer to do migrant work in cities. Compared with Yao, the current generation face fewer economic pressures from family. Their migrations are mostly driven by aspiration of urban life.

Yao's first job after she left the farm was in a duck slaughterhouse in Changyi city, Shandong Province. She was responsible for removing small feathers from the plucked duck's body by using a small clip. She woke in the morning around 4 a.m. and worked until 10 p.m. In addition to the long working hours, Yao suffered from rashes on her hands because of chemicals in the water used for cleaning the ducks. She could wear protective gloves but as workers were paid on a piecework basis, she chose not to so that she could work faster. In the first month at her first job, Yao earned CNY 600 (about USD 84). 'I was really excited with the money I earned. That's my first salary. But I also truly understood the hardship of life and making a living.' Her family did not have a telephone at that time so when she missed home, she had to call her neighbours' homes to be able to speak with her parents. She often could not help but cry when she heard her parents' voices over the phone.

When she was 18, she left Shandong and returned to her home village. She remained at home for two months and helped her parents in the cotton field before departing again, this time for Beijing to look for a job. 'I never planned to return to farming. I got tanned when helping my parents thinning the cotton flower. No girls want to be tanned. I liked Beijing and didn't want to be a farmer'. With the help of an employment agency, she started a new job at a Sony Ericsson factory where she worked on an assembly line producing mobile phones. She earned between CNY 600 (about USD 84) and CNY 800 (about USD 112) per month and remained at the factory for two years. In 2008, she shifted to a Panasonic factory where she remained for one year. Owing to the work experience in Beijing, Yao became more confident and talkative. She also felt pride in being economically independent. Of her CNY 1,000 (about USD 140) monthly wage, she only kept a small part and sent the rest of the money home. Meals and accommodation were provided by the factory, which helped to cut down her expenditure.

From 2008, when Yao was 21 years old, her father began to urge her to marry. In her father's mind, it was better for her to marry before her younger brother. 'My father called when I was in Beijing. He said, "how could your brother get married if you do not marry? If you don't find a husband, do not go to work anymore!"' It is part of the traditional social norm in the countryside of Hebei Province that older siblings should marry before their younger siblings to avoid bringing bad luck to the latter. Yao felt that she could not disobey her father. She quit her job in late 2008 and was soon engaged to a man that she met through a matchmaker. After the engagement, Yao moved to Weihai city in Shandong Province where she worked in an electronics factory for eight months. The hasty engagement foreshadowed future conflicts.

In 2009, Yao married and moved to her husband's village, Zhaizhuang. In rural China, following the patrilocal tradition, women usually move to their husbands' family after marriage. Their parents-in-law then will divide the farmland, house, and some other property with the new couple. This was not the case for Yao. For the first four years after their marriage, Yao and her husband remained in the house of her parents-in-law. Her husband's parents made all of the decisions on family financial issues and Yao and her husband had to hand over all of their wages to the parents. Yao's mother-in-law would not permit her to leave the village to work in a city. As a result, the young couple were not economically independent. Yao recalled: 'Life was so tough then. I didn't have money. I couldn't go out to work because my mother-in-law didn't like it. My husband mainly worked in his parents' vegetable greenhouse. I could only use my previous savings to buy new clothes.'

Her husband's family owned a greenhouse and did farm work there. Yao stayed at home and watched television every day. When all the family members worked in the greenhouse, no one talked with her. Her former workmate invited the couple to work at a factory in Weihai city. However, Yao's mother-in-law rejected the suggestion because she thought that the cost of renting accommodation in the city was too high. In 2010, Yao's first daughter was born and her only job was to care for the baby. For Yao, life became even more harsh and boring, especially since the baby was frequently ill and her parents quarrelled a lot. Yao related the struggles she faced during this period: 'We got married too soon to know each other well. In fact, I did not want to marry at that time. The marriage deprived my freedom. The engagement was made in haste and we did not love each other at the beginning. In the first several years I was in a bad temper and even thought to commit suicide.'

Things improved as the baby grew. In 2013, Yao welcomed a son and in the same year, her parents-in-law decided to divide the household. She thinks they saw the birth of a grandson as the real establishment of the young family's new household. Yao and her husband received 0.6 mu of farmland with a small vegetable greenhouse. They were not able to enlarge their scale of production at that time due to the lack of funds and land. They couldn't make ends meet and had to borrow money to send her daughter to kindergarten.

Thanks to a government subsidy that supported vegetable greenhouse construction, the couple had the opportunity to secure a loan from the Postal Savings Bank of China in 2013. They borrowed CNY 50,000 (about USD 7,000) for a period of one year. As they were unable to secure returns on their investment in the first six months, they had to borrow additional funds for daily expenses and to make interest payments. Yao remembers: 'It was too stressful and tough to spend that half of year. It is difficult to borrow money.'

The revenues from the sale of products grown in the new vegetable greenhouse were not as good as anticipated. The couple planted cucumbers but there was something wrong with the seedlings and the yield was low. 'Many people think vegetable greenhouse owners are rich. Actually, it is very difficult to manage.' Cucumber cultivation is also risky. In 2016, due to the severe smog, cucumbers in Yao's greenhouse were infected with bacterial soft rot and many withered away due to lack of sunlight. Many other vegetable farmers faced the same problem.

Yao never worked in the new vegetable greenhouse in its first year of operation – she spent all of her time taking care of the two children at home. Many villagers laughed at her, 'your son can walk and run now. They don't need your care anymore, why don't you work on your own land?' In Yao's mind, her children are more important than farming. The greenhouse environment is not good for children. She had a friend whose young daughter almost died after drinking pesticide in a greenhouse. 'As a mom, I just want to spend as much time as possible before they go to school. I wish my mom could accompany with me as much as possible when I was young, but she's always busy with the farm work.'

In 2016, Yao began farming in the greenhouse since her three-year-old son was enrolled in kindergarten. She went to the greenhouse every morning after sending the children to school. Her husband taught her how to plant cucumbers. He was responsible for applying pesticides, irrigation, and cucumber sales while Yao took care of all of the other jobs in the greenhouse on her own. To earn more money to support the family, Yao also worked in a small clothing factory in the township where she sewed schoolbags. She tells us that many women in the village manage the greenhouse by themselves when their husbands migrate to cities.

Yao's husband frequently attended training sessions on cucumber production. Yao did not accompany him as she felt that she could not understand the training contents. Her husband is responsible for cost management while Yao manages the revenues. Although she could manage the whole greenhouse operation on her own, she would rather handle the housework and leave the farming duties to her husband when he is at home. She is not interested in improving her farming skills. Despite her passion for freedom from the countryside, she accepts the social role for women to support their husbands and educate their children.

Yao feels that her life is steadily improving. With revenues from their vegetable greenhouse, she says that the family currently has no financial burdens. Her children are now in school so she has more time and energy to dedicate to farming. She is satisfied with her present life. Her relationship with her husband has also improved; although they sometimes quarrel, life is generally peaceful. The couple focus most of their efforts on their children's education, which differentiates them from other villagers. Overwhelmed with farm work, villagers in Zhaizhuang don't have enough time to pay attention to their children's education, and their grades suffer. Yao's ideas on education are influenced by her time working in big cities. The couple do not expect their children to attain great scores and instead focus on cultivating their hobbies and educational interests – they want their children to learn what they like. 'Do the scores matter? The most important thing is the process of study. Study depends on interest. If you don't enjoy study, the scores are useless.' She adds that the children nurtured under this model are no worse than others who are focusing on study only. Her daughter is a dancer and has even won a dance competition.

When her children are older, Yao plans to find another off-farm job to earn additional income to provide a better future for them. When asked which life is better, her present life or her earlier life as a migrant worker, she answered: 'It is incomparable. I worked outside for myself. Now, I have my husband and children. Even if I go back to be a migrant worker, I work for my children.' Throughout her education, migration, and marriage, Yao has struggled for freedom from her father, her husband, and her parents-in-law. In many cases, she has failed. Now being a mother of two children, she is trying her best to give her children more of a carefree childhood and allow them to pursue their freedom in the future. She doesn't have any inclination or bias on her children's future. 'I won't mind if they want to be farmers, as long as they like.'

Wu Haixia: A woman working in large-holding production
Changqi Li and Yanqing Li

Zhaizhuang village, Hebei Province

Wu Haixia and her husband planted 10 cucumber greenhouses. Except for the 3.7 mu contract land allocated by the village collective, they also rented an extra 6 mu from the village. Wu was born in 1980. She and her husband Zhangqun have two sons. The older son is 14 years old and in the second year of junior middle school, and the younger one is 11 years old in the fourth grade. Wu's natal family lives in Tatou village in the same county. Farmers in her village started growing cucumbers when she was seven or eight years old. At that time, every family needed help from their neighbours to accomplish large projects like building a greenhouse. Wu's family joined the other villagers in cucumber production and built a 30-metre-long greenhouse to grow cucumbers in 1987. After school, Wu would help with simple farm work outside of the greenhouse but she didn't know about the operations inside the greenhouse. It was also her responsibility to cook for her family and help with housework when her parents were in the fields. She has a brother who is two years younger than her, but she didn't care for her brother as they were around the same age.

Wu finished her primary and junior middle school education in her village. In her childhood, there was still a middle school at the village level. When her own children reached school age in 2011, the school had been moved further to the township or the county base. Wu was not a strong student and found school boring. Education was not the villagers' priority during that period and most young people expected to start wage work after completing junior middle school at age 16. Wu did not think too much about her future. Neither did she think about being a farmer. After completing her studies, she remained at home in the village for two years. Every day, she did some work in the small cucumber greenhouse, watched television, and waited until she was old enough to obtain a job beyond the village.

At the age of 18, Wu was able to buy a non-agricultural *hukou* (which means she is registered as an urban resident) through the relation of an aunt in Shanxi Province. She then found work at a pharmaceutical factory in Shanxi. Such a change from a rural identity to an urban identity had significant implications for Wu, as it does on all single rural women and men, then and now. For contemporary rural migrants, agricultural *hukou* still impedes their social integration and entitlement to many social services once they are living in an urban area.[1] The urban *hukou* registration was the big change for Wu, a dream to work in the city, and one that faded quickly. With a salary of CNY 300 (about USD 42) per month, Wu only saved CNY 500 (about USD 70) in four years of working in Shanxi. She was employed in a state-owned pharmaceutical factory where jobs were called 'iron rice bowls' because employment in state-owned or collectively owned businesses in the 1990s was stable. Nearly all of the factory workers were female and there were 50 people in a workshop. Wu worked in the processing workshop for 7.5 hours a day. Her job was to remove debris from the medicine by hand. When compared to the rigid labour conditions in Chinese factories today, Wu remembers a pretty good work environment and a very lively atmosphere in the workshop, with workers talking and laughing. Wu made some friends in the factory, but they have since lost contact with each other. Later, in 2002, Wu returned home to her village because the factory's benefits had fallen, and wages had not been paid for several months. Her younger brother had a similar bad work experience in a factory and there was often such news of 'employees unpaid' broadcast on television, which contributed to Wu losing interest in working outside the village. It was a time of change for state-owned enterprises and a great number of employees lost their 'iron rice bowl' in market-oriented reforms in the late 1990s. It was estimated that, nationwide, there were over 100 million employees in state-owned enterprises and departments in 1996, which was reduced to about 70 million in 2001.

In the first year after returning home from Shanxi Province, Wu did not take on another job. In late 2003, she married Zhangqun of Zhaizhuang village. There was little land that Zhangqun's family owned in the village and her husband's family had no greenhouse, only 3 mu^2 (0.49 acres) of land. The parents-in-law divided up the family property after the young couple's wedding and the latter got 1.6 mu (0.26 acres) of land. In the early days of their marriage, Wu's husband worked for the county's Grain Bureau, which also provided a kind of 'iron rice bowl' job in that era. However, after the Grain Bureau's dissolution a year later as a result of government institutional reform, he suddenly lost his job. He worked as a grain wholesaler for the next two years by virtue of his social network. During this time, Wu was responsible for childcare and maize planting. The birth of Wu's first son in 2004 brought her family another 533 m^2 of land. Two years later, in 2006, Wu and her husband built a cucumber greenhouse on their land after seeing the trend among their neighbours. They earned more than CNY 10,000 (about USD 1,400) in the first year of production. In Wu's view, the benefits of growing cucumbers are obvious when compared to the low wages in the county. Therefore, Wu and her husband gradually shifted to agriculture after their uneasy working experience in cities. In 2008, they rented in land from a neighbour and built their second greenhouse.

'It is not popular to work outside,' Wu always replied when she was asked if she would return to a salaried position off the farm. Since the 1980s, the tide of working away from farming as rural migrants has swept across thousands of villages in China. The limited arable land relative to population in most rural areas and low revenues earned from agriculture distracted many young people who migrated to urban areas for employment or higher wages. However, the booming cucumber industry has attracted young people to Zhaizhuang village and offered them stable economic benefits. Under the village committee's leadership, land was reconsolidated so that villagers were able to rent in more land for individual cucumber production. With the construction of a local market and provision of marketing services by the village committee, cucumber farmers could sell their products in a timely way within the village. The village has gradually become commercialized and specialized in cucumber plantations, which explains why these young people have remained in the village.

Once her husband decided to engage in cucumber farming, it was not easy for the couple to expand the scale. 'The poor do not have to divide up family property because there is no property to divide at all. We didn't have money when we split with my parents-in-law as they didn't have much money as well. We just started from scratch,' Wu recalled. Marriage and the division of land is both the birth of a new family and of a new family agricultural production and management entity. The husband and wife are the family's producers and neither had experience working in the greenhouse before marriage, rather they learned from their neighbours while growing their own cucumbers.

In 2007, Wu gave birth to her second son. Due to China's one-child policy, which has since been repealed, the couple paid a CNY 5,000 (about USD 700) fine in order to give their son a *hukou*[3] and they got 333 m² of land from the village collective.[4] The increase in family members put pressure on the family's livelihood – they needed additional income. Some village households in the same situation chose the 'half work and half till' mode which saw men go to cities for migrant work while women remain at home to farm. Wu and her husband chose to expand the scale of their cucumber production, inspired by the benefits brought by the harvest from the first greenhouse. In 2008, they built a second greenhouse next to their first one on land rented from other villagers.

Wu and her husband were the most important labourers in the greenhouse. Wu needed to take care of the children while tending to her responsibilities in the greenhouses. Her husband's mother sometimes helped her with the children, but she had to work in her own greenhouse as well. In the early days of their venture, there were no roller blinds to automatically roll up the covers on top of the greenhouse and the straw that covered the greenhouse needed to be wound up manually. This process was hard physical work and it took half an hour for a male labourer to complete the work for one single greenhouse. Such work needed to be done twice a day. Despite such hardships, the hard work is a good memory for Wu:

> When people rolled up the cover on the greenhouse, they could often see each other. People would stand on the greenhouse, working while talking to neighbours. After a busy day, people whose greenhouses were closed would find a greenhouse to gather and chat before it got dark, very lively. Because there were fewer greenhouses in the village previously, therefore people felt at ease and could rest at home after finishing the work. I really missed that time because people now are too busy to talk.

Availability of land has always been an issue in Zhaizhuang village. When Wu was married, she was allocated 533 m² of land from the village collective. It was a piece of reserved land in the village, used to adjust farmland distribution when a villager married or died. Since 2010, there have been no more reserved land allocations in the village as all farmland has been distributed. In 2012, to promote cucumber production and to make effective use of its land, the village collective actively planned two centralized vegetable gardens in the village, funded in part by government monies. The county's Bureau of Agricultural Development subsidized 50 greenhouses with CNY 60,000 (about USD 8,500) for each newly built greenhouse (the cost of a greenhouse is about CNY 80,000 to 100,000, equivalent to USD 11,200 to 14,000). All of the villagers who wished to have a new greenhouse could apply and the chance was decided by lot. Farmers' contracted land that was to become the new plantation location needed to be reassigned by the village collective. The grower/greenhouse owner would pay rent of CNY 1,000 (about USD 140) per mu per year to the land transfer household through the village collective. As the village's children grew older and entered school, the amount of money Wu's family needed also grew. When the option to rent land via the village collective was announced, Wu's family was among the first to submit their application. With stable revenue from cucumber production at that time, expanding the scale of planting would bring additional net income to the family. Thanks to the village's support and using their savings, Wu and her husband built three greenhouses on the south side of their house.

In 2013, recognizing that land would be increasingly scarce in the future, limiting their ability to expand their operations, Wu and her husband submitted a second application for land. They were successful and built five new greenhouses next to the first two greenhouses which were built in 2006 and 2008. At that moment they had 10 greenhouses in total. In order to build the five new greenhouses, they borrowed CNY 100,000 (about USD 1,400) from the bank and for a one-year period. In order to ensure that farmers would repay their loans on time, the bank required a 'three-family joint guarantee'; if one of the households could not repay their loan on time, the other two households would be responsible for the repayment. Nearly all small households in the village that took loans during the same period repaid their loans on time. The few who could not would borrow money from family, friends, and neighbours since the interest rate would increase to CNY 200 (about USD 28) per day after 365 days and any delay would impact their credit record. It happened that the weather was very good in 2013. Wu's family earned enough money with their 10 greenhouses in three months, and they quickly paid off the loan. The couple started with the 1.6 mu of land from Wu's parents-in-law and in less than 10 years, they were large greenhouse-holders in the village. In the village, each household plants three to four greenhouses on average. Wu's story is one of a successful entrepreneur but her momentum has remained her family:

> I have two sons and small land. The boys are growing up. They need money to go to school, go to college, and later buy apartments and get married. We need money, we need to plan and prepare for our kids. What can we do? We lost the job in cities and have no special

skills to earn good money. What we can do is to take any opportunity to have more land to plant. It's like gambling, if we lost the chance, we lost the money.

The birth of children and the enlargement of family size are the driving force for the couple's continuous expansion of production scale. The stable development of the cucumber industry has increased their confidence and the village's support and cucumber production-friendly policies have provided the couple with valuable opportunities. It is these domestic and external factors that have made Wu and her husband the large holders in the village.

Operating 10 greenhouses is not easy – it is like a small agribusiness – but Wu doesn't see herself as an entrepreneur. She would rather not spend time thinking about production. If she has time, she would prefer to spend it watching television, a favourite and relaxing pastime since childhood albeit with internet-enabled technology and many more functions. Wu has a smart phone, on which she uses WeChat and plays simple mobile games, but she does not find it easy to use; she often relies on her children's help. For example, videos on the mobile phone can be played on the television, but Wu doesn't know how to do this. She admits that she does not have much ambition to learn new production techniques either so it is her husband who is responsible for technical management and making decisions related to greenhouse plantation. As for families in the village where the husband and wife share responsibility for production, the common division of labour has the man taking on the role of manager, which includes pesticide application and cucumber sales, while the woman is responsible for specific work such as planting. This is the same for the Wu family. She does not apply pesticides because the barrel and the mist machine are relatively heavy for her, but also because she doesn't know how to mix pesticides and is ignorant of the various diseases encountered in the growth of cucumbers. Wu also pays little attention to economic news so it is her husband who needs to be attentive to new information on planting techniques and market conditions, selecting cucumber seedlings and pesticides, and solving trading problems at the market. Overall Wu remains in the cucumber greenhouse longer than her husband with specific tasks such as clearing up the greenhouse after a harvest, picking cucumbers, carrying cucumbers, and so on. After their expansion to 10 greenhouses, the couple could not meet the plantation's labour demands themselves. Hiring and managing wage labour is an important task in greenhouse production and this falls under Wu's responsibilities. She is more than capable of arranging routine work, just like a housewife manages domestic work in the home. With the couple's current division of labour, Wu does not think that her contributions to agricultural production are less than those of her husband:

> Our work is equally important and no one could do things on his/ her own. This is a kind of cooperation. My husband would be too

busy to handle everything without my assistance. Such labour division is not showing who's stronger and has more power. It's indeed to enhance efficiency. I don't like to think and fix problems, but I do things very quickly. Women have our advantage in the greenhouse work.

Wu shared that it is natural for many families in the village to adopt such a division of labour between men and women. However, there are also some left-behind women in the village who manage the cucumber cultivation on their own. Women have the ability to make independent decisions and manage production, but few women engage in decision-making and in the technical aspects of agricultural production because their opportunities to do so are often limited and despite having the capacity to do so, such efforts are despised by husbands.

'Greenhouse planting is like child rearing' – these are Wu's words of wisdom gained over many years of greenhouse planting. As a woman brought up in traditional Chinese culture, she treats her greenhouses like her children and exerts great effort to nurture the plants within. For farmers who grow cucumbers, a year does not begin from New Year's Day or the Spring Festival, but from the day when the cucumbers are planted. In July, the greenhouses will be sealed and the soil sterilized at a high temperature to prevent weeds. In August, the cucumbers will be planted in the cooler weather. To improve the soil's fertility and permeability, Wu would add corn straw into the land through deep ploughing. Given its specialization in cucumber production, there are very few corn fields in Zhaizhuang village and Wu would return to her natal village to collect straw. This is a reciprocal exchange between the villagers. Villagers can get straw in the fields for free if the landholders agree. In the past, the farmer would use a machine to thresh the straw into short rods, but this machine is no longer used. Instead, the straw is now smashed into pieces before being spread in the fields, which actually weakens its permeability. Chicken manure is also spread in the fields. Some farmers use wet chicken manure that has been sealed in plastic film to ferment and heaped up next to the greenhouses in the spring. Wu does not raise chickens, so she buys fermented chicken manure from agricultural materials stores and then spreads it on the fields. 'Using corn straw and chicken manure is a very local way to fertilize the land. For 10 month's production in a year, the land needs to be well attended. To prepare land with corn straw and chicken manure is very complicated, especially it stinks and dirty. But it's good and provides nutrition to the land.'

Wu and her husband buy cucumber seedlings from professional nurseries. Seedling varieties on the market are generally renewed every two or three years, and old varieties are then eliminated from the market. The variety of seedlings in Wu's family changes annually. In order to reduce the production risks, they plant different varieties in different greenhouses, and decide what seedlings to buy in the next year based on the current year's output. Wu doesn't know and care much about the varieties. She cannot tell which variety of seedlings is of better quality. She told us:

> I think seedling varieties are not that important. Seedlings cannot determine what they harvest, because the output of cucumbers is related to greenhouse management. The same seedlings would grow differently in different greenhouses. It's just like a child. He may not grow well if you look after him very carefully every day; he may grow very well if you raise him in hard conditions. So, as farmer, we need to gradually summarize the lessons and experiences and take care the cucumber differently. It's similar to raising the child.

If greenhouse planting is like child-rearing, then Wu is a 'partial' mother. She spends much more time and energy on the greenhouses than on her two sons who are now 17 and 14 years old. When her sons were young, there were only two greenhouses in her family. Wu was able to take care of both the greenhouses and the children. However, with the increase in the number of greenhouses, she spent more and more time at work and had no time to take care of her children – she didn't know whether her sons were playing computer games or were on their mobile phones at home. The couple decided to send one of their sons to a private school and another to a boarding school. The younger son could get decent care in private school while the older one was able to take care of himself in boarding school. Such an arrangement is not common in the village. Not only because tuition fees were higher in private school, but also parents usually prefer their children to be close to family. As busy parents, they thought this change was a better way for their sons to get the care they require as well as study supervision.

Without her children at home, Wu can concentrate on working in the greenhouses. Food and living conditions are nice at school, so Wu is not worried about the children. After returning from the greenhouses in the evening, she still has to complete basic housework. When the weather is fine, she will take the opportunity to air the boys' quilts so they can return with them to school in the fall. This type of small gesture is her way of expressing love to the children even though she is overwhelmed by farm work. Wu and her husband live a simple life when their sons are away. They eat steamed stuffed buns for lunch in the greenhouse, and buy ready-made dishes on their way home to eat for dinner. The couple sometimes doesn't cook for 20 days in a row during the busy farming season. Overwhelmed with busy farm work as well, Wu's husband is more aware of her hard work. He also helps a lot in domestic work, sharing the work of cooking sometimes or cleaning the house.

Wu may seem to be a boring woman. She has no family to care for, no time to recreate, and no leisure activities. Occasionally, she plays mahjong with other women, but the rest of her time is consumed by farming activities; even if she visits neighbours it's for greenhouse plantation. Wu is very tired after a day's work, and she would rather stay at home than engage in public activities in the village. Her parents' home is very close to Zhaizhuang village and she often shares a meal at their home. Wu will turn her focus off of the cucumber greenhouses only in important circumstances. For example, her mother-in-law was hospitalized in the provincial capital for more than four months in 2017 due to heart disease and mild uraemia. At that time, there was work to do in the greenhouses, and Zhangqun needed to apply pesticides. Wu had to shuttle from the greenhouses to the hospital every week.

Wu is not a smart businesswoman nor a miser. What she values is the importance of the cucumber greenhouses in sustaining her family, especially her two sons. She calculated money based on her children's subsistence demands. The 10 greenhouses can generate an income of CNY 150,000 to more than CNY 200,000 (about USD 21,000–28,000) annually, depending on the market price and the yield. The children's' tuition fees are more than CNY 20,000 (about USD 2,800) per year, which is a major expense for the family. Wu is also thinking ahead to expenses related to her children's marriage in the future, including buying apartments and cars for them, which she expects will cost about CNY 1,000,000 (about USD 141,000) :

> My older son doesn't study well. I felt sorry to him because I'm too busy to supervise his study. He always reports bad things such as making mistakes, losing something and so on when he calls me. I don't expect him to be some big figure, it's impossible for him to enter college. I'm prepared for the worst thing that they can't find a job and making a living in the city, and return to the village. If so, the cucumber greenhouse would be their last resort. That's why the land and the cucumber matters so much to me. It's related to the future life of my sons.

Wu imagines that her sons will marry when they reach age 22, like most young people in the village, and then give her grandsons. Wu's philosophy of life is do what others do, observing other people and following their decisions, as she does when plotting her sons' life paths. Wu's attitude to urban life is full of contradictions. On the one hand, she does not regret her life in the planting greenhouses where she is free to manage her daily life, but on the other hand, she cannot deny that she yearns for urban life, despite the accompanying restrictions. But after 12 years of working in the cucumber greenhouses, she is also afraid of the unknowns of urban life. She said:

> I could not imagine what kind of life I will live now without the greenhouse. If I was young, I'd like to try new things but now I'm accustomed to be a farmer. Maybe when I'm getting old and the life of my children are stabilized, I would keep two or three greenhouses and sell the extra ones. But before that, I will continue to grow cucumbers, as long as we can do it.

The work in the greenhouse consumes Wu's time, leaving her little opportunity to enjoy life, including in terms of interpersonal communication and personal development. Greenhouse planting began as her livelihood, but it is now her quotidian life. She not only gives her space and time to the 'child', but also plans her future around the greenhouses' operation. When asked why she chose to engage in agriculture and cucumber cultivation, she said, 'the life of my children and family would have been hard if I hadn't done so'. It seems that everything she does for the 'child' – her greenhouses – is, in fact, for her two sons.

Li Mei: Household reproduction of a left-behind woman farmer

Lu Pan and Dong Liang

Pingxi Township, Guangyuan City, Sichuan Province

Li Mei is 44 years old and lives in Dazhu village, Guangyuan City in Sichuan Province. The village is on top of a mountain, which takes hours to reach from the city. Li's family has 2.7 mu (0.44 acres) of farmland transferred to a company and now they only have 1 mu (0.16 acres) of hilly land to plant maize and vegetables. She also raised two pigs. Li's husband was a migrant worker in Ningxia with their older son who was 21 years old. Her younger son, who was 12 years old, was in junior middle school in the city. Li is a typical rural woman who has remained in the countryside and taken up farming as a profession. As a middle-aged woman, she's still 'young' among the farming population in her village since most adults have migrated within China in search of employment. Li has been married for 23 years and has two sons. Unique in her village, she and her husband have one of the only uxorilocal marriages – her husband married into Li's family. It was as difficult for rural youth in mountainous areas to find a partner in the 1990s as it is today. Li's husband grew up in a small village deep in the mountains. He had several unmarried brothers and the family's economic situation was unstable. He chose to marry into Li's family rather than remain single. In Chinese culture, especially in rural areas, men would reject uxorilocal marriage. It means their children would follow the family name of the mother while the father's lineage was interrupted.

Li dropped out of school at age 10 due to poverty. Her husband did not attend middle school either. Constrained by his education, Li's husband could only find jobs as a labourer in the city. He has been working on construction sites for over 10 years. Li has been separated from her husband for most of their marriage. Li is very shy to talk about her personal life and related emotions:

> Sometimes I'm worried that I can only live together with my husband when we are aged. We have to separate for such a long time. It's a bit desperate to think of it. If he stayed at home, like the first few years after we married, we can discuss on family issues and I have someone aside to talk. However, he couldn't, otherwise we won't have enough money to live. We have no choice. All I can do is to take care of our

kids and the household well to make my husband relieved when he's away. A woman has to uphold the family.

Li has never migrated to an urban area for employment given her poor health. Besides, her 12-year-old younger son is in middle school. As the couple only had a few years of schooling, they focused a lot of attention on their children's education. 'I'm afraid if I went outside of the village to be a migrant worker, nobody would take care of my son. Nobody would cook for him and wash clothes for him. My parents have passed away. If I left, he (the younger son) would be like an orphan.' Her younger son attended boarding school in the city and returned home every weekend. Li needs to stay at home to prepare food and clothes for him every weekend, which does not allow her to go to cities for long-term work. The younger son's annual education cost is around CNY 8,000 (about USD 1,100). 'I wish he could have a better future through education. I don't want him to come back to the village.' Li and her husband had the same expectations for their older son, who studied very hard at school and received his college diploma via correspondence in 2014. He studied engineering while working in a factory and paid the tuition with his wage. However, this education did not improve his job search chances. It's difficult for college students to find a job in the market, let alone a college student with correspondence education. 'All our hope is on our son. We [Li and her husband] only had very few years of education and we hope our son could have good education and good job. He studied very hard and worked very hard. He paid all of his tuition with his part-time job. Does college education become invaluable? Why he still could not get a decent job?' Li was very confused.

With the promotion and popularization of higher education, rural youth have more opportunities to go to college as long as they can afford the tuition. However, the quality of higher education and hence post-graduation employment opportunities cannot be guaranteed. For young people with a rural background who do not have a broad social network or strong social capital, higher education often does not offer them a promising future but rather leaves their families in poverty due to children's long-term education investment. Li's older son worked in a factory in Zhejiang province for two years after graduation and then joined his father as a construction worker. In 2017, father and son worked together on a construction project in Ningxia Autonomous Region, north-western China. Their daily salary was CNY 200 (about USD 28) to set up overhead wires as electrical power lines. However, the work is not very stable. They return to their hometown between projects. They usually rested for less than a month before getting jobs in another project.

Currently Li is very concerned about the marriage of the older son. Living expenditure in the countryside has been growing rapidly, especially the expenditure on rituals such as weddings and funerals, which is the typical 'fund of rituals' in the life world of Chinese peasants. 'When you participate in weddings or funerals of close relatives, usually the gift money is CNY 800 to 1,000 (about USD 112–140). If it's an ordinary relative, it would be CNY 200 (about USD 28) or 100 (about USD 14).' As a member of the community, a considerable part of household income has been used in such rituals. The wedding of Li's older son would be the moment to have her previous generosity repaid. In the previous year, Li started to build a new house to prepare for her son's wedding. It is a two-storey house with 12 rooms. The house's main structure was finished but it was still lacking windows, doors, and interior decoration. The family has spent CNY 260,000 (about USD 37,000) on the construction so far, and incurred a CNY 50,000 (about USD 7,000) debt. To complete the decoration, CNY 100,000 (about USD 14,000) more is needed.

> People in our area spend much money in building house. We earn some money in the cities and then put it into the construction. When the money ran out, we go outside once again to earn money and then come back to continue the construction. No villagers could build a new house in one time, the construction is done little by little and usually it takes many years. The wedding would cost around CNY 500,000, including building a new house and betrothal gifts to the girl's family. Of course, we don't need so many rooms for ourselves. But when prepare a wedding or funeral we need the rooms to host feast for friends, neighbours, and kinships.

Pressures of the son's marriage are not only due to the money but also to the difficulty of rural young men in finding a partner. Li's son was dumped by his girlfriend last year because the family was in the mountains and the girl's parents did not want their daughter to live in harsh conditions. 'All the young girls in our village are gone. Some are doing migrant work in the cities; some are married elsewhere. Even our local matchmaker could not think of a young girl to introduce to my son.'

It is very common for young men from Dazhu village to find a girlfriend during their time working away from home; some return with a new wife to their home village. Li's view is that this form of translocal marriage is not reliable. There were two 'runaway' young wives who were members of her natural village. One was from Qinghai Province and the other from Yunnan Province. They met their husbands during their time working in cities. When the women were pregnant, they returned to their husbands' villages for the delivery. After living a while in the village as the 'migrant' wives, they grew to feel dissatisfied with the area's poor living conditions. There were no recreational activities as in cities, and their husbands could not earn enough money to buy them beautiful clothes. They often ran away, leaving their newly born babies in the village. This new form of translocal marriage and the consequent risks have risen alongside the popularization of migration for rural youth. This marriage trend makes Li very concerned about her older son's prospects. She said: 'We could not afford to buy an apartment in the county for him. Without a stable job in the county, how could he pay the housing mortgage? Anyhow, if a rural young man doesn't have apartment in the county, it will be difficult for him to get a wife. Time has changed, without money everything becomes difficult.'

Li's older son failed in the civil servants' exam that the township government offers and he is preparing to take it a second time. 'My son works hard but who knows what will happen? It's very probably that he will follow the path of his dad, working as a migrant when young and returning home to farm when getting old.'

After marriage, Li and her husband began to make decisions for their own family and to farm by themselves. Li didn't know how to plant maize before – she even threw the seeds directly onto the field, not realizing that they needed to be sowed. She had no farming experience before marriage. Since her parents just had a small piece of land, they didn't ask Li and her younger sister to help with the farming. However, she's pretty sure that she would be a farmer as farming was part of the daily life for rural women in her time. In the late 1980s and 1990s, the county government was committed to agricultural extension in order to raise agricultural production. Through these services, Li learned skills related to seeding and gradually became capable of farming. 'Farming is like cooking. A new wife may think her cooking is not good. She can't make delicious food with the same materials as others. But when she cooked a lot, she became a good housewife.' Now Li is quite confident and proud of herself as a good farmer. Li and her husband had about 3 mu of land in the beginning after their marriage. When her husband was doing migrant work, Li opened up some wasteland around this land through her hard work and gradually had 5 mu of farmland to plant maize. In the late 1990s, the local government was promoting large-scale vegetable production and many villagers adopted cabbage production. The cabbage yields are very high and can reach between 4 and 5 tonnes per mu. Li also changed her crops to cabbage. As Li's husband is away for most of the year, she relies on mutual help from neighbours – they help her to finish the farm work and she repays the favour by providing her labour to them. As a left-behind woman and a farmer, mutual help within the community is important support for Li.

From planting maize to planting cabbage, Li's farming activities have been increasingly involved in agrarian transition of that area. Local government and agricultural policies play an important role in promoting agricultural industrialization. Take the marketing of cabbage as an example. Li mainly relied on intermediaries and brokers in selling cabbage in the 1990s. In around 2008, the township government encouraged farmers to join cooperatives in order to have more bargaining power and selling opportunities in the market. For Li, the village's vegetable cooperative is not as good as the government originally advocated. The cooperative failed to help smallholders to make more marketing profits.

> Before the formation of co-op in the village in 2007, wholesalers from different cities would come to buy vegetables. Some offered higher prices and some lower. We could sell vegetables to the wholesalers in the field and bargain for the price. Now as the government promotes

the form of co-ops, we'll sell our products through the co-op that monopolized the market now. No matter higher or lower the price, we have to sell to the co-ops. When the market was good, the co-op didn't pay us higher price. But when the market was bad, it didn't have good idea either to help us with marketing.

Another thing that puzzles is the 'visible hand' of the government in households' farm work. Li, and many of her fellow villagers, had taken for granted the autonomy that rural households have when planning their farming activities. Rural people could flexibly adjust or intercrop different varieties according to their own needs. With the large-scale migration over the last 20 years, however, many left-behind elderly plant maize as their main crop as it requires less labour. 'Now it's changed because the government asks us to plant vegetables for a uniformed landscape. Therefore, no maize cultivation is allowed. The land needs crop rotations to avoid soil disease, which we usually did before. (It is) only under the administrative management of monocropping that brings the problem of plant disease.'

To promote large-scale vegetable plantations, 300 mu of farmland was transferred to one company, which included Li's land. It was her best piece, adjacent to the main road with good irrigation and transportation. As the township government required, all the land along the main road should be leased to the company with annual rent of CNY 800 (about USD 112) per mu in order to maintain a uniformed landscape. The project involved land in several villages and the relevant village committees needed to persuade the households involved. Li said:

> I didn't want to transfer the land to the company but the government asked us to. If my neighbours have transferred their land but I didn't, they will gossip. I will be a bad person if the whole deal of transfer was suspended because of me. The minority has to obey the majority. But the land is really important for me. I need the land to produce food for my family. Besides, without land, what's the meaning of my stay behind? I have nothing to do!

After she transferred the land, Li used the rest of her farmland to grow vegetables for herself and her herds, including maize to feed two pigs, which are an important source of meat for her own family. Without sufficient land to farm to make a living, Li became a waged farmworker for the company to whom she transferred her land. She finds it very bizarre to work her former land as a contracted wage labourer. Zhang and Donaldson (2008) define this type of arrangement as semi-proletarian with Chinese characteristics. Li works for the company when she finishes the work on her own land for the day. The labour regime of wage labour is different. When she worked for her own family in the summer months, Li usually went to her land after 9:00 a.m., returned home for lunch at 1:00 p.m. and then continued in the field from 3:30 to 7:00 p.m. She can take about 3 hours lunch break to avoid the hottest time of the day. Now in her current situation, Li needs to work from 7:00 a.m. till 7:00 p.m., with a lunch break from 12:00 to 2:00 p.m. She needs to work in the strongest sunshine at noon. 'It was too tired to work for the company,' Li said. The year of 2017 is the third year of her land contract with the company. The contract states that rent should be paid in February. However, Li had not received the rent of CNY 1,600 (about USD 225) for two years. The company told her that it had no money and accordingly, she has not been paid her wages either. In summer 2017, she worked 20 days for the company, and the wages of CNY 1,800 (about USD 253) was not paid either. Li heard from neighbours that the company would not extend the land contract in the coming year. There is great uncertainty on the land issues in the village. Li feels like her status as a left-behind woman will last for years, not only to take care of her younger son but maybe later to take care of her grandchildren when her older son is married. For a left-behind woman like Li, her land and farming is her way of life and the way she reflects her love for her family. She is waiting for updates about the status of her transferred land and the possibility of being able to continue farming on that land for her and her family's benefit.

Yan Yuqiong: From woman farmer to rural elite
Dong Liang and Qirui Lin

Pingxi Township, Guangyuan City, Sichuan Province

Yan Yuqiong's family has 5 mu (0.82 acres) of farmland contracted from the village. Later she rented in 80 mu (13.1 acres) of land from villagers. All the land is used for vegetable plantation. Yan was born in 1972 in Dazhu village of Pingxi township. Her husband was two years older than her. The couple has two sons, the elder of which is 26 years old and began farming with Yan after his graduation from college in 2012. He is married with an eight-month-old baby. Yan's younger son is 19 years old and a college student.

Yan is the youngest of four children in her family. Her aunt and uncle adopted her when Yan was a year old because her parents were too poor to raise four children. Yan's aunt and uncle lived in the same village and had no children of their own. Child adoption between relatives in rural northern Sichuan Province was common and a way for poor parents to ensure their children's survival in tough economic times. Through this process, relatives also become more closely related. Yan left school after finishing her primary education at age 13 because her adoptive father died and her aunt could not afford the young girl's education. Yan then began farming with her aunt. She has remained in the countryside, never migrating to the city for work.

Before Yan was married, she and her aunt grew corn as a livelihood. She was keen to use corn seedling raising techniques that the local government advocated and the family's corn yield was higher than their neighbours. As she was an only child, Yan's husband married into her family. In the countryside, a household without sons implies an end to offspring and descendants, which means no descendants to worship ancestors and the family would die out. On the other hand, without male family members, it would be difficult for a family to survive in the countryside. The family would feel helpless in the village when facing some conflicts with others, just like a house without pillars. In such cases, uxorilocal marriage ensures survival and continuation for the family. For Yan, her uxorilocal marriage has provided her a higher domestic position when compared to other rural women in her village, which is one important factor in her success in agriculture. In 1992, after Yan gave birth to her first baby, she and her husband tried to start a business raising chickens. One day, she happened to see an advertisement in the *Sichuan Rural Daily* newspaper about a technique for hatching chicken eggs using kerosene lamps. She immediately contacted the provider and spent CNY 17 (about USD 2.4) for a copy of the technical guide. She asked one of her cousin brothers who was a carpenter to make several incubators as the guide instructed. In her first try, she bought 100 eggs and 90 chicks hatched. She gradually expanded the scale and sold chicks to local villagers, one chick for CNY 1.5 (about USD 0.2).

The techniques were not difficult to handle and some of her neighbours learned the operation from her. Several months later, after many other villagers acquired the same technique, Yan found the market for chicks was shrinking and she decided to raise pigs in her yard. Due to the risks of swine rearing such as diseases and price fluctuations, Yan frequently lost money. Raising pigs was also laborious work for her. Therefore, she decided to change to vegetable plantation. During our interview, she said confidently and proudly that 'I started the vegetable industry in our village'. Local villagers used to plant vegetables but mainly for domestic consumption. Yan first planted cabbage, potatoes, and asparagus lettuce (celtuse) for sale. She kept seeds for cabbage and potatoes and purchased asparagus lettuce seedlings from the local market. Before 2006, villagers were required to pay agricultural tax and provide grain to the state so Yan had to interplant corn with vegetables to make full use of her 5 mu of farmland. Yan's village is located on a mountain at an altitude of 1,100 metres. To sell their vegetables, Yan and her husband first had to carry their produce on their backs to the township market since they did not own a vehicle. They also sold vegetables to intermediaries who visited the village. At that time, the vegetable price was quite good because very few villagers planted vegetables for the local market. Between 2000 and 2005, Yan had made good money from vegetable production. After purchasing a motor tricycle, she began to transport vegetables by herself and sell in Guangyuan city. She did so in two harvest seasons of the year. It's about 50 km from her village to the city. Except for the vegetables planted by her family, Yan also collected vegetables of other villagers and sold them in the city. Bypassing the control of intermediaries, they can get a better price in the market.

While Yan was becoming more and more experienced in vegetable cultivation, many villagers between 30 and 40 years old began to migrate to cities. Their departure meant that Yan could rent the migrants' land and enlarge her vegetable production. She rented an additional 80 mu of farmland in her village based on oral contracts. The annual land rent is CNY 400 (about USD 56) per mu. Landowners had the option to take back their land at any time if they returned to live in the village. After scaling up her vegetable production, Yan began to hire labourers. There were two households in the village who worked for Yan for six months of the year.

From raising chicks to planting vegetables, Yan's husband has provided strong support to his wife. Many rural women don't have much decision-making power in their families due to patriarchal constraints. In contrast, Yan has enjoyed much more freedom when making family farming business decisions. One key reason is that Yan's husband, who married here from another village, does not have his own land in the village. In the countryside, farmland is collectively owned by the whole community and allocated to its native residents. Within a round of contract period (30 years), the community usually would not adjust land allocation in spite of population changes.

From 2006, along with the abolishment of the agricultural tax, the central government began to provide more subsides and created projects to boost rural development. County government officials started to advocate for vegetable production on land in the high mountains and provide subsidies for farming facilities. In 2007, the county government established a policy to grant subsidies for the construction of 10 greenhouses in Pingxi town; greenhouse contractors needed to also invest a small sum of money. When other villagers were still considering this option, Yan made a bold decision and applied to contract all 10 greenhouses. She planted vegetables such as eggplant, chilli, and cucumbers in the new greenhouses and made a healthy profit. The county government then provided more subsidies and advocated for villagers across the county to enter vegetable production.

In 2008, Yan set up a cooperative and registered her own vegetable trademark. In 2017, there were 78 household members in the cooperative. They belonged to different villages and planted vegetables on their own land (3 mu on average). The cooperative provided vegetable seedlings, fertilizers, and planting techniques to members at normal market price. At the end of the year, members can earn a bonus, which was about 20 per cent of their purchase. The cooperative sold vegetables for its members with a minimum protection price and could get government subsidies for the gap between the market price and the protection price. For example, market price for cabbage was 12 cents per kg and Yan could pay the cooperative members 20 cents. The gap was paid through government subsidy. Such an arrangement was to solve the selling difficulty of smallholders and stabilize their production.

In 2014, the cooperative sold 62,000 tonnes of vegetables and provided to its members over 500 tonnes of seeds, seedlings, and fertilizers. Its revenues that year were CNY 35.2 m (about USD 4.95 m) with a profit of CNY 1.23 m (about USD 173,000). The per capita income among members was over CNY 16,000 (about USD 2,000). Under the influence of Yan's cooperative, another six cooperatives were created. Among them, four of them qualified as a 'Model Cooperative in Sichuan Province' and the other two qualified as 'Model Cooperatives in Guangyuan City', according to a provincial government appraisal. Yan's cooperative was awarded the title of 'Model Cooperative in Sichuan Province' in 2009 and 'National Model Cooperative' in 2014. Yan was also elected as the Communist Party representative of the Tenth Provincial Party Committee in 2009.

Yan's cooperative is her career. She is quite busy providing a sales service for its members. In the busy season, seven or eight trucks depart with vegetables daily and each truck carries over 20 tonnes of vegetables. She can only sleep for three hours a night, 'earlier than 5 a.m., I begin to receive calls from villagers and vegetable purchasers'. Through the cooperative, local vegetables are shipped to wholesale markets in different cities across China, including Guangzhou, Chengdu, Chongqing, Nanchang, Nanchong, and Wuhan. The cooperative also has more than 20 stalls selling vegetables under its own brand in many cities.

Government support at several levels is very important for Yan's success. The greatest support from county government are infrastructure construction subsidies to help build venues for vegetable collection and cold storage. Yan had a venue for vegetable collection built on her land in front of her house. In 2008, she invested CNY 100,000 (about USD 14,000) to build a cold storage space with a subsidy of CNY 200,000 (about USD 28,000) from the local government. After the cooperative was recognized as a provincial model cooperative, local government granted Yan CNY 500,000 (about USD 70,000) for square and weighbridge construction. The local government also plans to invest about CNY 7 m (about USD 1 m) to construct a larger cold storage facility and Yan's cooperative could enjoy the user rights. The new facility could reduce the risks of market price volatility as Yan could store the vegetables for longer periods to ensure better prices.

'I didn't expect to be where I am today when I was young. My brother said I was courageous and dared to try anything.' After so many years, she is now at the centre of government attention. The county government often provides her with training opportunities, including to Zhejiang University, and invites her to visit modern agricultural demonstration parks. She uses modern means of transportation during these trips, including high-speed railways and planes, and has made friends with agricultural elites across the country, something that most rural women have no opportunity to experience. She has also become skilful in dealing with 'tricky' bosses and vendors, and she seldom suffers financial losses. Yan agrees that besides her continuous efforts in agriculture and a marriage of freedom and equality, the local government's strong support has been a key to her success. She adds:

> Actually, it's a kind of alliance. The local government needs a spotlight project or a demonstration as its performance. They will make it an example of our area and concentrate many favourable policies and subsidies in the cooperative. The cooperative will get benefits in return. However, the government would only provide support when

you already made some solid foundations in agriculture. If you're a starter, you will not have those support.

Although Yan has achieved success in the vegetable industry, she still faces challenges. In exchange for its support, local government officials expect Yan through her cooperative to advocate for more villagers to plant vegetables. When the market price is low, however, Yan feels quite helpless – the villagers refuse to sell vegetables at a low price and leave vegetables unharvested in the field. In 2008, due to the earthquake in Sichuan Province, many vendors refused to come to the village to purchase vegetables because it was dangerous. Instead, Yan had to collect the vegetables from villagers and arrange to have the produce sent by truck to wholesale markets in many cities, including Lanzhou and Chengdu. She shared:

> We have gained rich experience in planting vegetables. I have the confidence to say that I'm a good farmer. But I'm not a good business-woman. The biggest difficulty for vegetable industry is the volatile market price. It is quite hard to handle the market. We usually earn one year and lose in the next year. I can do nothing about the market price. I can only help villagers to sell vegetables at a price set by purchasers.

In Yan's view, one reason why the vegetable market was not good in 2016 and 2017 is the local government's promotion of large-scale vegetable production nationwide. In many places, governments are promoting agricultural indus-trialization. As vegetable production is not complicated and can produce profit in the short term, many local governments encourage smallholders to plant vegetables and provide them with subsidies for seeds, pesticides, and fertilizer. With such benefits, a growing number of businesses and companies are also becoming involved in large-scale cash crop production, especially in vegetables and fruits. For Yan, large-scale farming is not as beautiful as it looks:

> If one wants to make money, agricultural production should be the last choice. It is not easy. Many investors get stuck in agricultural investment. There are lots of greenhouses around, they look pretty nice but actually the owners can't make money. As for my own greenhouses, I have managed them for five years but lost money for three years. If I haven't got subsidies from local government, I would not have persisted until now.

As a rural woman who chose to remain in the countryside and engage in agricultural production, Yan is a successful woman farmer. Her success in agriculture operations benefits from several factors. First is the availability of land. When the household contract responsibility system was implemented in 1978, Yan was allocated pieces of land and later got the land of her aunt's family. From 13 years old, she started farming on her own land, which gave her more autonomy in agricultural production and more opportunities to innovate, such as her journey from growing corn to raising chicks and pigs and later planting vegetables. An important event in her agricultural operations was the opportunity to rent land as a result of the continuous outflow of labour from the countryside. Definitely, her success is the result of her hard work, initiative, and continuous learning and improvement, which urges her to constantly try new crops and operational approaches. Her success is inseparable from the strong government support that she has received to establish and develop her cooperative. The infrastructure improvement is another key to her success. Public investment in agricultural infrastructures and government support in incubating and enhancing young farmers is of great importance, as Yan's story confirms.

Reflections

The four cases of young women farmers are drawn from two different villages in two different provinces in China. The authors interviewed the women in August 2017 and July 2018. Dazhu village, where Li Mei and Yan Yuqiong come from, is a mountainous village in Sichuan Province in south-west China, which is a major source region of rural migrants. Zhaizhuang village, where Yao Hui and Wu Haixia come from, is an ordinary village in Hebei Province, which surrounds Beijing in northern China. The women's stories and experiences are different, even though these are drawn from the same two villages. Young women farmers are never a homogeneous group. Economic conditions, family structures, family demographic circles, and the characteristics of the women themselves all impact the diversified life experiences of this group. Nor do these four cases purport to represent young women farmers in China as a group. Such diversification, on the one hand, shows how little we know about the realities of young women farmers, while on the other hand, it reveals the complicated factors that trouble them in this transforming society. As young women, they are still burdened with traditional gender norms that the older generations usually enforce. As young farmers, they are facing new situations and challenges in the ever-changing political economy of agriculture. The intersectionality of gender, intergeneration, and political economy have shaped the dynamics of young women farmers, which further increases this group's diversity.

After reading Yao's story, readers may be astounded at the older generation's strong influence and authority on the young girl's life, especially in terms of education and migration. Boy preference still prevails in many areas of China where educating girls is considered as not a sound financial investment since they will leave the family when married. Furthermore, unmarried young girls should work to benefit their brothers and save money for their male sibling's bride price. That is why Yao's father halted her migration to Beijing, although she greatly benefited from that experience. Tradition holds that an unmarried older sister or brother brings bad luck to the marriage of the younger siblings. To guarantee a good marriage for

his son, Yao's father arranged her marriage in haste, which explains some
of Yao's conflicts with her husband in their first years of marriage. When
she married, the authority over Yao was transferred from her father to her
parents-in-law. It was Yao's mother-in-law's decision that changed the young
bride's trajectory as a migrant – she was asked to remain in the village for
reproduction and domestic work. Li's story shares some similarities with Yao
as they both remained in the countryside, largely for caregiving. Li first cared
for her father and later her children. Their stories challenge the mainstream
discourse on rural labour migration in the first decade of the new millennium.
In economics, their lower level of education and disadvantage in human
capital are often used to account for the smaller ratio of female migrants
in rural labour migration. Rural women are consequently seen as labourers
less qualified for paid work in urban sectors and instead they stagnate in
the countryside. The reality is that various factors influence family labour
division around migration. Besides the economic factors of skills acquisition
and labour market demands, traditional social gender norms continue to
be a principal determinant for left-behind women. In traditional Chinese
culture, the biological functions of giving birth and lactation have entitled
and consolidated women's gender role of population reproduction. Thus,
associated housekeeping activities and family care become women's exclusive
domain in the gender labour division. In rural families, a family's decision
for the wife and mother to remain at home is a continuation and represen-
tation of this traditional gender labour division. Under the gendered reality
of males migrating and females farming, the primary reason for women to
remain at home is not for farming or agricultural production but to care for
the elderly and children. Traditional gender labour division and the norms
of familism define women's roles and recognition in the domain of care and
housekeeping. Even the female migrants whose stories we have shared could
not escape traditional gender norms and had to change their migration status
according to family's care demands.

The traditional gender norms and gendered labour division also extend
to the production sphere of family farming. As the case of Wu Haixia shows,
the labour division of greenhouse operation in her household is another
application of the 'men outside women inside' model. Women's role of
caregiving in a reproduction domain was transplanted to and consolidated
in the production domain, only the object of care changed – from people
to plants. Just as women's care work in the domestic domain is often not
recognized because it is unpaid work without income contribution, the
'care' work of women in the production sphere also has biased impacts on
women. Within family farming, men are normally in charge of the technical
and marketing part of the operation while women are fixed to 'in-house'
production work. In-house work is more important to the quality of agro-
products; however, it is also more laborious and highly invisible. While men
have the chance to expand their social network and enjoy a bit of a social life
when engaging in market selling, women are gradually reduced to unpaid

workers on their own farms. It is true that the drudgery of family labour without wage calculation is key to the subsistence of family farms. With their own hard work and the right opportunities, Wu and her husband were able to expand their scale of production and became one of the large holders in the village. However, traditional gender norms still operate in the village arena despite women's successful farming experiences. It is impressive to see Wu's attitude towards plants and farming. She treats the plants as her own children, with care and tenderness. She treated farming with the same importance as the future of her own children as it provides funds for her sons' tuition and serves as a potential vocational backup. Being a large holder in agriculture, Wu's femininity made her more peasant-like in that she always places nature, family, and subsistence at the centre of her operations in farming. In this sense, the feminization of farming is never a symbol of backwardness for agricultural development.

Challenges for young women farmers not only stem from the traditional side of rural life in China, but also modern aspects. The overwhelming commodification of the modern economy, agriculture's capitalization, and the government's enthusiasm in promoting large-scale agriculture are the macro factors that influence young women farmers beyond their family domain. It is widely assumed that a new model of 'entrepreneurial farming' or a model of 'capitalist farming' are likely to become dominant. These processes clearly reconstitute farming on a new basis: land and labour are converted into commodities; farming is increasingly grounded upon multiple commodity flows; and finally, the units of production become part of overarching and complex financial operations (van der Ploeg 2009). In the pursuit of large-scale agriculture industry, local and county governments often exert administrative domain over agricultural production in the region, such as plantation structure and farmland use. This results in contradictions between rural households and local government. In the case of Li, her confusion over land transfer is a typical situation when rural households encounter commercial capital investment in agriculture. From an economic perspective, it is presumed that land transfer and moderate-scaled operation are favourable for optimizing allocation of land resources and raising labour productivity to guarantee food security and major products supply, and to promote technological extension and increasing peasants' income. Farmland transfer is increasingly common in rural areas. Informal land transfer usually occurs between rural households with an oral agreement, which is more flexible in terms and period of contract. Formal land transfer usually occurs between the village collective and external corporations or outsiders. Large-scale land transfers, to some extent, relieve the problem of agricultural deactivation, especially in areas with mass out-migration. However, for women farmers like Li, there are conflicts between land as a subsistence need for farmers and as a source of political performance for local governments. Li represents not only young woman farmers but all of the left-behind population like her who use land as an important source of livelihood. It's the source of the family's food and usually the source of money for left-behind women like Li whose migrant husbands cannot send remittances in a timely manner. Although Li does not understand why the government can make decisions for rural households about their contracted land, this is not a rare case in China's industrialization of agriculture.

Yan, who we learned about in the last case, is a so-called successful farmer. She started as a young woman farmer in her 20s when she could take the advantage of relatively equal gender relations in her uxorilocal marriage and the opportunity of the emerging commodity economy in the 1990s to gradually accumulate and develop her career in agriculture. While people admire her success and the government support that she has received, they usually overlook the uneasy experience of young women farmers in dealing with the market. Even though Yan is successful in the eyes of her neighbours, the fluctuating market is still a big challenge for her. The founding of Yan's co-op did not effectively relieve her marketing risks. When overwhelmed by the seemingly infinite market and in competing with enormous producers nationwide and even globally, Yan's co-op is too weak to change the disadvantage of farmers. This is one of the biggest challenges shared by many farmers in her region and across China. Beyond the challenges facing young women farmers due to their gender and age, they are also perplexed by the common problems that all farmers face.

Beyond the cases that this chapter presented, there are many young women farmers who have good stories from their personal and professional lives. Given the regional and individual diversity of young women farmers, it is almost impossible to make a general portrayal for the population. What is more important is to recognize the presence of young women farmers in agricultural and rural development as well as their intersectional social reality as young, woman, and farmer.

Notes

1. There is a dual household registration system in China that divides people into rural or urban registration according to their permanent residence. Provision of public services and public goods such as education, medical care, pensions, and other social policies differs for people with different *hukou*. Restricted by this system, rural migrants often would not be entitled to the same social welfare as urban citizens while working in the city.
2. Mu is a Chinese unit for land measurement, and 1 mu equals 0.165 acre; 1 acre equals 0.4 hectares.
3. *Hukou*, or household registration, is required when a child needs to go to school. It applies to all Chinese people.
4. Collective is a unique term in the Chinese context. In the countryside, land is collectively owned by all villagers of a single village. Each household has land contracted from the collective and can operate farming activities

independently. As the delegation of the collective, the village committee or villagers' team has the right to reallocate land based on the collective institution.

References

van der Ploeg, J.D. (2009) *The new peasantries: Struggles for autonomy and sustainability in an era of empire and globalization.* Earthscan Publications Ltd.

Zhang, Q.F., and Donaldson, J.A. (2008) 'The rise of agrarian capitalism with Chinese characteristics: Agricultural modernization, agribusiness and collective land rights'. *The China Journal* 60: 25–47. https://doi.org/10.1086/tcj.60.20647987

CHAPTER 6

No country for young women farmers: A situation analysis for India

Sudha Narayanan and Sharada Srinivasan

Introduction

In spite of their significant role in agriculture in India, women lack recognition as farmers and face structural barriers related to land ownership, access to resources and markets, and mobility, which are associated with high levels of gender discrimination and gender-based violence (Panda and Agarwal 2005; UNODC 2018). There is a stark absence of an intersectional analysis (based on age, disability, class, education) in the otherwise substantial body of scholarship on women in agriculture and the gender barriers that they encounter, tending instead to generalize a communal female experience. This lacuna is apparent in this current review of the situation of young women farmers in India. At the policy level, this silence is even more deafening; the predicament of young women farmers is something of a policy desert.

To be clear, there is not much information about young farmers in India in spite of the rhetoric of youth being a demographic dividend; we know even less about young women farmers (Vijayabaskar et al. 2018). In 2012, 56.6 per cent of India's rural youth in the age group 15–29 years derived their livelihood from agriculture, forestry, or fishing (GoI 2013; Vijayabaskar et al. 2018). According to a recent International Labour Organization estimate, female employment in agriculture was 57 per cent in 2018, compared to 19 per cent female employment in industry and 24 per cent in services (World Bank n.d.). Young women farmers' experiences are, however, lost between the two categories of rural youth and women. Even in the substantial body of work focused on women farmers in India, the generational aspects of women farmers are often under-researched.

This chapter presents an overview of the state of young women farmers in India as they navigate livelihoods in a sector that faces severe challenges. As outlined in the introductory chapter, young women farmers are a distinct analytical, and empirical category who merit attention. Besides being discriminated against compared to male youth, young women (farmers) are further likely more disadvantaged than older women in terms of access to productive resources and are relatively more constrained as economic actors, even though they tend to have more formal schooling and better access to information. Additionally, the trajectory of economic growth in India in recent decades has seen growing non-farm opportunities for young men rather than for young women (Binswanger-Mkhize 2012). While young women farmers in India share several challenges faced by their counterparts in other countries, they also face others that are specific to the social context of India, arising from gendered social norms across caste and class. This is not to suggest that these are uniquely Indian issues, nor is it the case that young women farmers across India are all alike. The principal issue is that we know little about young women farmers in India. This chapter focuses on who young women farmers are, what their (farming) experiences are, and the opportunities and challenges they face within broader socio-cultural and economic contexts. We argue that this knowledge is vital for the visibility and recognition of young women farmers as well as for sound, inclusive policies to support them.

We draw on existing data and literature to map the participation and situation of young women in agriculture. A brief discussion on a few methodological aspects related to defining, identifying, and counting young women farmers in official data and scholarly material is warranted. As set out in the book's introduction, the age group that we adopt for a young farmer is 18–45 years; and a farmer is someone who farms (not for wages) for a livelihood with access to land (owned, rented, or shared). But in India, such a group is not easily recognizable as policies designed for agriculture and/or youth have historically not addressed the issue of women farmers, much less young women farmers. This is despite the vigorous advocacy in India by a number of rights-based women's organizations, in particular, for the recognition of the rights of women farmers and several programmes that purport to economically empower women. Part of this challenge comes from the absence of a definition of a farmer in ways that render visible invisible work.

The National Commission of Farmers, which preceded a National Policy for Farmers, 2007, proposed a broad and inclusive definition of a farmer that goes well beyond mere land ownership to include activities beyond cultivation. Over a decade has passed, but this definition is yet to be translated fully into policy. Several advocates for women farmers have consistently urged the government to recognize women farmers – both those who own land and those working on others' lands – with a special focus on the most marginalized. Such an operationalization, they demanded, should include tenant farmers, livestock-rearing women farmers, fisherwomen, and women dependent on forests.

Advocacy groups proposed a National Policy on Women Farmers in 2008 to redress some of the perceived failures of the National Policy on Farmers, 2007, in providing a space for promoting women farmers (Krishnaraj and Dattatri 2008). In 2011, M.S. Swaminathan, member of the upper house of the national Parliament (2007–13) proposed the 'Women Farmers Entitlement Bill' that argued for recognition of women farmers irrespective of marital status and land ownership. Even as the bill lapsed in 2013, the Government of India declared the *Rashtriya Mahila Kisan Divas* (The National Woman Farmer

Day), to be observed annually on 15 October (PIB, 2017). Even though the category of young women farmers is missing in official data and scholarly literature, we argue that the question (and identity) of young women farmers is enmeshed in the larger question of recognition of women farmers. And it is vital to recognize and support young women farmers as such given their unique strengths, needs, and challenges.

This chapter is divided into four sections. By way of setting the context within which young women farmers operate, the first section documents the triad of challenges confronting Indian agriculture – an agrarian crisis, an apparent youth disengagement with agriculture/countryside, and an apparent feminization of agriculture. The second section draws on recently available data to estimate the extent of young women farmers and map the activities in which they engage. The third section reviews existing literature on the challenges and opportunities that young women farmers in India face. This section also addresses the extent to which policy in India addresses the specific needs of this group and reviews examples of a few approaches implemented by the state so far. We provide details on the data sets and literature that we reviewed in the respective sections. The fourth section concludes the chapter, introducing the case studies in the next chapter.

The triad of challenges

There is widespread agreement among researchers of Indian agriculture that it is in a state of crisis. Indian farmers' incomes today barely cover their costs of production; farmers tend to have high levels of debt and for a majority of them, agricultural income alone falls short of their consumption expenditure and costs of cultivation (NABARD, 2017). Wage income constitutes a significant share of total income among agricultural households (GoI 2013; Vijayabaskar et al. 2018), especially for smallholders. Among the many reasons for this apparent lack of profitability of agriculture, one serious structural issue has been the small and shrinking size of landholding. The average size of landholding has declined by half, from 2.28 hectares (ha) in 1970–71 to 1.16 ha in 2010–11 (NABARD 2014). Research has confirmed that the negative effects of the Green Revolution, which introduced high yielding varieties of rice and wheat, including depletion in quality of soils, increase in use of purchased inputs, and extensive extraction of groundwater through private investments (Reddy and Mishra 2009), has led to a process of capital intensification of agricultural production without commensurate increases in yields and/or returns. Accompanying these agro-ecological factors are a series of policy shifts such as reduced public investments in research and development, and a lack of technological breakthrough in rain-fed and drought-prone agriculture, which accounts for 60 per cent of the cropped area. Agriculture in India thus faces some stubborn problems that challenge the viability of smallholder farming, in a context where smallholders constitute an estimated 86.2 per cent of farmers in India.[1]

This challenge in turn exerts a strong push factor for youth to exit agriculture (Agarwal and Agarwal 2017). Studies have documented that many young men and women no longer want to remain in farming, preferring non-farm, factory jobs, especially in nearby urban centres (see Vijayabaskar et al. 2018 for a review of these studies; Sharma 2007; Sharma and Bhaduri 2009). Many parents aspire for their children to acquire routine (and if possible) secure jobs outside the farming sector, given the low returns associated with farming. While the continued non-viability of small-scale farming, successive subdivision, and fragmentation of land push children from such families to move out of farming in search of urban employment, rising costs of rural land make it challenging to expand farms to a viable scale and pose an obstacle even to those (youth) who might be inclined to become (new) or continue as farmers. Agrarian land ownership has traditionally been the prerogative of certain caste groups across the length and breadth of the country, making it extremely difficult if not impossible for those outside the acceptable caste groups to own land. At the same time, the stigma associated with manual work on farm, a marker of low (caste) status is another less documented reason for the youth to turn away from farming (Jeffrey 2010; Vijayabaskar et al. 2018).

Another apparent issue is the feminization of Indian agriculture, although the picture here is complex and different datasets do not always present a consistent picture. It is well documented that rural women are more likely to engage in agriculture (and other primary occupations such as forestry and fishing) than rural men. According to the National Sample Survey (NSS), in 1977–78, the figure was 88.1 per cent for women, and 80.6 per cent for men (see Table 6.1). Over time, the primary sectors, including agriculture, have declined in importance as a sector of employment for both men and women. However, the decline in the proportion of male workers was steeper than for women in the 1990s when India entered a phase of rapid economic growth. In 2009–10, only 62.8 per cent of the men were engaged in agriculture (a decline of 25 per cent), compared with 79.3 per cent of women (just over a 10 per cent decline) (Himanshu et al. 2011; Ghosh and Ghosh 2014). These trends are mirrored to some extent in data from the Indian Census at least until the 2000s, after which this trend is no longer apparent (Figure 6.1). One oft-cited reason for the feminization of agriculture is that there have been more employment opportunities in the rural non-farm sector for young men (18–26 years) than for young women, translating into a higher rate of exit from farming for young men relative to women (Eswaran et al. 2009; Binswanger-Mkhize 2012). Pattnaik et al. (2018) use four rounds of Indian Census data to demonstrate that the outmigration of men drives the feminization of agriculture. The Agricultural Census too shows that the proportion of operational holdings managed by women has increased over a five-year period, from 12.79 per cent in 2010–11 to 13.87 per cent in 2015–16. The corresponding figures for operated area are 10.36 per cent and 11.57 per cent respectively.

Table 6.1 Distribution of the workforce National Sample Survey (NSS), 2011–12

Group	Agriculture			Primary sector (agriculture, forestry, and fishing)		
(% of total; number in millions)	All workers	Cultivators workers	Cultivators labour force	All workers	Cultivators workers	Cultivators labour force
Men (over 45 years) (%)	75.3	89.4	89.3	75.9	89.6	89.6
(millions)	32.4	25.8	25.9	32.6	25.9	25.9
Men (18–45 years) (%)	65.0	81.4	80.0	65.6	81.6	80.2
(millions)	57.5	43.4	43.7	58	43.5	43.8
Women (over 45 years) (%)	84.1	91.9	91.6	84.4	92.1	91.8
(millions)	15	11.2	11.2	15	11.2	11.2
Women (18–45 years) (%)	78.3	89.2	87.8	78.5	89.3	87.9
(millions)	34.7	25.5	25.5	34.8	25.5	25.6
All (%)	72.1	86.1	85.1	72.6	86.3	85.3
(millions)	140	106	106	140	106	106

Notes: Workers are classified in the NSS based on usual principal status (UPS); that is, the status of a person engaged in any one of the activities mentioned above for 183 days or more (a majority of time) during the reference period, and usual subsidiary status (USS) that relates to the activity status of that person during the minor time (183 days or less) during the reference period, if the person was engaged in work during the minor time period. The USS of a person is recorded only if the person was engaged in that activity for at least 30 days. The table classifies a worker as being involved in agriculture based on a concept called usual status that considers principal and subsidiary status taken together (PS+SS). According to the usual status (PS+SS), workers are those who are accounted for as workers by either the UPS or USS criteria. We designate them as cultivators if the household they belong to reports having cultivated some land (irrespective of how they accessed that land) in the 365 days preceding the survey. These are expressed in absolute terms, but also as a proportion of all workers and of the labour force. For definitions please see NSSO (2013).

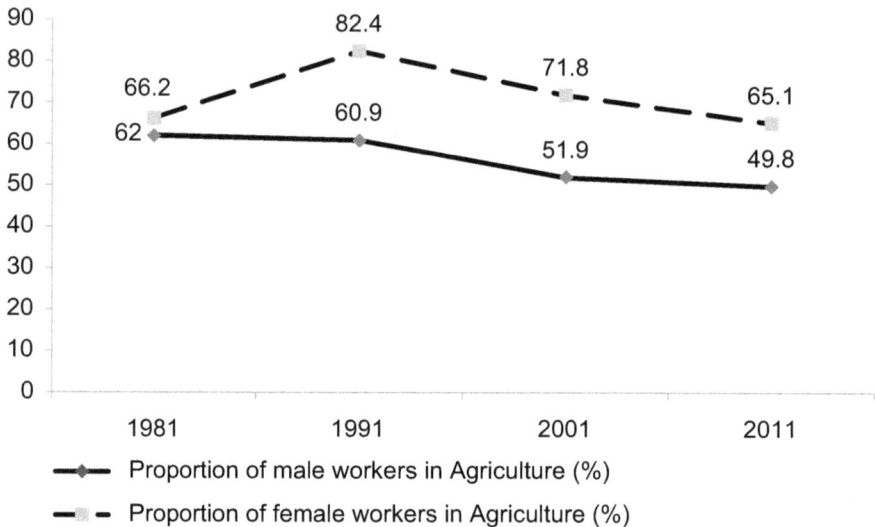

Figure 6.1 Women working in agriculture
Source: Based on Pattnaik et al. (2018)

Further, Pattnaik et al. (2018) point out that where participation of women in agriculture has increased relative to men, this seems to be correlated with indicators of poverty rather than of women's higher social or economic status, suggesting that the feminization of agriculture should be seen as the feminization of agrarian distress.

Counting young women farmers in India

In this context, what do we know about young women farmers in India? The decadal Population Census classifies individuals as main or marginal agricultural workers, but without publicly available data on their age; a quinquennial Agricultural Census focuses on operational holdings and their ownership, again without distinguishing age. Other than this, there are two decadal surveys on the situation of agricultural households (2002–03 and 2013) that sample agricultural/farm households but do not delve into the role of individuals other than a single brief question on whether or not the individual participated in agriculture a year preceding the survey. In the absence of other data, the main source for capturing specific trends by gender and age has been the various rounds of the NSS on Unemployment-Employment quinquennially (Table 6.1). These capture detailed information on employment status, sector of employment, spells of unemployment, and a seven-day recall of tasks undertaken. The NSS data are age-explicit and hence allow us to focus on the age of young farmers as we use in our study (18–45 years), disaggregated by gender. It also allows us to identify those from households that cultivate land, even if they do not own land. In terms of employment, the survey identifies those who reported agriculture as the principal activity as well as those who reported it as a subsidiary activity. In this section, therefore, we rely on these data to map the participation of young women (who are actively working and belong to cultivator households) in agriculture (Table 6.1).

Given these assumptions, there were an estimated 25.5 million young women farmers in India in 2011–12. In this period, as with earlier rounds, the proportion of workers from households operating land who depended on agriculture as a principal or subsidiary activity as cultivators and/or as workers was much higher for women than for men, and this is evident across age groups (Table 6.1). For example, 91.9 per cent of older women workers (over the age of 45 years) whose households operate land reported agriculture as their principal or subsidiary occupation (as opposed to 89.4 per cent of their male counterparts) and for younger women (18–45 years), the figure was 89.2 per cent (against 81.4 per cent of younger men in the same age group).The role of agriculture as a source of employment among those workers whose households operate land is therefore more important for women than for men. The numbers above also suggest that among households that operate land, agriculture is more important as an employer for older women than it is for younger women workers, although the difference is not substantial. This reflects that younger women have more opportunities than older women in the non-farm sector. This is evident from village studies as well. Padmaja and Bantilan (2014) draw on decades of data from specific villages in the Indian semi-arid tropics and note that the younger female age cohorts, for example, join off-farm employment in greater numbers, whereas women beyond the age of 35 tend to remain in agriculture in the rural areas even as rural-to-urban migratory patterns develop.

At another level, when one considers all agricultural workers (agriculture as primary and subsidiary activity), which is closer to the broad definition of farmers that the National Commission on Farmers proposed, not just those from cultivator households who operate land, the share of younger women is 2.34 times that of older women and similar to that of older men. Thus, given that a woman works in agriculture, it is more than twice as likely that the woman is between 18 and 45 years than she is older than 45 years. Younger women constitute just over a quarter of all workers in agriculture in 2011–12. Although there are 1.7 times more young male workers than there are young women workers (Table 6.1), this difference has been narrowing between 2004–05 and 2011–12 (not presented here). Differently, even if we do not directly identify young women farmers via surveys, given India's demographics, one would expect a majority of women farmers to be young.[2]

The data from 2011–12 also reflect a significant departure from previous trends, in that for the first time, India saw an absolute decline in overall female labour force participation (FLFP) across all sectors, including agriculture, to the tune of 19.16 million (Andres et al. 2017). According to them, the FLFP fell from 49.4 per cent in 2004–05 to 35.8 per cent in 2011–12. An estimated 53 per cent of this decline was from among the 15–24-year-olds (brought about in large part by those staying in school longer), about 32 per cent of this decline was among 25–34-year-olds, and about 15 per cent of this decline was among those 35 years and above (Andres et al. 2017). For a more recent analysis of FLFP, most researchers rely on a new set of surveys since 2017–18 called the Periodic Labour Force Survey, which measures FLFP differently (Deshpande 2023). These recent trends suggest an uptick in rural FLFP driven mostly by an increase in the share of the self-employed.

Regardless of the source of data, these numbers might still not represent the true extent of women's participation in agriculture for other reasons.[3] Rural women report domestic duties as the main or sole activity even when they are still engaged in specific agricultural tasks, especially caring for livestock, among other things. The status of work captured only documents someone as being engaged in agriculture if they spend either most of the time or at least one month in the past year on agricultural activities. Most likely, therefore, this is a lower bound of the estimates. These national data also mask important variations across region and social groups such as caste and class.

The social context of being and becoming young women farmers

In India, young women farmers' predicaments – lack of recognition as farmers, access to and control of land, little say in decision-making, and other factors of production and markets, mobility, skills, and training to pursue farming – reflect the intersection of gender and generation, embedded in the context of cultural norms related to caste, class, and religion across different regions (Dyson and Moore 1983). Young women's lives are embedded in the context of high levels of gender discrimination and gender-based violence particularly in rural India (Croll 2000; Rajan et al. 2017; UNODC 2018).

Gendered tasks

Nationally, within agriculture, women tend mostly to do manual work; non-manual work in cultivation is usually done by the men, as per activities reported in the NSS (not presented here). Women, both old and young, are also disproportionately involved in animal rearing activities. Women's participation in sowing, transplantation, weeding, and harvesting has been historically high. In the past decade, however, the use of machines for harvesting, and the emergence of weedicide as a popular way of controlling weeds, have reduced women's role in these activities. In contrast, ploughing, which was historically a man's task, is increasingly being undertaken by women. Men traditionally performed this work because of the strength required to use the plough and the cultural belief that women should not break the ground due to notions of impurity attached to menstruation and a belief that it would bring bad luck (Dube 1988; Kishwar 1987).[4]

Micro-level field studies confirm the gendered nature of tasks. Pattnaik and Lahiri-Dutt (2016) report from West Bengal and Gujarat that a larger proportion of women respondents were involved in harvesting, sowing, application of manure, and weeding, with only minor variation across sites. Few women involved themselves in marketing, pesticide spraying, or ploughing, an issue that we will return to later. Padmaja and Bantilan (2014) use long-term panel data mainly from the semi-arid tropics from 1975 to 2014 to document substantial variation in the tasks in which women engage. Despite differences, planting is more frequently practised by women, picking of cotton is done by women whereas ploughing is a male activity. They also observe that there is progressive feminization of labour and agriculture in the rural areas, but the patterns vary a great deal across sample villages. Anecdotal evidence from across the country indicates that norms around which tasks women and men undertake have changed over time. At the same time, there is evidence to suggest that drudgery-reducing tools and implements for what are considered women's tasks have been slow to come as evident in a scientist's remark that 'All we have given them is a sickle.'[5] Primary surveys of women farmers suggest that many of the tasks are extremely hard and implements and tools are inadequate to the task (Pattnaik and Lahiri-Dutt 2016), with serious health implications that we will discuss later.

Young women also shoulder a disproportionate amount of domestic work. For example, young women, especially daughters-in-law in rural areas, are often the first to rise and the last to go to bed (Narayanan et al. 2019), taking on roles ranging from fuel, food, and water collection as well as care for the elderly, the sick, and for young children – much more than older women do and often without the support of the men in the family. These responsibilities are especially acute if the woman is the household head or the family's main breadwinner. The familial obligation and interconnectedness between a farming lifestyle and farming jobs also mean that there is a fine line between whether an individual is doing work (compensated) or work in terms of household expectations (uncompensated, but expected roles and obligations). There are also instances where second wives of farmers are younger (Emran and Shilpi 2015), and therefore notably more vulnerable to exploitation and abuse within work and home settings, as are young daughters-in-law in general (Santhya 2011).

Agency and autonomy

Despite the large number of women engaged in agriculture, only a minority have a substantive role in decision-making. Given that most of these women are married, their status as young daughters-in-law in their marital homes is precarious, especially in north, central, and north-western India, which strongly embody characteristics of Kandiyoti's (1988) classical patriarchal belt.[6] Pattnaik and Dutt (2016), for instance, report that among women farmers that they interviewed, less than 3 per cent reported being involved in decision-making on major purchases or farm-related decisions. In Telangana, the number was higher. One-fifth reported participating in farm decisions, with 15 per cent reporting that the major say rests with them. Most of these were single women or from women-headed households (Ashalatha 2015). Quantitative work on women-managed farms often does not distinguish between supervisory and executive roles of women in farming (Chandrasekhar et al. 2017, for example). Those studies that do rely on self-reported involvement in decision-making in cultivation, which is often an unreliable measure because these survey questions ask merely whether women were involved (Mahajan 2019, for example).[7] Age hierarchies in patriarchal contexts also mean that younger women are far less likely to be consulted in these decisions than older women. In field surveys of rural households in Odisha and Bihar, Narayanan et al. (2019) note that while women in general might be marginalized from decision-making roles in agriculture and in having control over income, in some contexts, for example in Bihar, young women, especially daughters-in-law, were less likely to have a say relative to their mothers-in-law in decisions around cultivation and kitchen gardens.

Marketing in market yards is almost always undertaken by men while women typically engage in sales to traders at the farmgate or retail sales within the village (Ashalatha 2015). Younger women tend to face more restrictions on mobility and on interactions with men before marriage and upon marriage with men outside the immediate family, especially among castes higher in social hierarchy in rural areas in north, central, and north-west India where the practice of veiling is prevalent, disadvantaging younger women farmers. Few young women are therefore involved in marketing as these public spaces are overwhelmingly 'male' spaces.

This issue is stark in the context of animal rearing as well. Both livestock and backyard poultry rearing are often the responsibility of the (old and young) women in the household. They, however, tend to have little control over decisions around rearing or marketing and over the income that it yields. Where they do, there is some evidence that those dairy operations in India have higher productivity (Sneyers and Vandeplas 2015). There is also some evidence that when these activities are on a commercial scale, for example poultry reared in thousands in sheds, women's role in these activities tends to be lower (for example, Narayanan 2014 for poultry contracting in Tamil Nadu), presumably reflecting men's control when activities are associated with cash income (Mies 1988). Ashalatha (2015) notes that for dairy and livestock products (and vegetables) sold in local markets, women tend to have some say in decisions, but not if they were sold in non-local markets.

More broadly, women's status and aspirations can work to undermine family farming. Earlier work on women's status in India suggested that a greater demand for female labour in agriculture resulted in a relatively better status for women (Bardhan 1974, 1982; Miller 1981) but also that given the drudgery of farm work, women did not want to be married into landowning families (Jeffery and Jeffery 1996; Srinivasan 2017). Traditionally, land is owned by specific castes and, among large landowning families, women do not typically engage in farming but may undertake supervisory tasks. Another pattern evident is the withdrawal of women from labour with status mobility, especially upon (hypergamous) marriage. In a context where women have little incentive to farm (lack of ownership, control of land, decision-making), women's desire to marry out of farming stems from the hardships in farming as well as their aspirations for a good, urban lifestyle. The latter has been further spurred with the increase in school enrolments and rising educational aspirations among young women in rural India.[8] Young women who aspire to become and are farmers do so while negotiating these complex and oppressive social norms.

Limited access to land

Most crucially, despite the large numbers of women reporting that they work in agriculture, far fewer own the land that they farm. According to the India Human Development Survey, 83 per cent of agricultural land in the country is inherited by male members of the family and less than 2 per cent by their female counterparts. Women comprise over 42 per cent of the agricultural labour force in the country and yet they own less than 2 per cent of its farmland (Mehta 2018). A long tradition of patrilineal, patri-/virilocality leads to discrimination against daughters on land inheritance.[9] In several Indian communities, largely *Adivasis* (officially known as the Scheduled Tribes), daughters still could access some land in the parental village as an insurance against risks of marriage failures (Rao 2017, for example, documents these practices among the Santals in Jharkhand), even if in many cases the land eventually passes on or back to the male heirs. In these communities, marriage failures can actually prompt women to farm the lands that they receive in the parental home, providing a pathway into farming, even if temporarily. Along with other changes such as the practice of dowry, successive subdivision of land that leaves very small holdings for individual members of the household has put pressure on these customary practices and traditions since they further reduce the land available for male successors.

A 2005 amendment to the Hindu Succession Act 1956 ensures that daughters can inherit ancestral land. In practice, however, most women continue to not claim their share of land. One common rationale for this is that young women typically inherit movable property, often part of a large and increasing dowry (Srinivasan 2005). The gold, cash, and consumer goods transferred to a young bride is supposed to be in lieu of land for sons. But this is a false equivalence (see Agarwal 1994). A second reason is that the severity of patriarchal oppression in marital households necessitates maintenance of natal ties. Women trade their land inheritance right to the lifelong goodwill and support of their brothers. This issue particularly constrains young women farmers, whose name only ever gets recorded, if at all, on the land records in the marital home when the father-in-law or husband dies.

Limited access to land puts young women farmers at a disadvantage. The absence of recognition of women as farmers and using land ownership as a proxy for identifying a farmer marginalizes young women farmers. For example, many schemes in India targeting farmers require evidence of land ownership (for example for crop loans, to sell to the government procurement system, and so on). As long as the woman farmer's name is not on the land records, highly unlikely for young women, such support for agriculture is largely out of their reach. For example, Ahmad (n.d.) points out that the Rajasthan Farmer's Participation in Management of Irrigation System Act, which was passed in July 2000, brings the water user who is a land owner in the command area but as only 8 per cent of the landowners are women, they are unable to benefit much, even though women are the primary consumers and collectors of water in Rajasthan. Recent work on farmer suicides demonstrates that women farmer suicides are not recognized as such because of the invisibility of (young) women farmers, and the widows of farmers who commit suicide struggle to gain control over the (tiny) plot of land from money lenders and relatives, even as they try to cultivate the land to support themselves and their young children as well as paying off their husband's debts (Neelima 2018).

Access to other resources

There is empirical evidence from micro-level data that women have much poorer access, control, and ownership of land and other productive resources (Swaminathan et al. 2012; Lahoti et al., 2016) They also have inadequate access to public services, such as training, extension, and credit (Padmaja and Bantilan 2014). In a study on Gujarat and West Bengal, almost no woman farmers had ever met an extension agent and less than a fifth were aware of common agricultural programmes (Pattnaik and Dutt, 2016). Few women in Telangana were aware of crop insurance, for example (Ashalatha 2015). Young women farmers also have to contend with inherent male bias in policies and programmes, which are often presented in gender-neutral terms. Extension agents are usually men and their target group is also often men. Social networks that aid in dissemination of technologies are also often gendered so that knowledge disseminated to men tends to remain within the social networks among men (see Magnan et al. 2015 and Khan et al. 2016 for examples). If in particular these extension programmes are conducted outside the village, mobility restrictions as well as care responsibilities prevent younger women from accessing these opportunities.

The vulnerability of young women farmers

Recent work on women farmer health has drawn attention to the specific set of nutritional and health issues that women face. In general, existing evidence on women's empowerment in agriculture, represented by greater agency and access to resources, seems not to have a consistently strong correlation with women's own health. Insight into women's role in farming and their iron deficiency/rates of anaemia show a lack of access and consumption of nutritious foods compounded with the energy expenditures of women farmers; this also can result in the risk of lower average weights and poorer immune health (Subasinghe et al. 2014: 1–2). The age group that is most at risk is young women in rural areas who are burdened with (unpaid) economic and care activities along with discriminatory social norms around eating.

Leveraging Agriculture for Nutrition in South Asia (LANSA) studies on South Asian women working in agriculture suggest negative consequences on their health, but also that of their children, when pregnant women undertake strenuous agricultural work (Subasinghe et al. 2014; Rao et al. 2019). Field surveys from rural India also find that younger women eat last and least, and compromise their own nutritional needs, especially during times of scarcity (Lentz et al. 2019). There is documentation that some techniques of farming are less inimical to women's physical well-being than others. Sabarmatee (2013), for example, finds from an innovative analysis of pain and disease, that the System of Rice Intensification (SRI) entails less burden and fewer instances of water-related illnesses among women farmers. She found that in Odisha, transplanting operations go much faster in SRI rice production, with less painful labour for women. Also, weeding, traditionally done by women by hand, is facilitated with SRI because a mechanical hand weeder is used. This greatly reduces the time required and permits upright rather than bent posture. A study in Andhra Pradesh also found that mechanical weeders reduced women's labour time for weeding by up to 76 per cent, also reducing physical discomfort from this work (Mrunalini and Ganesh 2008). In some parts of India, men have taken over the task of SRI weeding because cultural norms expect them to do 'mechanical' work. A study in Tamil Nadu found that men's labour in rice cultivation increased for this reason by 60 per cent, while women's workload in rice production was reduced by 25 per cent (Thiyagarajan 2004).

Beyond these systematic issues associated with women's nutrition and health, there are concerns in India, as elsewhere, that women are likely to be disproportionately impacted by migration and climate change. But there is, as yet, little systematic research on the gendered impacts of migration and climate change on (young) women farmers.

Young women farmer case studies

In the next chapter, we present four case studies of young women farmers, two each from Tamil Nadu and Madhya Pradesh. While our study sample is not representative of young women farmers more generally across states and/or the country, we chose these four case studies to showcase the details of the experiences of young women in how they become farmers, what they do as farmers, and why they would like to continue farming. These four case studies were chosen from the 22 young women farmers that we interviewed in the two states.

In the villages that we visited in both states, when we asked for names of young farmers, women were not mentioned. This was the case even when we interacted with women who were active in farming. We therefore sought women between 18 and 46 years of age who were currently active in farming but not as wage labourers. Consistent with the literature, most of these young women in farming do not own land but have access to land to farm independently or with someone else (husband or other family members). We relied on our contacts to help identify young women who were part of family farms and contributed substantial labour to the family farm. In Madhya Pradesh, we reached out to members of women's self-help groups and constructed a list of young women farmers in the village – those who worked predominantly in farming even if they did not own or manage the farm themselves. In addition to young women farmers, we also interviewed older women farmers, young (and older) male farmers as well as women and men not involved in farming.

While the two states represent large ethnic, linguistic, and cultural differences, agriculture is an important sector in both states; both are major producers of several commodities in India. While in Tamil Nadu, agriculture's contribution to the State Domestic Product has declined rapidly, replaced by a vibrant non-farm economy, in Madhya Pradesh, agriculture continues to be the engine of economic growth with high rates of growth for over a decade.[10]

The social contexts within which women undertake farming in Madhya Pradesh and Tamil Nadu can broadly be characterized as belonging to the north–south socio-cultural and demographic regimes discussed earlier, with women in Tamil Nadu experiencing relatively higher autonomy, mobility, well-being, and status compared to their counterparts in Madhya Pradesh. Also, 25.1 per cent of the total population in Madhya Pradesh is tribal (Scheduled Tribes or *Adivasis*).[11]

In Madhya Pradesh, the young women farmers that we interviewed came from over 10 villages across two districts: Chhindwara, which is predominantly tribal and where cultivation of wheat and gram dominates, and Sehore, where soyabean, a cash crop, is the more popular crop grown. In Tamil Nadu, we focused on two districts: Erode and Thiruvannamalai. Erode and the rest of western Tamil Nadu or what is referred to as Kongunadu, has been the centre of the Green Revolution in the state as well as a region that has diversified extensively into industry and services based on investments of agrarian surplus. The region also has relatively higher farm holdings compared to the rest of the state, especially among the Kongu Vellalas, the numerically dominant caste in agriculture. Thiruvannamalai and other districts bordering Chennai, the state capital, have a strong agricultural economy based on tank irrigation and paddy cultivation. Urban expansion and poor tank management have eroded this economy in parts, but at the same time expansion of urban demand has led to

Table 6.2 Profile of young women farmers interviewed in India

	Tamil Nadu	Madhya Pradesh	India
Number of female farmers interviewed	11	11	22
Female farmers	11	11	22
Age started farming	16	13	14
Age farming independently	24	22	22
Mean age	38	37	37
% Under 35	45%	45%	45%
% Married	100%	82%	91%
% With >12 years' education	0%	9%	5%
% Working full-time	100%	100%	100%
% Full-time, primary income farming	91%	64%	77%
% Full-time, primary income – animal farmer	9%	0%	5%
% Full-time primary income – plant farmer	82%	64%	73%
% Full-time, primary income – farmer, not specified	0%	0%	0%
% Full-time, primary income – not farming	9%	36%	23%
% Farmers reporting that a family member in the household has title to land	82%	91%	86%
Average acres owned	1.56	12.99	7.84
% Farmers that have inherited land	64%	91%	77%
Average acres inherited	1.71	7.72	5.39
% Farmers likely to inherit land	27%	27%	27%
Average acres likely to be inherited	1.67	1.26	1.36
% Farmers renting in land	9%	0%	5%
Average acres rented in	2.00	0.00	0.20
% Farmers sharing land	9%	73%	41%
Average acres shared	7.00	3.84	4.11
% With access to community land	0%	0%	0%
Average of community land	0	0	0

a growing market for horticulture, which has in turn led to agricultural diversification and intensification on the periphery.

Despite the vastly different contexts of the two states, the profiles of our young women farmer respondents are quite similar (Table 6.2). Briefly, the average age of our sample is 37 years, comparable across both states. On average the women started farming as adolescent girls and started farming independently in their early 20s. Almost all of our respondents, except one, were married, again reflective of a larger pattern in which women are married off young and become part of their husbands' family farm. Our sample in Tamil Nadu is less educated than in Madhya Pradesh. However, a look at the female education attainment in the two states reveals that female literacy for the former is 73.44 per cent and 59.24 per cent for the latter (Office of the Registrar General 2011). Also, educational attainment for women in Tamil Nadu is higher than for women in Madhya Pradesh and the availability of off-farm opportunities are better for women in Tamil Nadu, especially if they have completed some schooling. In fact, it was hard to find single young women in farming given that women were either studying or working off-farm. Women who thus remain in or are entering farming seem to have low education levels. Another striking difference between the two groups is that whereas in Tamil Nadu, the respondents report that their primary income is from farming, in Madhya Pradesh, although the women spend most of the time farming, fewer report that it is their primary income source.[12] Beyond this characterization of our young women farmer respondents, there is significant diversity in their individual circumstances. Few have land exclusively in their name, and in many cases the farm is still in the name of the father-in-law (if married) or their parents and grand-parents (if unmarried). We draw on all of our interviews to understand the challenges in becoming a farmer and the predicament of young women farmers in the two study areas but use four specific case studies to detail young women farmers' lived experiences.

Notes

1. This refers to farmers owning land area less than 2 hectares as per the agricultural census, 2015–16.
2. Women in the age group 15–59 comprise 58 per cent of rural India's female population (Table C-14 Population in five-year age-group by residence and sex, Office of the Registrar General 2011b), with a median age of marriage of 18.4 years (for women in the age group 20–49) (Table 6.3.1 in IIPS 2016, 66). Close to 76 per cent of rural women in the age group 15–59 are currently married compared to other marital status (never married, widowed, separated, or divorced) (Table C-2 marital status by age and sex, Officer of the Registrar General 2011). First birth among women in rural areas occurs at a median age of 21 years (Table 4.9, NFHS, IIPS, 97). Additionally, we need to bear in mind that in socio-cultural and policy contexts across India, women do not exist as youth, but just as girls and then adults who marry and bear children. While policy and scholarly research do not specifically focus on young women farmers, for the reasons discussed here, a general focus on women farmers could be assumed to be largely about young women farmers who also undertake childbearing, rearing, and other care responsibilities in their marital households. Using these, we estimate that there are 25.5 million young women farmers and 11 million older women farmers. This is direct evidence that the question of women farmers is in large part about young women farmers.
3. A limitation of this data source is the absence of information on those under the age of 18 years.

4. These national trends represent an average and there exists substantial variation across regions, depending on cropping patterns and social norms.
5. R. S. Paroda at the Policy Forum on Social Transfers to Revitalize Rural India, co-organized by the International Food Policy Research Institute (IFPRI), Indian Council of Agricultural Research (ICAR), and the National Academy of Agricultural Sciences (NAAS), 26 April 2019.
6. The young wife in a context of severe patriarchal oppression is subordinate to the mother-in-law and will have to wait to become a mother-in-law herself to exercise power. This cyclic nature of patriarchy (Kandiyoti 1988) forces women who are junior in their marital homes to bargain in ways (son preference, for instance) that accentuate gender discrimination and their own subordination.
7. For example, many surveys ask who within the household makes decisions around cultivation with the options being, male, female members, or jointly. There is little clarity on what these categories and the responses represent.
8. Bourdieu (2008) writes persuasively about the role of the woman and her family in the demise of farming in France by choosing to marry into non-farm families.
9. There are several matrilineal communities in India, but we focus here on the dominant practice.
10. The agrarian context in both states is discussed extensively in Narayanan et al. 2024; Vijayabaskar and Varadarajan 2024; Narayanan 2024.
11. Detailed discussion on the agrarian contexts in the two states and field sites are presented in Srinivasan (2024).
12. We can only speculate that they see this as an intrinsic part of their 'duties' as it seems from the case studies (Narayanan 2024). This is also why many feminist economists say that the NSS typically undercounts women farmers because women tend to not report this.

References

Agarwal, B. (1994) *A field of one's own*. Cambridge: Cambridge University Press.
Agarwal, B., and Agrawal, A. (2017) 'Do farmers really like farming? Indian farmers in Transition.' *Oxford Development Studies* 45(4): 460–78. https://doi.org/10.1080/13600818.2017.1283010
Ahmad, N. (no date) *Women farmers and farm workers in Rajasthan*. Status Paper. Jaipur: Budget Analysis and Research Centre.
Andres, L.A., Dasgupta, B., Joseph, G., Abraham, V., and Correia, M. (2017) *Precarious drop: Reassessing patterns of female labor force participation in India*. The World Bank, Policy Research Working Paper 8024, Washington, DC: World Bank.
Ashalatha, S. (2015) *Women farmers: Land ownership and access to agriculture schemes in Telangana*. Hyderabad: Gramya Resource Centre for Women.
Bardhan, P. (1974) 'On life and death questions.' *Economic and Political Weekly* 9(32–34): 1293–1304.
Bardhan, P. (1982) 'Little girls and death in India.' *Economic and Political Weekly* 17(36): 1448–50.

Binswanger-Mkhize, H.P. (2012) 'India 1960–2010: Structural change, the rural non-farm sector, and the prospects for agriculture.' Paper presented at the *Global food policy and food security symposium series.* Center on Food Security and the Environment, Stanford University.

Bourdieu, P. (2008) *The bachelors' ball.* Cambridge and Malden: Polity.

Chandrasekhar, S., Sahoo, S., and Swaminathan, H. (2017) *Seasonal migration and feminization of farm management: Evidence from India.* Poverty, Equity and Growth-Discussion Papers No. 229. Göttingen: Courant Research Centre, Georg-August-Universität Göttingen.

Croll, E. (2000) *Endangered daughters: Discrimination and development in Asia.* London and New York: Routledge.

Deshpande, A. (2023) *Illusory or real? Unpacking the recent increase in women's labour force* participation *in India.* Centre for Economic Data Analysis (CEDA), Ashoka University, 15 December 2023. https://ceda.ashoka.edu.in/illusory-or-real-unpacking-the-recent-increase-in-womens-labour-force-participation-in-india/?print_page=true

Dube, L. (1988) 'On the construction of gender: Hindu girls in patrilineal India.' *Economic and Political Weekly* 23(18): WS11–WS19.

Dyson, T., and Moore, M. (1983) 'On kinship structure, female autonomy and demographic behaviour in India.' *Population and Development Review* 9(1): 35–60. https://doi.org/10.2307/1972894

Emran, M., and Shilpi, F. (2015) 'Gender, geography, and generations: Intergenerational educational mobility in post-reform India.' *World Development* 72: 362–80. https://doi.org/10.1016/j.worlddev.2015.03.009

Eswaran, M., Kotwal, A., Ramaswami, B., and Wadhwa, W. (2009) 'Sectoral labour flows and agricultural wages in India, 1983–2004: Has growth trickled down?' *Economic and Political Weekly* 44(2): 46–55.

Ghosh, M.M., and Ghosh, A. (2014) 'Analysis of women participation in Indian agriculture.' *International Journal of Gender and Women's Studies* 2(2): 271–81. https://doi.org/10.12691/ajrd-7-1-5

Government of India (GoI) (2013) *Report on youth employment: Unemployment scenario 2012–13,* Volume 3. New Delhi: Ministry of Labour and Employment, Labour Bureau, Government of India.

Himanshu, Lanjouw, P., Mukhopadhyay, A., and Murgai, R. (2011) *Non-farm diversification and rural poverty decline: A perspective from Indian sample survey and village study data.* Working Paper 44. London: Asia Research Centre, London School of Economics and Political Science.

International Institute for Population Sciences (IIPS) (2016) *National family health survey (NFHS 4), 2015–16.* Mumbai: IIPS.

Jeffery, P. and Jeffery, R. (1996) *Don't marry me to a plowman: Women's everyday lives in rural north India.* Boulder: Westview.

Jeffrey, C. (2010) *Timepass: Youth, class, and the politics of waiting in India.* Stanford: Stanford University Press.

Kandiyoti, D. (1988) 'Bargaining with patriarchy.' *Gender and Society* 2(3): 274–90. https://doi.org/10.1177/089124388002003004

Khan, M.T., Kishore, A., and Joshi, P.K. (2016) *Gender dimensions on farmers' preferences for direct-seeded rice with drum seeder in India.* IFPRI Discussion Paper 1550. Washington, DC: International Food Policy Research Institute (IFPRI). http://ebrary.ifpri.org/cdm/ref/collection/p15738coll2/id/130595

Kishwar, M. (1987) 'Toiling without rights: Ho women of Singhbhum.' *Economic and Political Weekly* 22(3): 95–101.

Krishnaraj, M., and Dattatri, A. (2008) *Women farmers of India*, 1st edn. New Delhi: National Book Trust.

Lahoti, R., Swaminathan, H., and Suchitra, JY. (2016) 'Not in her name', *Economic and Political Weekly* 51(5): 17–19.

Lentz, E.C., Narayanan, S., and De, A. (2019) 'Last and least: Findings on intrahousehold undernutrition from participatory research in South Asia.' *Social Science & Medicine* 232: 316–23. https://doi.org/10.1016/j.socscimed.2019.05.024

Magnan, N., Spielman, D.J., Gulati, K. and Lybbert, T.J. (2015) *Information networks among women and men and the demand for an agricultural technology in India*. IFPRI Discussion Paper 1411. Washington, DC: International Food Policy Research Institute (IFPRI). http://ebrary.ifpri.org/cdm/ref/collection/p15738coll2/id/128949

Mahajan, K. (2019) 'Back to the plough: Women managers and farm productivity in India.' *World Development* 124: 104633. https://doi.org/10.1016/j.worlddev.2019.104633

Mehta, A. (2018) 'Gender gap in land ownership', *Business Standard*, 17 April. https://www.ncaer.org/wp-content/uploads/2022/08/Gender-gap-in-land-ownership_Anupma-Mehta_Business-Standard_Tuesday-17-April-2018.pdf

Mies, M. (1988) *Patriarchy and accumulation on a world scale: Women in the international division of labour*. London and Atlantic Highlands: Zed Books.

Miller, B. (1981) *The endangered sex: Neglect of female children in rural north India*. Ithaca and London: Cornell University Press.

Mrunalini, A., and Ganesh, M. (2008) 'Work load on women using cono weeder in SRI method of paddy cultivation.' *ORYZA: An international journal on rice* 45: 58–61. https://www.indianjournals.com/ijor.aspx?target=ijor:oryza&volume=45&issue=1&article=013&type=pdf

National Bank for Agriculture and Rural Development (NABARD) (2014) 'Agricultural landholdings pattern in India.' *Rural Pulse* 1 (Jan–Feb).

NABARD (2017) *NABARD All India Rural Financial Inclusion Survey 2016–17*. Mumbai: NABARD.

Narayanan, S. (2014) 'Profits from participation in high value agriculture: Evidence of heterogeneous benefits in contract farming schemes in southern India.' *Food Policy* 44: 142–57. http://dx.doi.org/10.1016/j.foodpol.2013.10.010

Narayanan, S. (2024) '"I had to bear this burden": Youth transcending constraints to become farmers in Madhya Pradesh, India'. In S. Srinivasan (ed.), *Becoming a young farmer: Young people's pathways in farming – Canada, China, Indonesia and India*. Cham, Switzerland: Palgrave Macmillan. https://link.springer.com/book/10.1007/978-3-031-15233-7

Narayanan, S., Lentz, E., Fontana, M., De, A., and Kulkarni, B. (2019) 'Developing the Women's Empowerment in Nutrition Index in two states of India.' *Food Policy* 89: 101780. https://doi.org/10.1016/j.foodpol.2019.101780

Narayanan, S., Vijayabaskar, M., and Srinivasan, S. (2024) 'The youth dividend and agricultural revival in India'. In S. Srinivasan (ed.), *Becoming a young farmer: Young people's pathways in farming – Canada, China, Indonesia and*

India. Cham, Switzerland: Palgrave Macmillan. https://link.springer.com/book/10.1007/978-3-031-15233-7

Neelima, K. (2018) 'Widows of farmer suicide victims in Vidharba.' *Economic and Political Weekly* 53(26–27): 24–31.

National Sample Survey Office (NSSO) (2013) *Key Indicators of Employment and Unemployment in India, 2011–12*, NSS 68th Round, NSSO, Government of India.

Office of the Registrar General (2011) 'Census tables' [website]. https://censusindia.gov.in/census.website/data/census-tables

Padmaja, R., and Bantilan, M.C.S. (2014) *Feminization of agriculture in the semi-arid tropics: Micro-level evidences from the village dynamics studies in South Asia*. Patancheru: International Crops Research Institute for the Semi-Arid Tropics.

Panda, P., and Agarwal, B. (2005) 'Marital violence, human development and women's property status in India. *World Development* 33(5): 823–850. https://doi.org/10.1016/j.worlddev.2005.01.009

Pattnaik, I., and Lahiri-Dutt, K. (2016) 'Feminization of Indian agriculture: Status of women farmers', presentation at the *MAKAAM National Convention of Women Farmers, Bapatla, Guntur, Andhra Pradesh, India, 17–19 March 2016*.

Pattnaik, I., Lahiri-Dutt, K., Lockie, S., and Pritchard, B. (2018) 'The feminization of agriculture or the feminization of agrarian distress? Tracking the trajectory of women in agriculture in India.' *Journal of the Asia Pacific economy* 23(1): 138–55. https://doi.org/10.1080/13547860.2017.1394569

Press Information Bureau (PIB) (2017) 'Women can propel the country towards second Green Revolution and change the landscape of the development if they get opportunities and facilities: Shri Radha Mohan Singh' [press release], 15 October, Ministry of Agriculture and Farmers Welfare, Press Information Bureau. https://pib.gov.in/newsite/PrintRelease.aspx?relid=171730

Rajan, S.I., Srinivasan, S., and Bedi, A.S. (2017) 'Update on trends in sex ratio at birth in India.' *Economic and Political Weekly* 52(11): 14–16.

Rao, N. (2017) *'Good women do not inherit land': Politics of land and gender in India*. London: Routledge.

Rao, N., Gazdar, H., Chanchani, D., and Ibrahim, M. (2019) 'Women's agricultural work and nutrition in South Asia: From pathways to a cross-disciplinary, grounded analytical framework.' *Food Policy* 82: 50–62. https://doi.org/10.1016/j.foodpol.2018.10.014

Reddy, D.N., and Mishra, S. (eds) (2009) *Agrarian crisis in India*. New Delhi: Oxford University Press.

Sabarmatee, S. (2013) 'Understanding dynamics of labour in System of Rice Intensification (SRI): Insights from grassroots experiences in Odisha, India.' Presentation of PhD thesis research, Wageningen University, Netherlands. http://www.sri-india.net/event2014/documents/presentations/Presentation_2.pdf

Santhya, K. (2011) 'Early marriage and sexual and reproductive health vulnerabilities of young women: A synthesis of recent evidence from developing countries.' *Current Opinion in Obstetrics and Gynecology* 23(5): 334–39. https://doi.org/10.1097/gco.0b013e32834a93d2

Sharma, A. (2007) 'The changing agricultural demography of India: Evidence from a rural youth perception survey.' *International Journal of Rural Management* 3(1): 27–41. https://doi.org/10.1177/097300520700300102

Sharma, A., and Bhaduri, A. (2009) 'The "tipping point" in Indian agriculture: Understanding the withdrawal of the Indian rural youth.' *Asian Journal of Agriculture and Development* 6(1): 83–97. http://dx.doi.org/10.22004/ag.econ.199072

Sneyers, A., and Vandeplas, A. (2015) 'A gender gap in agricultural productivity? Evidence from the dairy sector in India.' Presented at the *International Association of Agricultural Economists Conference 2015, Milan, Italy, 9–14 August 2015*. https://ideas.repec.org/s/ags/iaae15.html

Srinivasan, S. (2005) 'Daughters or dowries? The changing nature of dowry practices in South India.' *World Development* 33(4): 593–615. https://doi.org/10.1016/j.worlddev.2004.12.003

Srinivasan, S. (2017) 'Cross-region migration of brides and gender relations in a daughter deficit context.' *Migration and Development* 16(1): 123–43. https://doi.org/10.1080/21632324.2015.1083723

Srinivasan, S. (ed.) (2024) *Becoming a young farmer: Young people's pathways into farming in Canada, China, India and Indonesia*, Rethinking Rural Series. Palgrave Macmillan, Open Access. https://link.springer.com/book/10.1007/978-3-031-15233-7

Subasinghe, A.K., Karen, Z., Walker, K.Z., Evans, R.G., Srikanth, V., Arabshahi, S., Kartik, K., Kalyanram, K., and Thrift, A.G. (2014) 'Association between farming and chronic energy deficiency in rural South India.' *PLoS ONE* 9(1): e87423. https://doi.org/10.1371/journal.pone.0087423

Swaminathan, H., Lahoti, R., and Suchitra, J.Y. (2012) 'Gender asset and wealth gaps: Evidence from Karnataka', *Economic and Political Weekly*, 47(35): 59-67.

Thiyagarajan, T.M. (2004) 'On-farm evaluation of SRI in Tamiraparani Command Area, Tamil Nadu, India.' Presented at the *World Rice Research Congress, Tsukuba, Japan, 4–7 November 2004*. http://sri.ciifad.cornell.edu/conferences/wrrc/wrrcppts/wrintnseveraju.ppt

United Nations Office on Drugs and Crime (UNODC) (2018) *Global study on homicide: Gender-related killing of women and girls*. Vienna: UNODC. https://www.unodc.org/documents/data-and-analysis/GSH2018/GSH18_Gender-related_killing_of_women_and_girls.pdf

Vijayabaskar, M., Narayanan, S., and Srinivasan, S. (2018) 'Agricultural revival and reaping the youth dividend.' *Economic and Political Weekly* 53(26–27). https://www.epw.in/journal/2018/26-27

Vijayabaskar, M. and Varadarajan, R. (2024) 'Becoming/being a young farmer in a fast-transitioning region: The case of Tamil Nadu'. In S. Srinivasan, (ed.), *Becoming a young farmer: Young people's pathways in farming – Canada, China, Indonesia and India*. Cham, Switzerland: Palgrave Macmillan. https://link.springer.com/book/10.1007/978-3-031-15233-7

World Bank (no date) 'World Bank Data: India.' https://data.worldbank.org/country/india

CHAPTER 7

With a little help: Young women farmers' experiences in India

Sharada Srinivasan and Sudha Narayanan

We present four case studies of young women farmers in India, two each from Tamil Nadu and Madhya Pradesh. As outlined in the previous chapter, the case studies offer an in-depth view into how young women become farmers, their experiences as farmers and the challenges they face. They highlight similarities but also differences across the respondents. The concluding section draws implications from the four case studies to reflect on experiences of other young women farmers in this study but also what they illustrate of young women farmers' experiences more broadly.

Tamil Nadu
Shanti[1]

Shanti is getting ready one early morning to get to her coconut grove of 1.5 acres.[2] She has hired a person who has offered the best price to pluck the coconuts and buy them. This time the hire picks 900 coconuts. If there were no water shortage, she would have had 1,000 coconuts. She usually keeps about 30 coconuts for her own use. She keeps track of the trees that have few coconuts and doesn't let him climb those as it costs INR 15 (USD 0.20) to climb each tree. These few coconuts eventually fall by themselves, which are for her own use. Shanti always gets someone who offers the best price for the coconuts unlike her father-in-law who always gave the opportunity to the same person even if the price that he received for the product was lower. This she has to do, to make sure she gets a good price each time.

The coconut grove needs a regular supply of water, and every six months the trees need fertilizer. Shanti buys fertilizer from a local store. With the shortage of water in the last two years, the yield has dropped considerably. But she will continue to nurture the coconut trees so she can earn a regular income to live off. The coconut grove is not labour demanding.

Shanti is 36 years old and belongs to the landowning caste, Kongu Vellala (KV) Gounders. She lives with her husband and daughter. Her husband suffers from severe physical and mental disabilities and cannot help her with farm or household work. They have a daughter who is 19 years old and attends university. Shanti is keen to give her daughter a good education and marry her into a good family. She is determined that her daughter should have a better life than her. Shanti lost her father when she was 10 years old. Her natal family did not own much land. When one of the largest landowning families sought her hand in marriage for their son, her mother and maternal uncles decided this was in her best interest even though the husband had severe disabilities. She was married off when she was 16; she had no say in it at all. She was very young and didn't know what to expect. Post-marriage, she lived in the same village as her natal family, with her husband and in-laws. Her daughter was born after two years of marriage.

Until her father-in-law's death, Shanti worked with him on his land. After his death, her husband's share of 9 acres is entirely her responsibility. Five acres come from her mother-in-law's side and is held jointly in the young couple's names. The remaining 4 acres (out of the total 10.5 acres from her father-in-law) is in the name of her husband alone. Since she finds it difficult to manage all of the land, she leases out 5 acres. Of the remaining 4 acres, 1.5 acres comprise the coconut grove and 2 acres are for sugarcane. The last 0.5 acre was all rocks, but she has now cleared the area and it is ready for farming. She paid nearly INR 3 lakhs (USD 4,000) to prepare the land. Due to the aforementioned drought-like situation, though, she has not cultivated sugarcane, as it is a water-intensive crop.

Shanti received 0.75 acre of land from her father. Her father had two wives and she is the only daughter with two older stepbrothers. Initially her brothers did not talk to her but now they do. She sold her share of the land to them and shared the money with her mother who works as an agricultural labourer.

Growing up, Shanti did not engage in farming at all even though her father owned land and her mother has done some farming.

> It was when my daughter was born. My father-in-law decided to teach me all about farming. He got me ready to be a farmer on my own and he did let me become one after I turned 23 ... I am married into a farming family, so I had to take up farming not out of my own will but out of necessity. Given the hard work and not knowing what to do, I didn't like it at first but have a liking for it now.

Shanti realizes the value of owning land; almost every KV family owns land. If someone here didn't own land, they lease it in (*kuthagai*). It takes a year for sugarcane to be harvested, three months for corn, and three months for sesame seeds.

Leasing out of land is almost entirely based on trust; landowners would lease out their land only to people they know well. A written agreement is not common. Nowadays, such agreements are for a maximum of three years, after which the land is leased out to a different person. This, Shanti explains, is due to the law (land to the tiller) that entitles a person who has cultivated the same land for 10 years or more to own the land.[3]

Shanti attended teacher training, and she would have liked to teach classes five or six at a private school. The salary would be about INR 5,000 to INR 6,000 (USD 66–80) a month. It's not a big amount, but she would have loved to teach. 'With my teacher's salary, I would have to spend on the bus fare and work for somebody. I wanted to work on my own land instead, I don't have to be afraid of anyone in my own land, '*nane raja, nane manthiri* (I'll be king and counsel)'. In her view, this is the best reason for deciding to farm on her own.

The income from farming was okay until two years ago. It was good enough to put food on their plate and pay for her daughter's education. With the water shortage, Shanti had to take out a bank loan using 5 acres of land as collateral to run the household. 'I have 9 acres of land, it's worth a lot of money, but there is no cash in hand. It feels like I have so much butter in my hand but can't eat it all.'

She also recalls her father-in-law giving away some land to the government to build a road through his land. With not enough extra earnings from farming, she is not able to repair her own home, which was built 100 years ago on 15 cent land and is in dire need of repairs. She now lives in rented accommodation. People around her always think that she has a lot of land and that she is doing well but they do not understand that everything needs money to maintain.

At 36, Shanti is a young farmer; the women farmers in her area are older than her. Most of the younger women are married and have children; some unmarried women work the land, but as wage labourers. Women in her age group typically do not farm on their own. Most of the agricultural labourers are much older. Men get paid INR 400 (USD 5) and women get paid INR 200 (USD 3) as daily wages.

When she started farming by herself, there were relatives and other people in the surrounding area who wondered if she could farm and, if she did, would she be able to outperform them. If she does well, they get jealous. Shanti does not let these things bother her.

Shanti feels that any person who works on the farm is a farmer, be it a man or woman. A lot of people have land and treat it as a business but don't get in and work. They are farmers. She feels that people who don't own land but work in the fields should be called farmers. Many women work on their husbands' farms even if they don't own the land. It's only correct that their wives are also called farmers.

As a woman, she doesn't feel inferior to male farmers: 'I think it's all in the effort you put in, and the produce we get. I am educated, I can ask people for advice and get help to get my work done.'

Once when she cultivated 2 acres of sugarcane, she sold the harvest to a local factory. It usually took three months to get paid. Swallowing her pride, she requested that the factory pay her sooner considering her circumstances and they did. If she does not know something, she asks the people around her.

When she needs farming advice, she asks people she knows the same question and decides on the best information that suits her farmland. She does not watch any television shows on agriculture. She does watch YouTube videos to learn about organic farming, which is an area she is interested in trying in the future. She and her stepbrothers share a WhatsApp group, which she uses on her phone to talk with them when in doubt. She does not, however, have anyone to physically help her on the farm.

Shanti has not met anyone or attended any training programmes that the agriculture department offers. She did travel to meet someone once to secure a subsidy for drip irrigation, which she has not yet been able to implement due to water shortages. A lot of people in her area are interested in drip irrigation and some have installed the necessary infrastructure, but it is not of much use in light of the water scarcity. If she had it installed and working, it would save her a lot of time going back and forth to the fields to water twice a day, for about an hour each in the morning and evening. She usually rides on her two-wheeler to get to the farm.

Shanti says that she is not part of any *vivasaya kuzhu* (farmers' group) as these groups are aimed at farmers who have 3–5 acres of land. What she did not mention is that these groups consist mostly of male farmers.[4]

There are loans available for farmers. In her view, it's good to understand how the loans work. Farmers can receive an interest-free agricultural loan for 13 months from the banks. Shanti pays off this loan at the end of the term and applies for another 13-month loan a week later. If she does not pay off the loan on time, interest is charged from the very next day. She makes sure that she keeps track of the loan period dates.

Shanti is a lone woman farmer. When she married, she knew that her husband was incapacitated. From what she was told, her husband was not so modern and she assumed that he could probably still take care of the land. When she moved into their marital home, she soon realized that her husband could do nothing: 'I was so scared and felt very bad for myself. It was my father-in-law who made me a farmer and guided me while he was alive. My mother comes and helps me in the farm whenever she can.'

Sometimes, Shanti finds it difficult to find good help from labourers as they ask for a lot of money, a common grievance among farmers. She also asks labourers who work on her stepbrother's farm to work for her. She doesn't find it difficult managing them: 'I am nice to them, treat them with respect, give them coffee and snacks. I also let them rest a bit in between their work. When my mom comes, she also rests, so it's only fair that I do the same with all labourers as most of them are elderly. When I do this, they are certain to come back and work for me.'

Shanti takes all key decisions related to farming and the household, after weighing the pros and cons. Sometimes her husband remembers things well and at other times he acts like a three-year-old. He cannot work as he does not have the capacity or knowledge. In this scenario, Shanti has to take care of everything: attend to farming, talk to people, and attend festivals and events – be it a wedding or a death ceremony – which male members of the household often undertake.

She told us: 'I have to take the initiative and arrange for my daughter's wedding too. I have to represent myself and my husband in everything, good and bad.'

Shanti articulates a few disadvantages that she experiences as a female farmer. If she needs something right away, she cannot ride her two-wheeler in the night. She also cannot ride with a man on her two-wheeler; for example, she cannot offer a ride to a male labourer from her stepbrother's farm to bring him to work on her land. At night, a lot more preparation goes into travelling to the farm to turn off the water. 'I am very scared to go in the night, I leave the motor room light on, remove all my jewellery … I am nearly in tears to leave home in the dark of the night, I am in constant fear.'

Shanti also explains that everyone knows that her husband is incapacitated and that she manages all matters by herself. Many are sympathetic and helpful. When she goes to the market which is an all-male space, she is often helped by other men there. When she approaches a man to help her or takes a man's help, sometimes they try to take advantage of her by making sexual advances or seeking sexual favours. This reveals that gender norms shape these seemingly mundane activities, which impact the work of running a farm for her as a woman farmer.

Shanti cannot engage in off-farm work or engage in any other side businesses; she has only her land to work with to turn things around and live a good life. Recently she has spent INR 1.5 lakhs (USD 2,000) to prepare 1 acre of rocky land to be fit for farming. She plans to sell this piece of land, which she hopes will fetch about INR 50 lakhs (USD 66,000). A few years ago, this would have been worth INR 1 crore (USD 133,000), but she was not willing to sell then. She is now planning for her daughter's wedding. She plans to buy a new house worth INR 30 lakhs (USD 40,000) as well as jewellery. She would also like to gift a car worth about INR 10 lakhs (USD 13,000) to her daughter. She does not wish her daughter to suffer like she did and would like her daughter to marry well. As their only child, Shanti's daughter will inherit all of her parents' land.

> My daughter doesn't know farming now as she is focusing on graduating her BSc. She is most welcome to get into farming with her husband if she wishes. It's not a bad occupation once everything is in place. It is calming to look at the greenery in one's own land.
>
> Once my daughter is married, I want to start organic farming in a small way for my personal satisfaction, not for money. I want to grow fruit trees in 2 acres, and teak in another acre. I would like to cultivate a lot of organic vegetables to market them.

Shanti's hope is that farmers will earn better from their produce with much needed government support. Currently it is the intermediaries who are making the most profit from farmers' harvests. She feels that there is a change coming as the government is asking farmers not to sell their land.

A part of Shanti still wants to pursue employment as a teacher for which she has already trained. She would need to pass an exam to become a government schoolteacher. The age of retirement for women in public sector jobs is 58 years so she hopes to be able to teach for at least 10 years. If this were to happen, she would lease out their land (*kuthagai*).

Will Shanti become a full-time farmer growing organic vegetables, and fruit and teak trees, and tending to her coconut farm that she has nurtured throughout her married life? All of this will depend on nature, the benefits that the government has to offer, and the price that consumers are willing to pay for farmers' produce.

Parvathi

Parvathi is 40 years old and belongs to a middle class Kongu Vellala (KV) family. In many ways her family is typical of the KV community – the family owns land and also has a secure non-farm income. She lives with her husband in a house adjacent to her mother's house. She says: 'I fondly remember pulling out weeds with my two brothers from the fields when I was young. I was interested in farming but my parents didn't let me put my feet on the soil. I lived like a queen.'

She recalls that when she was young, her dad cared only about her, not his sons. He didn't even talk to them. He wanted her to study, but Parvathi was not keen; she used to think, 'we have so much land, why bother to study'. Those were the days when only half of the girl population attended school. Now, how did this girl who enjoyed life being pampered by her father, become a full-time farmer?

Parvathi was married when she was 15 years old. She was happy with her married life, and gave birth to two children. Her husband holds MSc and MEd degrees, and worked as a teacher. When she was 25 years old, her second child (a son) was in kindergarten and they lived in a rental house. The house owners were a bank manager and his wife, Mala, who was a farmer.

Mala was very active with domestic chores, took care of her kids and her husband, and was a full-time farmer. At 40 years old, she worked much harder than most men. After her morning chores at home, she was ready to farm at 7:00 a.m. Mala became very interested in farming and credits Mala for making her a full-time farmer. Mala used to say to her: 'You are born into a farming family, your husband has land, you should learn to farm on your own; it gives a lot of satisfaction, you will have money of your own.'

It was around this time that Parvathi lost her maternal grandfather, who took care of all the farming for his daughter, her mother, an only child. Her dad had fallen into bad habits and did not take care of any farming. Her mother felt that her two sons should study and not depend on farming or be negatively influenced by their father. Both of Parvathi's brothers are married and live in cities. One of her brothers is a college professor and another works in the software industry.

Parvathi decided to step out of the comfort of her house and help her mother with farming, being inspired by Mala. She says with pride: 'I wanted to help my mother like a son would. This was in 1997–1998, my brothers were studying in the city. I learnt to ride a two-wheeler.'

She started farming when she was 25 years old, and in 1999, when Parvathi was 27, she started full-time farming on her own, a development that didn't happen so easily. Her father-in-law leased out the 5 acres of land that rightfully belonged to her husband. The couple then bought 3 more acres with her husband's earnings. She had to fight with her father-in-law to take care of these 3 acres on her own. There were doubts that she could manage on her own. In the first year he helped Parvathi and since then she has been farming on her own.

Parvathi has tried different crops – banana, paddy, sugarcane, turmeric, and tapioca. She says that all farmers in the area have cultivated paddy, sugarcane, and tapioca for over 20 years. Over the last 10 years, banana cultivation has picked up. For paddy crops, farmers used to rely on canal irrigation. The water supply came to a standstill with the drought, following which many farmers, including herself, suffered a loss in paddy cultivation. This loss led her to try banana cultivation and, after the first year, she decided it was cost effective. She asks her neighbours who cultivate banana for advice as well as the agriculture department.

She manages the farm by herself. She decides what to cultivate, hires labour, purchases the inputs (fertilizers and manure), and keeps track of planting, watering, harvesting, and marketing.

When she was young, she remembers that farmers used to cultivate mainly cotton and turmeric. Both are labour intensive. Most farmers are now giving up on growing these crops due to labour shortages and the costs and work involved. Other crops are relatively easier.

The only organic farming that Parvathi does now is the paddy that she grows in half an acre of land for household use. For all other crops, she uses fertilizers. Most farmers are able to manage only when they use fertilizers. Yield is higher; half of the yield helps to take care of the farm and the other half helps them survive. Her brother's friend undertakes organic farming on 2 acres of land. Production is lower compared to when fertilizers are used. She explains:

> If one person decides to convert to organic farming, it's not enough. All farmers in the area should work towards it. If I decide to go organic and the neighbour uses fertilizers in their land, some of it gets washed on to my land. This I feel is not 100 per cent organic. Everyone should have the resources and the time to convert to organic farming. It takes about three years for the entire land to become totally organic after all the effects from the fertilizers are washed away. About 50–60 per cent of people here are aware of organic farming. They all hesitate to switch as the yield is not enough for survival.

Parvathi learned to farm from her mother and father-in-law. She asks her neighbours and friends as well as agriculture department staff for farming information and advice. Some share this information willingly; others do not. She is very eager to share information when someone asks her. She is especially keen to help other women farmers – she visits their fields and takes them to the agriculture staff that she knows to find a solution when she cannot provide one herself. Several other women farmers in this village spoke about Parvathi's support in helping them to deal with family members' resistance to their farming, providing knowledge and skills, and accompanying them to the market or to the agriculture department.

She does not watch YouTube videos, but she does read *Pasumai Vikadan*, a Tamil-language magazine on matters related to agriculture. She thinks that most of the (success) stories reported in the magazine are not true. She believes that there is nothing like talking to a farmer in person, understanding how farming works for them, the costs involved, the hardships that they face, and what really works for them.

She recalls the farming that her maternal grandfather and her mother engaged in:

> My *thatha* [grandfather] did not use any medicine [fertilizer] for his crops, he used only dung from cows and goats that he owned. There were two permanent employees who worked on the land. The two months when they did not have work on the farm, they went around and collected leaves of native plants (*erukkai elai, kolunji*) and stored them with organic waste. They also collected the leaves and fruits that fell from the neem trees and used all this while preparing the fields for paddy cultivation. These days we don't have anyone to do all that.

Parvathi is very determined to harvest at least a kilogram more than other farmers. For this to happen, she strictly follows watering and manure schedules. She also explains that banana plants have to be cut at the right time, otherwise they ripen and are difficult to sell.

She also makes sure that she sells her produce to the five people that she has been dealing with over a long period of time. The one with the best price takes the farm produce. They have to use her measuring scale. She also allows her neighbour farmers to use her scale to buy or sell their produce. She decided to do this because she had heard a lot of stories of intermediaries who cheated farmers by using a faulty scale. This is remarkable as not all farmers, let alone a woman farmer, can stand their ground with the intermediaries.

Parvathi says that she can bargain for a better price only if she has produce that other farmers do not. If every farmer has the same produce, this is a big drawback.

Parvathi takes pride in going to the auction all by herself: 'My inspiration for farming came from Mala. I have made myself very confident, if I feel that way, people stand aside and let me do my business in *yelam* [auction]. I don't feel shy like most women do. Earlier I took my dad and my husband, now I go on my own. I always ride a vehicle; I can take 100 kg like men do by myself in the vehicle.'

At the auction, the prices for produce and cows are determined in certain ways. For cows, bidders touch certain fingers and say a price. For bananas, she says that if a buyer raises his eyebrows, the price is lower; if he opens and closes his eyes, then they will take the bananas. In a government tender, to get the price that she wants, Parvathi has to pay a 6 per cent commission. Once farmers offload their produce, they are also charged for loading and offloading, so in all she pays 7 per cent, which she says is a big loss for her.

Parvathi says that if nature cooperates, the farmers don't get a good price for their produce; if there is a good price, they don't have enough water to get a good harvest. She feels that if a farmer can decide the price, agriculture would be an ideal occupation as one doesn't have to depend on anybody for benefits. But right now, for small farmers who are totally dependent on farming, even eating becomes difficult. She says people engaged in farming treat their crops like babies, treat them like they have life, and don't mind the hardships that they endure, but not earning enough hurts.

The real benefit is for the big farmers who own 100–200 acres. Small farmers like her have to pay a bribe even to get a farmer card. According to Parvathi, there are no big farmers in her area; the largest area of land owned by a single family is 15 acres.

Parvathi strongly feels that the government should do more to help farmers: 'They have to get us a good price for our harvest. They should make sure that government officials and staff don't take bribes from farmers. We don't need any assistance from the government, but if they help and do everything fairly, existing farmers can have a better life and more farmers or new, younger farmers will choose agriculture as their main occupation.'

There is also a shortage of electricity, but she says that the government can help individuals in rural areas to secure electricity via solar power. Free power is given to industries; agriculture is as important. She says that one can live without those industries but not without food from agriculture.

Parvathi assures us that women farmers are eager to farm even if they don't own land. But they are neither given the freedom nor allowed to take any important decisions pertaining to what and how crops should be cultivated. She says: 'If men farm on their own and lose, it is okay, but if a woman loses, you would hear, "I knew this would happen," from her own family members. Men are dominant, so society thinks a man can be anyway, but if a woman is bad, she cannot bring up her family.'

She says that women should be encouraged, motivated, given confidence, and not put down; for a woman farmer to flourish, the entire household has to cooperate.

The 10 acres of land her mother owns will go to her two brothers. Her mother gave her some land to build her own home, which is in Parvathi's name. The house is now worth INR 60 lakhs (USD 80,000). She does not have any farmland in her name – she farms 8 acres of land that are in her husband's name.

Parvathi is aware that there is a law that says land has to be shared equally between a daughter and son. But she loves her brothers and does not want to demand her share of land. In an interview with us, Parvathi's mother explains that as a woman who owns land, she cannot deprive her daughter of her share but she also has to think of her sons. 'I am obliged to give my sons their share of land but I definitely want to give my daughter some land.'

As far as her children are concerned, Parvathi explains that 60 per cent of her husband's land would go to their daughter and 40 per cent to the son, even though her daughter is not interested in farming at present, because she feels that girls always care and show more affection to parents. But it becomes difficult if they don't find the right life partner.

She says that girls have to be made independent; they should not suffer due to lack of finances. She married her daughter to a farming family who own 10 acres. She intends to buy an additional 3 acres of land for her daughter.

In the coming years, Parvathi would like to lease more land, but she cannot find any nearby. Ten families live off her land. She also supports the education and other expenses of Palanichamy's son. Palanichamy, a Scheduled Caste labourer, stays on the land. She also pays his son when he works on the farm. She hopes to be able to support more families if she had additional land.

Parvathi would like for her son to become involved in farming and he has shown some interest. If he marries a girl who is not interested in this lifestyle, then it's his choice. Parvathi is also keen on bringing her husband into farming. He used to go to the farm when he was younger before he moved to teaching and leased out his land. Her husband recently retired from his job as a government school headmaster and earns a good pension. She wants him to start helping her with the farm soon. This would be very helpful for Parvathi as there is a lot of work involved in full-time farming.

Besides encouraging other women to take up farming, Parvathi has slowly brought one of her brothers into farming. She has helped him to lease in 2 acres of land and he is now managing it, albeit on a part-time basis.

Madhya Pradesh
Suman

There are not many in the village who share Suman's trajectory. Even though her parents had a small patch of land, less than an acre, it barely supported the family and her parents did not farm. She married into a family that had 11.5 acres of land. Her in-laws did not farm much either due to water constraints and because the undulating fields made for poor yields. Suman, like others in her marital household, used to migrate often for work, just as she had done in her parental home before marriage. In fact, much of her early life involved migrating for work. Suman never attended school as a child and because her parents were very poor she was forced to work to bring in some money. In her words:

> My parents ... migrated a lot and farmed a little ... my cousins wanted to take me to school with them and I did go for a day but the very next day my father took me to work. I started working as a

maid for different houses for some years. I discontinued after I got married. Such was the situation in my parents' house that all three of us [sisters] could not study. Even when I got married, I migrated frequently and worked long hours as hired labour in cities.

Suman says that her parents were not educated enough to realise the importance of educating her and they regret it now: 'It would have helped me in taking decisions in life; maybe I could have become an *anganwadi* [nutrition] worker. But nothing can be done now.'

Farming was not what Suman aspired for when she was younger. She was married at the age of 15, not uncommon in her community, and she continued to migrate for work periodically, earning a daily wage of INR 150–200 (USD 2–3). However, after her son was born, about two years after her marriage, she preferred looking for work in the village. At this time, she became a *Panchayat* member (village administrative committee) for a five-year term. This proved to be a turning point for Suman. Farming, she says, was mostly her decision. Although her husband's parents used to engage in a bit of farming, the main initiative to become a farmer came when she was part of the Panchayat. Other Panchayat members suggested to her that since her in-laws' land was near a stream, a well on the farm might provide a reliable supply of water. Suman then took advantage of a state government scheme called *Kapildhara*, under the MGNREGA (Mahatma Gandhi National Rural Employment Guarantee Act), to construct a well.[5] Some villagers then suggested that she sow maize and wheat since the farm had access to water. Suman worked as a hired labourer for a while and saved enough to install a motor for the well. She also started putting away money as savings by joining a savings and thrift group called the Parath Mahila Samuh in the village. At that time, she did not really obtain much information from the state agriculture department and in the first season she mainly learned from her peers. 'That is when,' says Suman, 'I started farming and stopped migrating'.

Suman says that she learned the basics of farming slowly over time and was fortunate to have found support from a large foundation (established as part of a corporate social responsibility initiative). The foundation, active in that part of Chhindwara District, was forthcoming with technical information about farming. After acquiring basic farming skills, Suman sought to diversify into other crops and also try out new techniques. She started growing vegetables. Until the early 2000s, maize, millet, and rice were the major crops in the village. Then local farmers shifted to soybeans since the yield is high. However, since about 2015, as the soybean yield has decreased, there has been an increase in millet and maize production. These crops too depend on rainfall. She adds that the farmers keep changing their crop choices based on the prices that they can fetch in the market. In general, she and her husband market their harvest in a nearby town, selling mainly to traders based there. Her experiments as a farmer have had mixed results. Though she started with organic farming, she decided to use chemicals, seeing others in the village use them. The results were disappointing. She feels that the chemical fertilizers that are commonly used affect the soil quality and crop yield negatively but also decrease the immunity of people consuming that produce in the long run. 'We require more of it every time now and more labour to take care of the land,' she says. Now with the help of the foundation, the farmers in the village have begun vermicomposting in their fields and many use fewer chemical inputs than before.

She says that the corporate foundation has also made an effort to start beekeeping and dairy farming initiatives in the village but that did not continue, according to her, because of a lack of response on the part of the villagers. Parath Mahila Samuh's efforts to engage locals in poultry farming also failed to bear results for the same reason. Consequently, enterprising farmers like Suman lose out on opportunities.

She adds that the help and support that such organizations advance have been crucial given that the agriculture department officials from the state or district hardly ever visit the village. Farmers like her travel to these organizations' offices to meet their staff when they need assistance or information. These bodies also offer training sessions in vermicomposting and in the construction of retaining walls. Some farmers in the village have also learned land levelling techniques and have benefited from these new and practical skills.

Today, they are a family of seven: her in-laws, husband, two sons (aged 19 and 13), and a daughter (aged 16). 'We take our decisions together as family,' says Suman. 'My husband takes my opinion into account for everything, be it farming, food … anything.' Her parents-in-law help her out with housework and farming when she is away on errands or at meetings. Her own parents' response to her efforts as a farmer has also evolved. Suman says, 'I am more industrious and enterprising than my siblings and my parents realize that now – now that they can see that things are changing.' She adds that her parents also regret not sending her to school since they now believe in her capabilities. They rely on her for support and advice for many matters in their own lives. 'What I have realized is that it's essential to be educated, not only for better work opportunities but also for better marriage prospects. So we made sure that we educated our kids.'

According to her, a successful farmer is one who has all of the resources such as machines, water sources, knowledge about technology, and of course, sufficient income earned solely through farming. There should be no need to migrate to make ends meet. She adds that someone who has a small farm does not really count as a farmer. Someone with produce from 15–20 acres of land is a successful farmer.

Despite her transition to being a farmer, the odds are still stacked against her, coming as much from her identity as a young woman farmer as from the larger challenges for agriculture in the region. Things are not easy, she says. It is very difficult to find and hire labour in the village because locals prefer to migrate to cities where they are paid a higher wage. Farmers like Suman cannot afford to pay as much and the family ends up doing all the work themselves. She says, 'One day's worth of work takes two days to complete but there is no way out.'

Suman recently took a loan from Parath Mahila Samuh and opened a tea stall in the village. She noted, 'My husband works there while I take care of the land and migrate for work if I get some time. I have joined another group started by the foundation, which has 10 women members currently.' She says that while such groups incentivize them to save, she still refrains from borrowing because of the fear of default. The couple want to buy a tractor but she feels that it would be risky to take a loan given their financial situation. In case of emergency, she borrows from the Parath Mahila Samuh, which charges a 2 per cent interest rate; otherwise she has to go to local money lenders who charge 5 per cent. The agriculture department in the state provides a 50 per cent subsidy to farmers to purchase farm equipment. She says that she has been planning to fence her fields and buy pipes for irrigation, but even with the subsidy, the expense would be INR 25,000 (USD 300), which she cannot afford at the moment.

Suman does not own the land that she farms – it is still in the name of her father-in-law whose own father bought the land. However, she and her husband have recently purchased 5 acres of land in Suman's name, renting out 3 acres of their land in order to pay for the registration of this new acquisition.[6] The acquisition of land has since provided the basis of her efforts to be a successful farmer. There is not much land that she can inherit from her own parents, nor from her marital household. Even if she could, norms of inheritance are not particularly supportive of women gaining access to land. Suman says, 'Women do have a claim to their father's land legally, but most choose to give up their share for their brothers. Women who insist on their share are generally ostracized from the family.' She explains that women lay claim to parental land only if their parents and brothers are willing to share. Otherwise the tendency is to give their share to the brothers to avoid creating discord in the family. The parents believe that the woman has land in her marital home and hence she does not need to take her inheritance from whatever little land the parents have. But it is different if you are buying or selling the land within family, she adds. That is fine. She explains that people from outside the village buy land from the farmers at lucrative rates. In general, she adds, most people prefer to work on their own farms rather than rent land since people in the village have a tendency to go back on the oral contract that was agreed on since these contracts are based on trust and not legally enforceable.

She believes that there is a need to improve social cohesion in the village. There is also a need to educate the village's children. However, the biggest problem for farming, according to her, is water scarcity. These are the challenges faced by farmers in her village at large.

Kamla

Kamla's story is a contrast to Suman's. Kamla faces most of the constraints that other young women farmers such as Suman typically face; in addition, Kamla also farms in a context that is highly resource constrained and where there is little by way of support to farmers, especially to those who are not part of dominant social networks within the village. This is her story.

Kamla is a 25-year-old woman farmer from an *Adivasi* (Indigenous) community. She can't recall exactly when she started farming but says she was probably just eight or nine years old. Her entry into farming was a matter of course. The youngest of three siblings, her parents were poor with just an acre of poor-quality land and they migrated frequently to find work. They were reluctant to send Kamla to a distant residential school, the only available facility at that time. Consequently, Kamla never went to school. She started helping her parents with farm work, learning the tasks by observing others who farmed, and accompanied her parents when they migrated for work. Even as a child, she was involved in many farming operations, including assisting with tilling, sowing, and harvesting. When a new road was built connecting a nearby town, opportunities in the village expanded. Her parents stopped migrating and started farming full-time, finding work within the village when required. As a child, she dreamt of becoming a doctor and still regrets that she could not study.

Her two older brothers – she can't recall how much older they are – did study, but they stopped attending after completing primary and secondary school respectively and started working as drivers in Panduna, a nearby town, where they settled as adults. Their departure left her with the responsibility of taking care of her parents and also of the little cultivable land that they own – a farmer on her parents' land.

Kamla married in 2015, aged 23, and relocated to a village a few hours away to live with her husband and his family. Her husband lives with his parents, a married older brother, and a younger brother and sister, the youngest of whom is around 22 years old. Her husband's family owns a 4.5-acre farm and the family farms this land jointly. She and her husband farm one part of the family plot and are involved with the operations for the entire farm. However, since most of her husband's family migrate for work, the responsibility for the farm and its operations rests mainly with her and her husband. She is now a farmer twice over.

She finds it challenging to divide her time between the two households (natal and marital) and two tasks – farming and domestic and care work. In general, she spends a week at her marital home and 15 to 20 days in her natal home. Sometimes on these visits, she takes the two bullocks[7] that her husband's family owns to her parents' farm to work the field. Kamla says that her husband is very supportive. He visits her parents intermittently to help with the farm. In contrast, her brothers offer no support, monetarily or otherwise.

Although Kamla identifies herself as a farmer, she and her husband continue to rely on migration. She has migrated about eight times in the past two years and each visit has been at least a week long. She earns about INR 200 (USD 3) per day for work like the construction of a linter roof (a roof that supports weight around doors and windows). She spends around INR 1,000–1,200 (USD 13–16) per week on food when she stays in the city and the rest she saves for the two households – her husband's and her parents'. She adds that most farmers her age have to look for some off-farm activities to make ends meet.

Kamla shares many constraints that other young women farmers face. For example, in her narrative, she never refers to the two farms she works on as hers; indeed they are not hers. Although her brothers left farming and she farms her parental land, there is little chance that she will inherit that land. The land is still in her father's name. When the time comes – and there has been no explicit discussion on when, there usually isn't such a conversation within the family – the land is divided equally among the siblings, but the sisters generally give up their share of land to the brothers. Kamla adds that daughters can keep the land depending on their situation but adds that they usually do not. She says what women farmers here commonly say: 'The brothers help out in kind or cash if the sisters are in need of help.' In her marital home, the land belongs to her father-in-law and will be divided among the husband and his brothers upon his passing. Yet, it is not only whether or not one gets any land; it is also about the quality of the land they might inherit. Kamla notes with concern: 'The part of land that my husband and I work on currently is quite barren while his brothers have more fertile land. If they get that after the division of land, then we will be stuck with the barren part; with farming and migration.'

The other constraint is a familiar one. In her marital household, as daughter-in-law, she is expected to shoulder the bulk of the domestic and care work, in addition to farm work. Further, there is not much scope for her and her husband to retain their earnings, as they contribute all of their earnings to the expenditure of two households and to farm expenses. Yet, she has no role in decision-making in either household. As she puts it: 'My father-in-law makes all the decisions. He gets urea, seeds, etc. and we give him the money. My parents make all the decisions for their land.'

Her aspirations are somewhat ambivalent. She identifies herself as a farmer and is motivated to diversify her crops and get a higher yield and be more profitable – qualities she associates with being a better farmer. At the same time, she also feels that there are insurmountable constraints to farming. Water is at the forefront of her concerns. She adds that if there were enough water then perhaps they would not have to migrate and could sustain a living on the farm itself. On her parental land, they grow maize and a bit of *kutki* (millet) and flat beans. Maize and gram are the crops grown on her marital farmland, but they grow gram only if it rains since their land is not irrigated. She follows: 'We don't sell much; we get around five to six big bags of produce (80–100 kg) but we sell maybe 10 kg since most of it is consumed at home. We go to Tamia to sell it to the shopkeepers and then buy spices and oil from the market. We don't end up saving anything because everything is so costly.'

She also faces challenges in accessing loans. She says that there are no money lenders that she can approach in times of need. According to her, there is a provision for loans at low interest rates for individuals above the age of 50 years in the village, but her parents have not been able to make use of this facility. For additional income, she works in others' fields, migrates, or tries to find work under the MGNREGA, if at all. Occasionally, the couple rent out the more fertile parts of their land. Of the MGNREGA, Kamla says: 'We don't depend on it because it is difficult to get and even when they do get it, there are times they don't receive the payment ... we can formally complain against this but the fear of being ostracized from the village prevents me from pursing this matter further.'

She laments too that she has not received any help or guidance from any government official or agency or even the corporate foundation that has been quite active in the region. Although she has attended a couple of sessions on innovative farming techniques that the foundation has offered, the teachings have not been of much benefit to her because of the paucity of water. She has inherited a few tools from her mother but has to rely on the prominent farmers in the village from whom she rents the tools required for farming. She emphasizes that only those who are associated with the Gram Panchayat or know those in the village administration benefit – they are the ones who receive work provided under MGNREGA and who do not feel the need to migrate. The members of the village's women's savings group are also decided based on how well connected one is. Those generally excluded from this network migrate and/or start poultry and dairy farming. Kamla herself has two cows, two oxen, and some poultry on her husband's farm. There are three calves at her parents' farm that they bought recently. She continues:

> We do not even get information about any scheme or any assistance given by the government. There are a select few in the village ... people with larger land holdings and better connections ... who ensure that others do not get information about the new schemes. People are too involved in their own farms and tend not to share even among themselves ... We generally get all the information when we go out and meet others and see what they are doing.

Kamla and her husband started using urea just five or six years ago; until then they had been using manure. She notes that maize yields, for example, are better now, the plants stronger, and the cob bigger. She says, 'I noticed that people were using urea when I started going out of the village for work. I learn the most from my peers, some within and some outside the village.'

Another major constraint is access to land, which Kamla says is a sensitive issue. There isn't much land around and people generally do not sell. Several people in the village have encroached forest land. Encroachment is common, it seems. Kamla recounts:

> If someone has captured land then it's not possible to get it back because people get violent over it. My mother-in-law has been taking care of her parents' land for a long time (since she has no siblings or

relatives in her natal village), but the neighbours have been trying to illegally capture the land by threatening to beat her up. We have tried going to the *tehsil* (district administration) and they charged us Rupees 2,000 to 3,000 to settle the dispute but nothing has come of it yet. This is just one example of the issues that we face here.

For Kamla, expanding the farm is difficult. She and her husband are directing efforts to secure the land that belongs to her husband's mother. If this does not materialize, she and her husband plan to open a small shop, preferably in a city, once they have saved enough. For this reason, her husband encourages her to learn sewing and tailoring. She reiterates her lack of education as a major impediment in getting better job opportunities. She says that she favours city life to village life because of easier access to basic amenities. But she also realizes that moving away from the village would mean that there would be added expenses like food and accommodation. While she dislikes the village life, she likes the simple and clean environment in the village. While she still wishes to study, she is bogged down by responsibilities and non-availability of a school where someone her age could study.

According to her, a successful farmer is one whose produce is good and who makes profits from farming. With the constraints that she faces, Kamla is open to the prospect of shifting fully to non-farm activities, even though she identifies herself as a farmer. She stresses water constraints and the availability of work as the primary reasons why she and her husband would settle in the city.

Reflections

The four case studies highlight several similarities and differences and echo several themes outlined in the previous chapter. First, young women farmers in this study demonstrate that they take farming seriously and are knowledgeable and passionate about farming. This is significant because women are not socialized to take over the land or lead farming, an advantage that many young male farmers enjoy. Their success depends on family support even without independent access to land. Most of these women began farming when they were as young as eight or nine years old, assisting their parents or grandparents on the farm. This usually involved simple tasks such as assisting with harvesting and weeding or grazing cattle. One young woman farmer in the second field site, Sehore, in Madhya Pradesh, says, 'we watch and learn, I did what my grandmother did'. When not from a farming family, a young woman typically learns from the in-laws or picks up these skills from her peers.

Second, most young women farmers in our study as well as more broadly seem to become full-time farmers typically after marriage. This is especially the case in recent years with daughters being sent to school and then being married relatively young. While landowning caste groups such as KV Gounders in Tamil Nadu send their daughters to study – keeping them away from farming – and marry them to men who have non-farm jobs, the presence of land and the practice of farming in their marital homes draw many young women into farming. The support from husbands and sometimes more importantly from fathers-in-law – as the land is in their name – is crucial.

Third, as the previous chapter and case studies illustrate, even when women engage in full-time farming, land ownership eludes them. Yet, most of our respondents did not identify this as a barrier. Further, many rationalize this by emphasizing that the support offered by their brothers was more important than their formal rights to land. One woman farmer in Madhya Pradesh suggested that even if her brothers were fine with her claiming her share of land, it would be unfair to the wives of her brothers, who might have given up claims to their own inheritances for the sake of their brothers. Both the fact that women do not demand their lawful share and that they do not acknowledge this to be a barrier reflect the deeply entrenched social norms governing land inheritance and gender relations discussed in the previous chapter. Even the instances when women do inherit land, it is driven by family-specific or at times region-specific informal norms. Across some caste groups in Tamil Nadu (not discussed here) property is equally inherited by sons and daughters although even here there are wide variations. Even within the KV caste discussed here, there are instances of land being passed on to daughters (mainly in the absence of sons), but it is never the norm. Legal support for equal rights has, however, enabled women to stake claims, although this is highly unlikely.

Fourth, the limited access to land for young women farmers has important material consequences. Because formal ownership of land is often linked to being recognized as a farmer in the eyes of the government, most women farmers are not recognized as farmers. Too often, the criterion for eligibility for a large number of government schemes remains title to land; those in the family who have ownership rights thus mediate a young woman farmer's access to government support. This can potentially be a large constraint. We saw this in the case of Kamla Ukey, whose parents were eligible for a farm loan, although she managed the farm. Or in the case of Suman Parteti, where the well under the *Kapildhara* scheme would be granted to her father-in-law, since he was the legal owner of the farm. In most of the villages, acquiring land through leasing in or purchases is near impossible given the rising cost of land. Some women, as suggested in the case studies, do manage to do this, thus increasing their ability to become landowning farmers.

Fifth, some of the young women we interviewed, especially in Tamil Nadu, enjoy quite high levels of freedom to pursue farming on their own. Among certain landowning caste groups like the KV, it might be possible for women to become full-time farmers as men are in full-time non-farm employment. In the case of Madhya Pradesh, both men and women pursue plural activities and combine farm and non-farm activities, most likely on account of the limited opportunities for employment in the non-farm sector for men and women alike. In these cases, the autonomy of the young women farmers seems relatively limited.

Sixth, besides lack of land ownership young women farmers face several other challenges. Access to training and techniques can be challenging for young women farmers. For example, a young woman farmer in Sehore, Madhya Pradesh, who has completed a Master's degree and identifies herself as a farmer, describes: 'The agriculture extension officials who visit the village meet only the male farmers. It is hardly ever the case that these male farmers then discuss the matters related to farming with women in the house who also farm along with them … their role has been reduced to just providing assistance with no decision-making power.'

In the case of Madhya Pradesh, some women have taken up farming and acquired a set of skills with the support of state and central government programmes, and corporate social responsibility initiatives. Societal support seems important as well in the form of learning from one's peers. Tamil Nadu's young women farmers seem more equipped to access the latest techniques via social media. In contrast, the young women farmers in Madhya Pradesh continue to rely on more traditional forms of extension and peer group support.

Seventh, the young women farmers in our study clearly demonstrate that being and becoming a farmer does not absolve them of their domestic and care work. Some of our case studies illustrate this clearly and here too, unless they have some support from other (and older) family members in sharing responsibilities for household chores or farm work, the dual responsibility of farm and domestic work can be overwhelming. Kamla and Shanti's life stories as farmers establish the intersection of age and gender wherein women straddle multiple identities and responsibilities across different patriarchal relationships – from daughters to daughters-in-law to parents, between natal and marital households. Attending to farm and household work and care responsibilities can also crowd out opportunities. For example, a young woman farmer and mother of two small children in Sehore, Madhya Pradesh, says that she would have loved to diversify into dairy but that cattle 'needed timely care – feeding and providing drinking water'. With her childcare responsibilities, acquiring and maintaining cattle was out of the question.

Eighth, young women farmers also face substantial difficulties in negotiating male spaces, such as the market. In particular, they experience severe limits to their mobility because of public spaces being male dominated. Relative to older women, younger women face more obstacles travelling out of the village. In our study, we found that when women went to the market, they were accompanied by their male spouses or other male members of the family. In general, when itinerant traders are the main buyers of produce, prices are often set by these traders. The problem of managing a farm can be acute for young women farmers who are single or widowed. Procurement of inputs, hiring of labour, and selling of output represent a formidable challenge. Not all are able to accomplish these without a hired male farm manager or male relative. A young widowed farmer in Sehore told us: 'Who cares that a woman is alone or needs help?' suggesting that there is no state support for individuals like her. She relies overwhelmingly on a hired manager who shares expenses incurred on cultivation and shares the produce while taking responsibility for all purchases and sales.

We also note differences in terms of class and community support in mediating this process of negotiating male-dominated spaces. While Shanti, with relatively lesser social and land endowments, struggles to negotiate, Parvathi seems to be relatively more successful in such negotiations. In fact, interestingly, Shanti, despite being a joint owner of land, finds it a lot more difficult to access such spaces compared to Parvathi, who is confident about her ability to bargain with intermediaries for better prices. This highlights the importance of social networks in mediating and coping with gender-related vulnerabilities. Many recent initiatives such as self-help groups have aided young women farmers in their attempts to navigate male-dominated spaces. A young woman farmer in Sehore says: 'More than that (i.e., a savings group), it is a platform for women to meet and discuss their problems … this has really enabled women to present their opinions in front of men and outsiders.'

Often these social networks also determine access to government programmes or other external support from corporate foundations or self-help groups. A young woman farmer from a marginalized caste or tribe is often triple marginalized. In the case of Madhya Pradesh, several programmes that are tailored for tribal communities have provided lifelines to these young women farmers, as have the corporate foundations operating in tribal-dominated districts. In Tiruvannamalai, the second study site in Tamil Nadu, a non-governmental organization (NGO) provides training in organic farming to smallholder Dalit women farmers, assisting them with market access and training them to produce organic manure. In such cases, however, their smaller landholding sizes (1–3 acres) and lower caste status prove to be barriers.

While collective mobilization does help women farmers to overcome some of the limitations imposed on them by their gender, caste, and economic status, their prospects in farming continue to be constrained by these very institutions. In conclusion, it is useful to go beyond our study to seek a policy setting that would be conducive to and supportive of young women farmers.[8] Initiatives that focus on women's collective access/right to land simultaneously challenge the family farm as the unit of organizing production and offer the potential to weaken caste hierarchies, status, and patriarchal relations that undergird the family farm (Agarwal and Agrawal 2017; Vijayabaskar et al. 2018).

In this regard, perhaps the two most transformative policy initiatives for young women have been the establishment of a Directorate of Women in Agriculture[9] and the organization of women into self-help groups under the National Rural Livelihoods Mission. The former has actively engaged in research and developing technologies for women in agriculture and the latter, like the NGO-run self-help groups, is often regarded as offering a platform for young women to organize themselves. Such groups can redress some of the disadvantages that young women farmers face in accessing information and training (Raghunathan et al. 2019, for example). Similarly, programmes such as the Mahila Samakhya,[10] women's self-help groups, and one-third reservation for women in Panchayats are useful to focus on women's needs more broadly. These initiatives focus on providing training and finance to support livelihoods. Many have actively provided platforms for extension training, production, and marketing. Although not specifically framed with young women farmers in mind, as we have shown in the previous chapter, they are likely focusing on the vast majority of young women, albeit on married young women.

Notes

1. Actual names are not used for the four cases of young women farmers.
2. 1 acre equals 0.4 hectares.
3. This is, however, a perception among landowners because of the enormous costs involved in eviction of tenants. In Tamil Nadu, there was an effort to pass such a law in the 1970s, but it did not get Presidential assent. However, the laws for eviction are hard to enforce and this has led to fear that leasing out to unknown persons may pose problems.
4. This was evident in a farmers' group that we met during fieldwork. We did not explicitly request to meet young women farmers. It was an all-male farmers' group with whom we interacted.
5. *Kapildhara* is a state government programme to support the construction of wells on land owned by those who belonged to the Scheduled Castes/ Tribes and marginal farmers. The labour for the wells' construction was provided by the Mahatma Gandhi National Rural Employment Guarantee Act (MGNREGA), a workfare programme that entitles each rural household to 100 days of unskilled manual work and prescribed wages, based on work completed.
6. The registration fee while not substantial can still be a burden and renting out land for a year would likely cover these costs.
7. Castrated bulls are referred to as bullocks, used as draught animals.
8. In 2018, the Government of India committed to allocating 30 per cent of the funds to agriculture in the Union Budget to schemes supporting women in agriculture. Rai (2019), however, points out that there is not much that is specifically directed to women farmers. Further, recent budget allocations in 2019 have not conformed to this commitment of 30 per cent.
9. The Working Group on Agricultural Research and Education constituted by the Planning Commission for the formulation of the Eighth Five Year Plan (1992–97) recommended the establishment of a National Research Centre for Women in Agriculture (NRCWA). Accordingly, the Indian Council of Agricultural Research established the NRCWA in 1996 at Bhubaneswar, which was upgraded to the Directorate of Research on Women in Agriculture (DRWA) in 2008, with a sub-centre in Bhopal.
10. The Mahila Samakhya programme, launched by the Government of India in 1988, aimed to promote education and empowerment of rural women in rural areas, especially from socially and economically marginalized groups.

References

Agarwal, B., and Agrawal, A. (2017) 'Do farmers really like farming? Indian farmers in transition.' *Oxford Development Studies* 45(4): 460–78. https://doi.org/10.1080/13600818.2017.1283010

Raghunathan, K., Kannan, S., and Quisumbing, A.R. (2019) 'Can women's self-help groups improve access to information, decision-making, and agricultural practices? The Indian case.' *Agricultural Economics* 50: 567–80. https://doi.org/10.1111/agec.12510

Rai, S. (2019) 'Where is the money for women farmers?' *IDR Online*, 22 March 2019. https://idronline.org/contributor/sakshi-rai/

Vijayabaskar, M., Narayanan, S., and Srinivasan, S. (2018) 'Agricultural revival and reaping the youth dividend.' *Economic and Political Weekly* 53(26–27). https://www.epw.in/journal/2018/26-27

CHAPTER 8

Young women and farming in Indonesia

Aprilia Ambarwati, Charina Chazali, Isono Sadoko, and Ben White

General background

Agriculture is important in Indonesia, not only to provide food for its 270 million population (BPS 2021), but also as the country's single largest source of employment. Despite urbanization (57 per cent of the population), in 2020 more than 30 per cent of the total (rural and urban) labour force, and more than 50 per cent of the rural labour force, reported their main occupation as agricultural, far outstripping the two next largest sectors of trade and manufacturing. While women were somewhat more diversified into the trade and manufacturing sectors, still close to 30 per cent of all employed women reported agriculture as their main occupation (BPS 2020, 2021). The qualification 'main occupation' is important, as pluriactivity – diversified income sources – is a general feature of economic activity of both richer and poorer, both men and women, in rural areas. Contrary to general perceptions or expectations about rural youth, agriculture still employs a much higher proportion of young rural people – both women and men – than industry or any other sector, and this proportion has been relatively stable in recent years.

To understand the position of young women in agriculture in Indonesia, we first provide a general picture of agrarian structures. The next section then summarizes what we know about the changing position of young men and women within these structures, including: the age and gender of farmers, modes of intergenerational transfer of farm land and property, young people's apparent turn away from agriculture, and patterns of rural youth labour mobility between places and sectors.

Agrarian structures

Indonesia's agrarian structure reflects its historical legacy of large-scale, formerly colonial plantations (in such crops as rubber, tobacco, sugarcane, tea, coffee, and more recently oil palm) alongside some 28 million smallholder farms. Today's plantations are either state-owned (many former Dutch and Belgian companies nationalized under the Sukarno regime in the late 1950s) or owned by domestic conglomerates and domestic–foreign joint ventures. Some plantation crops have expanded and others contracted in the last 20 years, but all are dwarfed by the rapid expansion and huge area of oil palm plantations.

Indonesia is the world's biggest producer of oil palm, which now covers more than 18 million hectares, mainly in Kalimantan and Sumatra, with a target of expansion to 29 million ha, larger than the total area devoted to food crops. About 70 per cent of total crude palm oil production is exported. Big corporations have 'grabbed' large amounts of land where the occupants do not have formal ownership certificates and the Ministry of Forestry claims land jurisdiction. Most of the oil palm is formally or informally under the control of big plantation actors, sometimes operated on classic plantation lines, sometimes combining this with smallholder contract farming schemes. About 10 million people (2 million workers and their families) now live in the oil palm zones and depend on the plantations for income once the land frontier is closed. This level of employment (with only one worker per five hectares) is very low, even compared to other plantation crops; in rubber, for example, the ratio is closer to 1:1 (Li 2017). The large-scale plantation sector as a whole offers few attractive labour or career opportunities to young people. Wage levels and labour conditions in this sector are generally very poor, and women are commonly employed only in low-paying plot maintenance work (Li and Semedi 2021). One study focusing on young people's prospects in the plantation sector (Li 2017) concludes that once land frontiers are closed, opportunities for plantation-related wage work are very limited, and the corporations make no provisions for either land or jobs for the next generation. Women have disproportionally borne the costs of customary land loss, and dispossession has not only reproduced existing patriarchal structures but also undermined more gender-equal ones, most notably women's customary land rights (Julia and White 2011; Levien 2017: 1124).

Staple food production and horticulture, in contrast, are dominated by smallholder agriculture, and there is also a significant minority of smallholders growing export crops, independently or on contract. Farm sizes in the smallholder sector tend to be very small: at the last Agricultural Census (2023), around three-quarters of Indonesia's 26 million smallholder farms were under 1 ha and more than half were under 0.5 ha, as shown in Table 8.1.

The Centre for Social Analysis's (AKATIGA) study of 20 rice-producing villages in Java, South Sulawesi, and Lampung found varying degrees of land concentration and landlessness. Large land ownership in rice-producing villages generally leads not to large farm sizes or capitalist farming, but to increasing rates of tenancy (particularly share tenancy) as the larger owners parcel out their land to sharecroppers (Ambarwati et al. 2016; for a broader historical view of this pattern, see White 2018). In one of the five sample villages for our study of young women farmers (Kulon Progo – see below), more than half of all rice farmers were share tenants.

Table 8.1 Smallholder farm sizes, Indonesia, 2023

Farm size (ha)	Number (millions)	% of total
<0.1	7.4	26
0.1–0.19	4.0	14
0.2–0.49	6.3	22
0.5–0.99	4.2	15
1.0–1.99	3.8	13
2.0–2.99	1.5	5
≥3.0	1.3	5
Total	28.4	100

Source: BPS 2023

Compared to Indonesia's 'Green Revolution' period of the 1970s and early 1980s, smallholder farming in Indonesia currently receives little government support. Much of the available support (such as subsidized seeds, fertilizers, and pesticides) does not reach small farmers, particularly (but not only) those tenant farmers who do not own land.

Pluriactivity – household livelihoods composed of a combination of farm and non-farm activities – has been common for a long time, at least in densely populated regions, among both large- and small-farm and landless-worker households. In general, larger farmers transfer surpluses into investments in relatively high-return, non-farm activities such as trading and shopkeeping, agro-processing, and transport, while small farmers and landless farm workers transfer labour without capital into low-return activities (often providing less per day than agricultural wages) such as petty trade, handicrafts, or non-agricultural wage work.[1]

To our knowledge there have been no previous studies of young women farmers in Indonesia. However, several recent local-level studies of rural youth in different regions have reached broadly similar conclusions about young rural women's attitudes to, and experiences of, migration and farming. After leaving secondary school or college, young rural men and women aspire to find salaried work and financial security, but for the great majority, education does not fulfil its promise of secure employment. Both those who remain in the village, and those who return after a period of migration, do not disassociate themselves completely from agrarian-based livelihoods although they express reluctance to becoming full-time farmers. Lack of access to land – a problem for all, but particularly so for young women – and declining land productivity for those who do obtain land, may drive them to a growing reliance on non-farm work but they continue to sustain intergenerational farm reproduction, in a pattern that Rigg et al. (2016, 2020) note is now common in much of East and South-east Asia (see among others Schut 2019 for Flores; Griffin et al. 2024 for South Sulawesi; Nugraha and Herawati 2015, Yuniarto 2016, and Woodward 2020 for Java).

Table 8.2 Changing age of smallholder 'farm heads',[7] 1983–2023

Age group	1983	2023
<25	3	1
25–34	22	9
35–44	31	22
45–54	25	28
>55	18	40
Total	100	100

Source: BPS 1983, 2023

Table 8.3 Age and gender of 'farm heads' in smallholder farming, 2013

Age group	% of all farm heads	% male	% female	Total (millions)
≤ 24	1	90	10	0.23
25–34	12	94	6	3.13
35–44	26	93	7	6.89
45–54	28	89	11	7.33
55–64	20	85	15	5.23
65+	13	79	21	3.33
Total	100	89	11	26.14

Source: BPS 2013. Comparable age-specific data from the 2023 Agricultural Census are not yet available

Young men and women in Indonesian agriculture

Age and gender of farmers

Some data on the age and gender structure of Indonesia's farming population are shown in Table 8.2 and Table 8.3. Table 8.2 shows that the average age of 'farm heads' (the self-defined 'primary farmer' or *petani utama* in farm households) has been rising significantly between 1983 and 2023. In the space of four decades between 1983 and 2023 the proportion of farm heads under age 35 more than halved, while those 55 years and older more than doubled. But Table 8.2 also shows that even in 1983, the proportion of farm heads under 25 years of age was very small (only 3 per cent). At that time, most boys in rural areas were leaving school at age 15, and girls often at age 12. So in the past, too, there was a long gap between the age of leaving school and the time at which young people could take over management of a farm. Looking at these statistics, we can ask: are today's farm heads being forced to continue farming into their old age because of the lack of successors – this is the most commonly assumed explanation – or are they living and/or staying healthier longer, with little or no social protection for the aged, and therefore not ready to hand over farms to the next generation? Is the problem that the old cannot stop because the young are unwilling to start, or that the young are unable to start, because the old are unwilling or unable to stop, or to transfer a part of their tiny farms to their children? Or is there another, more complex dynamic at work, as Jonathan Rigg argues based on his research in Thailand, meaning that these are the wrong questions to ask and that we need to reconsider the way we think about ageing and occupational change, about what is a farmer and what is farming (Rigg et al. 2020). We will return to this point later.

In the 2023 Agricultural Census only 11 per cent of reported farm heads were female, as shown in Table 8.3. This number undoubtedly underestimates the reality due to prevailing discursive cultural barriers which render both young and older women farmers invisible, as will be discussed further below. The percentage of female farm heads was highest among those aged 55 and above, suggesting the influence of divorce and/or widowhood.

Young women and land: modes of intergenerational transfer of farm land and property

> It is clear that multiple problems are generated by women's limited access to land ownership and land inheritance (FAO 2019: 30).

In Indonesian law there are no formal barriers, and in most regions no customary barriers, to women's ownership and inheritance of land. In most parts of Indonesia, both men and women have rights – though not always equal rights – to own and inherit land and other family property. But there are some notable exceptions, such as our two case-study villages in West Manggarai district, Flores (see next chapter) where women cannot inherit, and some other regions where inheritance goes through the female line. Where both sons and daughters inherit, shares are sometimes equal, sometimes daughters receive less than sons.

In Kupang (East Nusa Tenggara, eastern Indonesia), Ruwiastuti et al. reported in the late 1990s that male children generally inherit more land than daughters. Daughters may keep the land they are cultivating after marriage but when they die the land reverts to their parents or male siblings or their descendants (Ruwiastuti et al. 1997: 30). In Western Lombok (West Nusa Tenggara), customary inheritance rules follow the saying *nina nyenyon mama melembah* (the woman carries one load on her head, the man two loads on a shoulder-pole); that is, male heirs receive twice the share of female heirs.[2] In some cases where landholdings are too small to be further sub-divided, daughters do not receive a share, but depend on their brothers or other male heir(s) to give them a share of the harvest (Ruwiastuti et al. 1997: 30). In some regions such as Aceh (northern Sumatra), daughters are entitled to a smaller share of landed property than sons, under Sharia law (FAO 2019: 29).

Large-scale data on land ownership by gender (and age) are scarce, and probably not very accurate. A USAID report (cited in FAO 2019: 29) found that in Java, 65 per cent of land held by married couples was registered in the husband's name. Data from the 2012 Indonesia Demographic and Health

Table 8.4 Percentage of rural men and women aged 15–49 by type of land ownership, 2012

	Men %	Women %
Self-ownership	34	14
Self and joint ownership	2	3
Joint ownership	28	32
Having no land	36	52
	100	100

Source: BPS et al. 2013, Tables 13.4.1 and 13.4.2

Survey suggest that about 52 per cent of rural women aged 15–49 own no land (either in their own name or jointly) compared to 35 per cent of men, and only 16 per cent of women landholders report owning land in their own names, compared to 36 per cent of men (Table 8.4) BPS et al. 2013. A portion of those 'having no land' are likely younger men and women who still have some prospect of inheritance.

Unequal access to land also means unequal access to formal credit through land entitlements (FAO 2019: 30). There are also many cultural barriers – both in the bureaucracy and in rural community relationships – to women's discursive and material recognition as farmers in their own right. They are poorly represented in the local public sphere, for example in local leadership and decision-making positions as well as in institutions tasked with supporting small farmers, including membership of cooperatives and farmer groups and access to their facilities (FAO 2019: 31). At the local level, these organizations may play important roles in decisions on, for example, seed varieties to be planted, and planting and irrigation schedules (FAO 2019: 33).

We have not found any ethnographic studies on the processes of inter-generational farm transmission through the transfer of land before (*hibah*) or after (*warisan*) the owners' death.[3] AKATIGA's study in rice-producing villages in Java and South Sulawesi found that land could be transferred either when a son/daughter is married, or when the parents became sick or too weak to continue farming, or on the parents' death. Children waiting to inherit land may either stay in the village and help on the farm, or (more frequently) migrate to various non-farm occupations. Cases where children had been able to become independent farmers (rather than farm helpers) while parents were still living were rare. When grown-up children help on the parental farm, the parents may give them a share of the harvest (Nugraha and Herawati 2015: 33–34). In some cases (for example, our respondents Yaya, Partini, and Grace in the next chapter), the potential successors enter a standard share cropping arrangement with their parents or parents-in-law, bearing all of the costs of cultivation and handing over one-half of the harvest. Share tenancy, thus, can sometimes represent a phase in the process of devolution of land rights between the generations.

Young people's apparent aversion to the idea of farming futures is partially related to the image of farming as occupation and of rural life generally, but economic and structural issues are certainly also an important cause. The AKATIGA researchers have been studying these issues since 2013, in 12 rice-producing villages in West Java, Central Java, and South Sulawesi. In most of these rice-producing villages, the landholding structure means that most young people have no realistic prospect of becoming farmers, or at least not while they are young. Landlessness is widespread and less than half of farmers own the land that they cultivate. The only people who have some chance of owning land while they are still young are those who come from wealthy landowning households. But they typically go to university, and aim for a future in a secure, salaried job; their parents also have the resources to get them into these jobs. They may look forward to inheriting and owning land, but as a source of income through rent; they may have no interest in farming it themselves.

Meanwhile, young people growing up in smallholder farming families may eventually inherit a piece of land, but their parents have too little land to hand over part of it to their children while they are still young. They may be in their 40s or 50s when they finally receive land from their parents. And for the many young people whose parents are landless, there is only the prospect of becoming a sharecropper or farm labourer, unless they can find another way to access land. For these young men and women, unless they find a spouse who already has access to land, the only possible way to become a farmer is to find work first outside agriculture (and often outside the village) and hope to save enough money to buy or rent some land (AKATIGA and White 2015; see also Chazali et al. 2024, Ambarwati and Chazali 2024, White and Wijaya 2024).

Plurilocality and pluriactivity in the life course of rural youth

Given the fact that so many rural young people have either no prospect of inheriting land, or the prospect of a long wait before they can start farming independently, it is not surprising that so many young rural men and women decide to migrate to various kinds of paid jobs or informal-sector work, both within Indonesia and sometimes overseas including Malaysia and the Gulf countries. Young people's decisions to farm or not to farm, and to stay in the village or to migrate, are not permanent decisions. Many of today's older farmers themselves migrated when young, and returned when they had saved money or when land became available.

In our sample of 109 young farmer respondents (discussed in more detail below), 59 per cent of young male farmers and 31 per cent of young women farmers had prior experience of migration for work before turning to farming. But there is significant regional variation: only one-third of sample young farmers in our two Flores villages had migration experience, compared to three-quarters of those in the three Javanese villages. After graduating from secondary school, young women may try to find work in factories, in petty trade, as shop assistants in urban areas, or as domestic workers both in Indonesia and abroad. Men are less visible in factory and trading sectors, but more in the construction sector and various informal-sector activities such as *ojeg* (motor-cycle taxi) driver. In Indonesia, as Rigg and his colleagues (2020) found in Thailand, it is increasingly inadequate to categorize rural people – especially the young generation – in binary categories such as 'farmer/non-farmer' or 'rural/urban' as national population and labour-force statistics do, when so many of them span both.

There are many reasons why leaving the village may seem attractive, and farming futures unattractive, to young people. Mass media often portray the rural world and farmers as backward and poor. But many dimensions of rural life are changing fast. In many villages connectivity is now as good as in the cities; motorbikes are cheap and common; and all young people are busy with Facebook and Instagram accounts. Young men and women engage actively with global ideas and global youth lifestyles, and with the rapid progress of these and other rural infrastructures, they may now feel that it is more possible to enact a modern youth lifestyle. All this may make them look at rural life and farming differently to how their parents did.

Methodology and introduction to the five sample villages and young women farmers[4]

The case studies we present in the following chapter are drawn from field research conducted in three study villages in Java (Central Java and Yogyakarta), and two study villages in West Manggarai, as shown in Figure 8.1. In these villages we interviewed 109 young farmers, including 49 young women farmers. We first introduce the five villages, and then describe the field methodology, including the selection of the 109 young farmers from which we have drawn the nine young women farmer cases discussed in the next chapter.

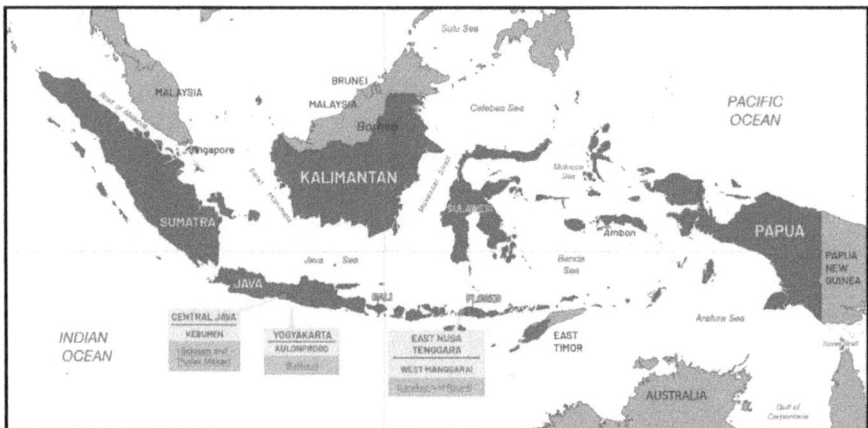

Figure 8.1 Sample villages in Central Java, Yogyakarta, and West Manggarai
Source: Indonesian maps from www.cia.gov (adapted by the authors).

Sidosari, Pudak Mekar, and Kaliloro (Java)

Our three sample villages in Central Java and Yogyakarta[5] reflect the character-istics of the region: densely populated, with very small farm sizes, significant rates of landlessness, and long histories of pluriactivity and out-migration – not always permanent – of young people. In all these villages, both sons and daughters inherit land. Sidosari is a village in Central Java's lowland rice-bowl region with good canal irrigation. Pudak Mekar is closer to the southern coastal area (Indian Ocean) where almost all of the farm land is rainfed (*tegalan*). These villages are located in Kebumen District, around 165 kilometres south of the provincial capital, Semarang. The two cases from these villages are of Tasniah and Jamini, with their different aspirations when they were young, and different experience of pluriactivity. Kaliloro (in Kulon Progo District, Yogyakarta) is a rice-growing village with good canal irrigation located between the river Progo and the Menoreh foothills, some 35 kilometres north-west of Yogyakarta city. The three cases that we have chosen – Yaya, Partini, and Menik – with their different experiences of migration prior to farming, access to land, and (non)-recognition as farmers, illustrate the range of generational gender and class constraints that young women farmers face.

Langkap and Nigara (West Manggarai, Flores)

Langkap is an upland village directly adjacent to the Mbeliling forest, currently being developed as an ecotourism village. Nigara is also mainly an upland village, but one of its hamlets is far separated from the rest in the lowland part of the village, which has irrigated rice fields. This hamlet is part of an area that was developed as a rice-growing area since the Suharto era (1967–98). These villages have a combination of rice fields and dry land farming as well as a system of customary tenure in which land can only be allocated to men.[6] Our two cases from these villages, Grace and Noya, illustrate how they started farming, the division of labour, and gender constraints in accessing land and farming resources.

In both of the West Manggarai study villages, some small-scale land grabs – not massive or spectacular, but no less important to those who experience them – can be observed in recent years. Almost half of all customary land within these two villages has already been sold by villagers, facilitated by the head of their customary community, to national or international private investors who plan to develop tourist resorts in these areas.

Sample selection and interview methods

In many villages, as already mentioned, young farmers are former migrants and turn to farming only in their late 20s or early 30s. If we had restricted our sample to the standard United Nations' definition of 'youth' (ages 15–24), we would have missed many young farmers. Furthermore, as we wanted to explore the experiences of young farmers, we did not want to have a sample only of those who had just recently begun farming. All the farmers aged 40 or over in our sample had started farming while in their 30s, and many of them in their early 30s or late 20s. The oldest age at which a respondent had become an independent farmer, among our 109 young farmers, was 38; the average age of starting was 24 years, and the modal age 27.

In all the research locations, the young men and women respondents were selected by a combination of information from key informants and snowball techniques, as described further for each location below. Data collection was based mainly on qualitative techniques, including semi-structured interviews, but also included a short household survey questionnaire. The life-history method inspired our semi-structured interviews, with a focus on key moments over the respondents' life course in the process of becoming a farmer.

In Kebumen, we conducted in-depth interviews and a small-scale survey with 29 young farmers (11 female and 18 male). To find and select the young farmers, we asked a local non-governmental organization (NGO) for help. In discussions with village officials, the NGO made a list of farmers under 45 years of age from different hamlets, and the size of their farms. We tried to contact and interview all of those on the list. In this list, however, young men were dominant (reflecting the bias of the NGO and village officials). We then added more cases, mainly women, based on information from our initial respondents, and achieved a better balance.

In Kaliloro village, we interviewed 30 young farmers (6 women, and 24 men). We began by identifying farmers aged below 45 (mostly men) from a survey of some 400 households that Ben White and Hanny Wijaya had conducted the previous year. After meeting and interviewing these young farmers, we asked them to help us identify others, especially women. In this village, young women tend to be involved in non-farm activities such as small trading or shopkeeping, domestic service, or wage work in nearby factories within commuting distance (by motorbike). For these women, involvement in farming is minimal as they are busy at least six days per week. Many young men migrate over longer distances, to big urban complexes like greater Jakarta and Tangerang (West Java). The great majority of our young farmer sample, therefore, are ex-migrants. The six young women respondents are all farmers in their own right (i.e. they manage as well as work on their farms). Other women farmers manage the farm together with their husbands, and in all such cases, we tried to ensure that both were interviewed, whether together or separately.

In the two villages in Flores, we interviewed 50 young farmers (18 men and 32 women). This gender imbalance may seem curious, as these are the villages where – in contrast to Java – women cannot inherit or own land in their own right. But they are indeed, in many cases, the *de facto* primary farmers while their husbands and brothers are busier with non-farm work, inside or outside the village. We found the first young farmer respondents with the help of a village official and an active member of the local farmers' group. These respondents then helped us identify further respondents, and so on. We also interviewed several older farmers, parents of our young farmer respondents, mainly to obtain information on intergenerational changes in farming practices and intergenerational transfers of resources and farming knowledge.

In all of the villages, we tried to identify and interview respondents from different geographical locations within the village, as location may be an important influence on farming and other economic activities (for example, in relatively remote neighbourhoods compared to those close to the main road). In Nigara (Flores), with its unique settlement conditions spanning irrigated lowland and dryland upland areas at quite some distance from each other, we interviewed respondents from both locations, although many of the respondents who are living in the upland area also have a garden house (*rumah kebun*) in the lowland area where some family members stay during the peak seasons of activity in rice farming.

For the duration of the research period, the research teams stayed with villagers and complemented the interview-based methods with participant observation by taking part in everyday activities. We often engaged our young respondents in informal conversation while joining them in day-to-day activities in and around the house. In this way, they felt freer to tell their stories because they did not feel they were being 'interviewed'. These conversations often happened in the kitchen while preparing food, in the early evening when women like to sit together and chat, or while enjoying the evening meal together. This made it easier for the researchers to discuss delicate topics such as intergenerational and inter-sibling relations and inheritance.

All the young women farmers we interviewed in Kebumen and Kulonprogo were married. Some of those we interviewed in Flores were single, and in these cases, their older (mainly male) siblings or neighbours sometimes interrupted and attempted to correct their answers. When this occurred, we tried to return to the respondents later to ask more questions. But in some cases it was not possible to elicit information on sensitive topics such as relationships within the household and with parents and kin.

In all research locations, in the case of married young farmer couples (where both were active farmers), we tried to interview them both. In such cases, to complete the structured questionnaire (on landholdings, family structure, and other basic household-level data), we tried to interview them together. For the subsequent in-depth interviews, we tried, where possible, to interview women separately, as they felt more comfortable telling their stories outside their husbands' presence. The depth of information obtained varies from case to case. For instance, in Flores, women carry out almost all stages of farming, but their husbands or male siblings own the land. Therefore, sometimes the women farmers did not really know the details of how their husbands or siblings obtained the land. They also sometimes felt hesitant when they were speaking about their parents-in-law.

Some general conclusions drawn from this chapter and the case studies will be found at the end of the next chapter.

Notes

1. Alexander et al. (1991) give some historical examples of this pattern from the late colonial period; White and Wiradi (1989) give some examples from Java in the 'Green Revolution' period.
2. Compare the same principle *sepikul segendong* (a [man's] two-basket shoulder-pole load, a [woman's] one-basket load), often reported as customary practice in parts of Java, but not always followed.
3. A recent exception is Firman et al.'s (2018) micro-study of succession models in smallholder dairy farms in Pangalengan, West Java. This study found that the transfer of the whole dairy farm before (*hibah*) or after the owner's death (*warisan*) were both rare. More common were various modes of gradual parental facilitation of the potential successor's access to a number of cows and support services from the dairy cooperative.
4. All of the names of people and villages in this chapter are pseudonyms.
5. Yogyakarta is administratively a Special Region, geographically located in southern central Java.
6. Widows in Langkap village also receive a piece of customary land from the head of their customary communities.
7. 'Farm head' (*petani utama*) in this table and Table 8.3 is defined as 'the farm holder who represents the [farm] household. The farm holder selected was the highest income earner from agricultural undertaking among the farm holders within the household. If there were two farm holders with the same income, then the [one with] the largest activity in agriculture was selected' (BPS 2013: 78).

References

AKATIGA and White, B. (2015) 'Would I like to be a farmer?' *Inside Indonesia* 120 (April–June). https://www.insideindonesia.org/editions/edition-120-apr-jun-2015/would-i-like-to-be-a-farmer?

Alexander, P., Boomgaard, P., and White, B. (eds) (1991) *In the shadow of agriculture: Nonfarm activities in the Javanese economy, past and present.* Amsterdam: Royal Tropical Institute Press.

Ambarwati, A. and Chazali, C. (2024) 'The long road to becoming a farmer in Kebumen, Central Java, Indonesia'. In S. Srinivasan (ed.), *Becoming a young farmer: Young people's pathways into farming – Canada, China, India, Indonesia*, pp. 361–82. London: Palgrave Macmillan (Open Access).

Ambarwati, A., Harahap, R.A., Sadoko, I., and White, B. (2016) 'Land tenure and agrarian structure in regions of small-scale food production.' In J. McCarthy and K. Robinson (eds), *Land and development in Indonesia: Searching for the people's sovereignty*, pp. 265–94. Singapore: National University of Singapore Press.

Badan Pusat Statistik (BPS) (1983) 'Agricultural Census 1983, Series B: Result of Sample Census.' Jakarta: Badan Pusat Statistik.

BPS (2013) *Agricultural Census 2013, Report of the 2013 Agricultural Census* (Complete Enumeration). Jakarta: Badan Pusat Statistik.

BPS (2020) *Keadaan Angkatan Kerja di Indonesia Agustus 2020* [*Labour force situation in Indonesia August 2020*]. Jakarta: Badan Pusat Statistik.

BPS (2021) *Potret Sensus Penduduk 2020* [*A portrait of the 2020 Population Census*]. Jakarta: Badan Pusat Statistik.

BPS (2023) *Agricultural Census 2023: Complete Enumeration Results* (Edition 1). Jakarta: Badan Pusat Statistik.

BPS, National Population and Family Planning Board (BKKBN), Ministry of Health (Kementerian Kesehatan), and ICF International (2013) *Indonesia Demographic and Health Survey 2012*. Jakarta: BPS, BKKBN, Ministry of Health (Kementerian Kesehatan), and ICF International.

Chazali, C., Ambarwati, A., Huijsmans, R., and White, B. (2024) 'Young farmers' access to land: Gendered pathways into and out of farming in Nigara and Langkap (West Manggarai, Indonesia)'. In S. Srinivasan (ed.), *Becoming a young farmer: Young people's pathways into farming – Canada, China, India, Indonesia*, pp. 337–59. London: Palgrave Macmillan (Open Access).

Firman, A., Budimulati, L., Paturochman, M., and Munandar, M. (2018) 'Succession models on smallholder dairy farms in Indonesia'. *Livestock research for rural development* 30: 176. http://www.lrrd.org/lrrd30/10/achma30176.html

Food and Agriculture Organization of the United Nations (FAO) (2019) *Country gender assessment of agriculture and the rural sector*. Jakarta: FAO.

Griffin, C., Sirimorok, N., Dressler, W., Sahide, M., Fisher, M., Faturachmat, F., Muin, A., Andary, P., Batiran, K., Rahmat, Rizaldi, M., Toumbourou, T., Suwarso, R., Salim, W., Utomo, A., Akhmad, F., and Clendenning, J. (2024) 'The persistence of precarity: Youth livelihood struggles and aspirations in the context of truncated agrarian change, South Sulawesi, Indonesia'. *Agriculture and Human Values* 41: 293–311. https://doi.org/10.1007/s10460-023-10489-5

Julia, and White, B. (2011) 'Gendered experiences of dispossession: Oil palm expansion in a Dayak Hibun community in West Kalimantan.' *Journal of Peasant Studies* 39(3–4): 995–1016. http://dx.doi.org/10.1080/03066150.2012.676544

Levien, M. (2017) 'Gender and land dispossession: A comparative analysis.' *Journal of Peasant Studies* 44(6): 1111–34. https://doi.org/10.1080/03066150.2017.1367291

Li, T.M. (2017) 'Intergenerational displacement in Indonesia's oil palm plantation zone.' *Journal of Peasant Studies* 44(6): 1158–76. https://doi.org/10.1080/03066150.2017.1308353

Li, T.M. and Semedi, P. (2021) *Plantation life: Corporate occupation in Indonesia's palm zone*. Durham, NC: Duke University Press.

Nugraha, Y., and Herawati, R. (2015) 'Menguak Realitas Pemuda di Sektor Pertanian Perdesaan'. *Journal Analisis Sosial* 19(1): 27–40.

Rigg, J., Salamanca, A., and Thompson, E.C. (2016) 'The puzzle of East and Southeast Asia's persistent smallholder'. *Journal of Rural Studies* 43: 118–33. http://dx.doi.org/10.1016/j.jrurstud.2015.11.003

Rigg, J., Phongsiri, M., Promphakping, B., Salamanca, A., and Sripun, M. (2020) 'Who will tend the farm? Interrogating the ageing Asian farmer'. *Journal of Peasant Studies* 42(2): 306–25. https://doi.org/10.1080/03066150.2019.1572605

Ruwiastuti, M., Fauzi, N., and Bachriadi, D. (1997) *Penghancuran Hak Masyarakat Adat Atas Tanah* [*The destruction of indigenous people's land rights*]. Bandung: Konsorsium Pembaruan Agraria.

Schut, T. (2019) 'The promises of education and its paradox in rural Flores, Eastern Indonesia'. *Focaal* 83: 85–97. https://doi.org/10.3167/fcl.2019.830109

White, B. (2018) 'Marx and Chayanov at the margins: Understanding agrarian change in Java'. *Journal of Peasant Studies* 45(5–6): 1108–26. https://doi.org/10.1080/03066150.2017.1419191

White, B. and Wijaya, H. (2024) 'Pluriactive and plurilocal: Young people's pathways out of and into farming in Kulon Progo, Yogyakarta, Indonesia'. In S. Srinivasan (ed.), *Becoming a young farmer: Young people's pathways into farming – Canada, China, India, Indonesia*, pp. 383–414. London: Palgrave Macmillan (Open Access).

White, B. and Wiradi, G. (1989) 'Agrarian and non-agrarian bases of inequality in nine Javanese villages.' In G. Hart, A. Turton, and B. White (eds), *Agrarian transformations: Local processes and the state in Southeast Asia*, pp. 266–302. Berkeley: University of California Press.

Woodward, L. (2020) *Poverty, vulnerability and social protection programs: Implications for young people in mountain Java.* PhD thesis, Murdoch University, Australia.

Yuniarto, P.R. (2016) 'Adaptasi strategis dan kewirausahaaan para pekerja migran Indonesia di desa asalnya'. *Journal Analisis Sosial* 20(1–2): 165–82.

CHAPTER 9

At the intersection of class, generation, and gender: Young women farmers in Java and Flores, Indonesia

Aprilia Ambarwati, Charina Chazali, Roy Huijsmans, Hanny Wijaya, and Ben White

Introduction to the case studies

This chapter explores the experiences of seven young women farmers in Central Java and Yogyakarta – regions where women can inherit land in their own right – and West Manggarai (Flores), where women are dependent on male kin for access to land. The research locations, and our methodology, have been described in Chapter 8 (Ambarwati et al. 2025). In presenting the cases we take a life-course perspective, drawing particular attention to intersecting structures of gender, generation, and class in matters of access to resources, pluriactivity, and recognition as farmers. The seven young women farmers that we introduce come from both poor and elite backgrounds, and include both those with, and those without, histories of out-migration prior to farming. In the final part of the chapter, following the case studies, we reflect on the insights gained and their broader implications for promoting gender equality and younger-generation interests and needs in future agrifood systems. The two most important areas for attention, we argue, relate to access to land for young women (would-be) farmers, and the need of young women (would-be) farmers for recognition and support as farmers in their own right, in both formal and informal institutions, and in society.

Kebumen, Central Java and Kulon Progo, Yogyakarta[1]
Tasniah (Sidosari village, Kebumen district)

Tasniah (32 years old) is married to Marto (35 years old) and has a seven-year-old daughter. Tasniah was born in a neighbouring village. She was a bright student and when she completed secondary school at age 17, she wanted to continue her studies and train to be a teacher, but the family could not afford the costs. She then asked her parents to pay for a three-month sewing course.

After that, she decided to help her parents in the rice fields, and also earned money as a farm labourer, giving all the money she earned to her parents. Then when she was 21, a neighbour invited her to take a job as sales girl in a clothing shop in Bandung city (roughly 300 km from Sidosari village). Her parents agreed because Tasniah, as the first child and also the first of three daughters, was expected to contribute income to the family, and also because many young people from Kebumen district were working in Bandung; they felt she would be safe in the city.

Tasniah was happy working in Bandung, earning her own money and being able to buy things that she needed. At the same time she felt constrained, as she was living with her neighbours from Sidosari and did not feel free to go out with friends. Also, to earn the money that she needed, she had to work overtime and still had to pay for her lodgings, food, and transport for her visits home. Her monthly earnings at the time were only Indonesian rupiah (IDR) 500,000 (USD 36),[2] of which she sent about IDR 200,000 (USD 14) to her family.

After three years in Bandung, Tasniah became interested in job vacancies for factory work in Jakarta. She asked her parents for permission to apply, but they refused as they thought it was too far away (Jakarta is 430 km from Kebumen or 6–7 hours by train), and asked Tasniah to return home to help them in the village. She followed their wishes and went back to the village: 'I felt sorry for my parents if I would refuse their request, especially as I'm the oldest child. The oldest child has to work to help the parents pay for their younger siblings' education and find money to repair the house.' In the village, she helped her parents weaving bamboo, and she met Marto. He was often migrating for work, but frequently fell ill and had to spend his earnings on medical treatment, so he decided to return and work in the village. They married in 2009 when Tasniah was 24 years old and immediately registered for the annual lottery of village-owned land (for rental).[3] After a year's wait, it was their turn to obtain a piece of land; the first time, Tasniah remembers, they borrowed all of the rental money from Tasniah and Marto's relatives.

When she is not busy with farm work, Tasniah is weaving bamboo strips that her husband then uses to make *caping* (the typical Indonesian peasant's conical hat). She also earns wages planting rice for other farmers. Besides making *caping* Marto helps with the farm, and works as a wage labourer on other people's land at harvest time (usually 2.5 months per year). The couple raises goats (three adult goats and six kids), which Marto mostly looks after while Tasniah takes care of their daughter and does the housekeeping. The *caping* sales provide the most regular income, although the earnings are low. Farming is more profitable, but the income is intermittent; there is also perpetual insecurity about access to rental land as rental agreements are typically short term, usually one year.

The general opinion among women farmers in Tasniah's village is that independent farming should begin upon marriage. Tasniah says: 'We are independent farmers after marriage, managing everything ourselves, especially if we're living apart from the parents. But "independent" doesn't always mean you have your own land. It's good when you get land from your parents. (For me) it was the village land that helped me to make a start as a farmer.'

Tasniah's parents own a very small rice field (490 m² or one-twentieth of a hectare). They are both still in good health and handle the cultivation themselves. As the land is still needed for their subsistence, Tasniah has never asked them about the prospect of inheritance, neither has she ever discussed the matter with her younger brother or sister. She expects that her parents' land will be divided among the children after they die. Until this time, she will have to find other ways to access land.

At the time of our research, Tasniah and Marto cultivated 2,632 m² of rented irrigated rice fields. The first plot of 602 m² is village land, rented for IDR 387,000 (USD 28) per year. Tasniah says that this land is very useful, as the rent is lower than the market rate, but next year it will transfer to another farmer. They rent a second plot of 1,400 m² from a farmer in the neighbouring village at IDR 3.6 m (USD 257), paid in advance, for two years. The rent is relatively low, as a home-based brick industry formerly used these fields as a clay supply so the couple had to level the land before they could plant. A third plot of 630 m² belongs to a village official who charges IDR 1.25 m (USD 89) per year for its rent.

Young landless tenant farmers like Tasniah and Marto have no guarantee of land access in the future. Continuation from year to year depends not only on the landowner's decision, but also on the harvest. Only if the harvest provides a good surplus are they able to pay for a new rental agreement. Despite this uncertainty, the couple needs to request a continuation of the rental agreement long before the harvest; doing so late may mean that the owner has already rented out the land to another farmer.

It is Tasniah's dream to own some farmland. This became evident when she mentioned that her neighbours received a subsidy from the village government to build a house. 'I don't need a housing subsidy,' she says, 'a simple house like ours is enough. It would be better if the government gave us some farmland. That could be our capital.' Rising prices have put land purchase increasingly beyond her reach and that of many others. At present, the price can be as high as IDR 180,000 (USD 13) per square metre, which amounts to almost half a billion rupiah (USD 71,500) for the amount of land that they are presently farming.

As a landless farmer, Tasniah finds raising working capital a perpetual challenge. Lacking collateral, Tasniah and Marto usually borrow money from their relatives to pay most of the land rent. For her, this is the best way as the loans are interest free and can be paid back in instalments. The money generated through their *caping* sales is used for daily food expenditures and their daughter's pocket money at school. Part of the rice harvest is used for subsistence, and part is sold in order to pay off debts and for savings. When there is money saved from selling part of the rice harvest, Tasniah buys young goats for breeding. The money earned from selling goats is put aside to pay the land rent and school fees. Young goats fetch around IDR 300,000–400,000 (USD 21–29) while full-grown goats can fetch IDR 700,000–800,000 (USD 50–57). The animals thus function as a convenient form of saving because they can be sold at any time, and the young couple can generate a relatively large amount of cash quite quickly should land become available for rent. Tasniah would also like to buy a cow as they fetch higher prices.

Tasniah and Marto don't have a bank account. Tasniah doesn't see the point of having a bank account when they can convert virtually all of their savings into goats. However, she just learned from a village official that one of the government banks now provides farmers with a 'Farmer's Card' (*Kartu Tani*) that can be used to buy cheaper and more easily available fertilizers. This is attractive because her husband usually buys fertilizer from a shop in the market near the village at the regular price. Moreover, sometimes the village shop runs out of supplies and then Marto has to travel to the sub-district town to purchase fertilizer. However, Tasniah is not sure whether she will apply for a Farmer's Card. Although it was announced that all farmers qualify for the card, she has understood from fellow villagers that those who own land are given priority to receive the card. Another complicating factor is that in their applications, farmers have to provide data on their land, its location, and the commodity to be grown. The uncertainty characterizing Tasniah's access to land does not allow her to provide such data with any degree of certainty. Given her situation, neighbours advised her she should just borrow a landowning farmer's card. But she is scared that she would be discovered and get into trouble.

Not owning land also makes Tasniah reluctant to participate in *arisan* (rotating credit groups) as a way of saving. Her uncertain land access makes her worried that she might not be able to make the monthly contributions. In addition, the money she earns from wage labour during the harvest season is needed to feed the family.

Next to financial challenges, Tasniah is also confronted with more common farming problems such as crop pests and water supply. She finds it difficult to find advice about how to tackle these problems. She isn't aware of the existence of the agricultural extension service and doesn't know any agricultural officials. For this reason, in case of problems with pests or seeds, her husband will seek advice from one of the (male) farmers who works more or larger plots of land. These farmers usually have more and better access to information because they have more government support. Tasniah and Marto also ask older farmers, tapping into their farming knowledge based on many years of experience. Looking to the future, Tasniah will not forbid her daughter to become a farmer, but hopes that she will first have more experience working outside the village.

Jamini (Pudak Mekar village, Kebumen district)

Jamini (33 years old) was born in Pudak Mekar. She lives with her husband and 11-year-old daughter. At age 15, Jamini decided to leave school to work in Jakarta as a domestic servant. She left for the city one week before the junior high school final exam because she thought that earning money was more important than completing her studies. She says: 'For villagers, it's common for children to work. We need to work to survive.' Jamini left the village with both her parents' blessings. A broker who was well-known in her village for recruiting young villagers for informal work facilitated the teenager's migration. After one year in Jakarta, she took a chance and signed a two-year contract to work in Singapore as a housemaid. Unfortunately, her employer's child was very naughty and Jamini could not handle the childcare, and asked permission to return to Indonesia. As Jamini had not completed her contract, her employer would not cover her travel costs, and she had to use a good part of her earnings to pay for her return to her village. The remainder of her earnings she used to buy a cow.

After returning to the village, Jamini started to make *keset* (doormats made of coconut fibre). *Keset* are typically made by women (both younger and older) and are one of the main non-farm livelihood sources in Pudak Mekar. In 2003, at the age of 19, Jamini decided to migrate internationally for a second time, this time to Malaysia and again to work as a housemaid. She completed her two-year contract but did not want to extend because she wanted to take a break from migrant work. With her earnings, Jamini bought a small residential plot and built a small house in her village. It was after she had returned to the village that she met her husband, Lasno. They married in 2005 when Jamini was 21 years old and after that, Jamini decided to remain in the village.

Lasno was born in Angsana village, near Pudak Mekar. He completed elementary school but did not continue to secondary school. When he met Jamini, he had just returned from Selat Panjang, Sumatra, where he had worked in a sago processing factory. The young couple decided to stay in Pudak Mekar because Jamini already had a house there, even though she had no furniture. Lasno used his earnings to furnish the house. This is contrary to what most men do, Jamini says. 'Men often do not bring money back from overseas. From my salary, I could buy a cow, buy a small house-garden plot and build a house. But men mostly spend their money on cigarettes and playing around.'

After marriage, Lasno worked as a *bawon*[4] harvester each rice harvesting season while Jamini continued to make mats and take care of the cow. At first, Jamini and Lasno's parents did not provide them with land for cultivation because they were still able to work on their own. At the time of the interview in 2017, Jamini's parents were still working on their own land of almost 1,400 m^2.

In 2009, Lasno's parents gave the young couple use of 420 m² of land,⁵ which was located in another village nearby. Jamini explains: 'This rice field has not been given to us yet, it still belongs to my in-laws. My husband and I were told to manage it and give them a little if the harvest was good.' For the past three years, Jamini has also rented 560 m² of rice fields from Lasno's aunt for IDR 250,000 (USD 18) per season. This land is also located in another village. Jamini chose to plant both of these plots with chillies, peanuts, and vegetables because the soil is sandy.

Jamini defines herself as a farmer. She insists that she is not just helping her husband. In fact, over the past five years her husband has been busy working as a sand digger, leaving much of the farm work to her. Since she was six years old, Jamini's father often asked her to guard the rice crop by chasing away *manuk* birds. While doing this, she saw how farmers worked and learned about farming by observation. In addition, her mother often asked Jamini to help out with peanut and corn planting.

However, during the past four months, Jamini has missed one planting season (three months) for lack of inputs. Over the past five years, they have invested most of their income as working capital in sand mining. Although this was Lasno's decision, Jamini argues that they discussed it together. They purchased a small boat and digging equipment with a bank loan. This acquisition means that Lasno does not have to work for other people and can earn a net income of around IDR 100,000 to 200,000 (about USD 7 to 14) per day. Another reason why Jamini agreed to postpone planting is because the harvest had failed twice due to uncertain weather conditions and pests. Jamini says: 'If you are a farmer, sometimes the result is bad. But if it fails twice in a row, it is difficult. When I started farming, I was able to predict the weather and, on that basis, decide on the right moment to plant vegetables, fruit, and chillies. But now the weather is like *nasib* (fate). During the dry season, the rain still came until the crops were rotten, and growing chillies is not cheap.' It is usually her husband who decides what pesticide brands to use, but they are not very effective now. Often, she must buy more seeds because pests like snails destroy the young plants in the first month, even though they have been sprayed with pesticides. She will sow the seeds again after the snails have come and gone. She says that there are no active women's groups for farming in Pudak Mekar, and other farmers also face similar problems.

Despite these setbacks, Jamini is planning to ask for a loan from her family to continue farming for the coming season. She still feels that farming is the safest job, referring to her parents' experience; they are still working on their own land in their old age. At present, her husband is still young and can dive into the water every day. Jamini says: 'One day I will buy rice fields, my husband will not be as strong as now for digging sand. If I am old like my parents later, I want to plant and produce crops by myself.'

As for the prospect of inheriting land from her parents, Jamini thinks that the land will not be divided. She thinks that the land will be too small if divided among the six heirs. She predicts that the one who will receive the land will take care of the parents' funeral. Jamini says:

> If my father dies, and there are no savings, the children should be able to pay the *syarat* (the funeral ritual), including paying for every *tahlilan* day (inviting neighbours to pray together for the deceased), and buy two goats if the deceased is male, etc. If you ask me now, I don't know who can afford it, maybe we should get some loan. But this would be different if my parents gave information to us if they had savings to pay their own funeral, therefore they will also inform us who will get the land.

However, she has never asked her parents about it.

Yaya, Partini, and Menik (Kaliloro village, Kulon Progo district)

The timing of 'becoming an independent farmer' is gender-specific. All of the seven married women farmers that we interviewed became independent farmers only after marriage, while 4 of the 25 young male farmers interviewed had become farmers while still single, receiving land from their parents either free or on a sharecropping basis.

Yaya, an in-migrant to Kaliloro, was born in the neighbouring hilly district of Samigaluh. She is an orphan with no close relatives. She was around five years old when both of her parents died. Her grandmother then cared for her until she had finished primary school. At age 12, she left her grandmother's home to work in a small household enterprise run by a woman neighbour making *slondok* (a ring-shaped fried snack made of cassava). Her employer adopted her and supported her education for a further six years until she completed (vocational) secondary school with a qualification in secretarial work. During this period, she helped her adopted mother making *slondok*, collecting fuel wood, and doing the laundry and other household tasks. She was not involved in rice farming, as her adopted mother had only a mixed garden planted with bamboo, cassava, coconut palms, and various other tree crops. She did help in the garden, weeding and harvesting. After completing secondary school, she left the village to work in the Yogyakarta region, first as a shop assistant and then in a *bakso* (meatball and noodle soup) food stall. She hoped to find a factory job in Jakarta, but since the only factory jobs available through the Labour Office were far away on Batam (an island close to Singapore), she did not pursue this plan further. At the age of 20, after working for two years, she met and married Jarwo and moved to Kaliloro. It was then that she learned the ins and outs of rice farming: 'If I hadn't married Jarwo, I probably wouldn't have become a farmer.'

Yaya is now 24 and has a son aged four years. Jarwo is two years older than Yaya and the son of the neighbourhood[6] head, Widyanto, who is remunerated with 0.6 hectares of village-owned irrigated rice fields (*pelungguh*[7]) in place of a salary. He does not farm this land himself but parcels it out to seven farmers with rental or share-tenancy agreements, each getting a small plot of about 700 m² (0.07 ha).

Yaya – who as we will see, is for all practical purposes the farm manager – has no land of any kind in her own right and depends completely on access to her father-in-law's land. Before receiving any land for planting from Widyanto, she spent about three years learning the skills of rice farming, after a middle-aged woman neighbour, a landless wage worker, invited her to join her planting and harvesting rice for wages in the neighbours' fields. Soon after moving to Kaliloro, Widyanto also asked Yaya to help with various tasks in his rice field, including hoeing. 'He taught me to make the bunds around the fields and to *ler-ler* (levelling the inundated field after ploughing) – that's usually men's work but at that time Jarwo had no interest in helping on the farm, so I took his place.' After about two years – four rice-planting seasons – she felt competent in all of the tasks from land preparation to harvest, including hoeing, preparing the seed bed, transplanting, applying fertilizer, weeding, and applying pesticides. Besides learning from her father-in-law, Yaya often asked advice from farmers on nearby plots, mostly older men; she felt relaxed about this and was not shy of asking for help on technical matters.

After these two years of marriage and learning to farm, Widyanto offered them the use of 1,000 m² of his *pelungguh* land, which a neighbouring tenant had previously been cultivating. Yaya explains that Widyanto had two reasons for this: 'First, now that I had a child, he said that we had to have extra income besides what Jarwo earned as a tractor operator and construction worker. Second, he said that the tenant was not a good farmer.' And more recently, since becoming too sick to farm, he has asked them to take on cultivation of his own 700 m² field, which he inherited from Jarwo's grandfather. The young couple do all of the work on this plot and provide all of the cash inputs, but give the entire harvest to Widyanto without receiving a share. This situation is not uncommon for young couples, who work on their parents' land without compensation, hoping to eventually benefit from the land.

In 2017 Widyanto allowed them to become share tenants on another 700 m² plot of his *pelungguh* land, as he was not satisfied with the previous tenant. A condition of the tenancy was that the ripe, standing crop should be sold in the field to a *penebas* buyer who then brings his own harvesting crew. 'It will sell for about IDR 2.5 m (USD 179) – half of that goes to us, but the cash costs are about IDR 0.4 m (USD 18), besides our own labour.'

Yaya was happy to take up farming, and Jarwo was now also willing to help in the fields. At the same time, they began building their own house, next door to Widyanto. 'The house-plot is inherited from Jarwo's grandfather and still registered to him. We're building the house in stages; it still isn't completely finished.' The breeze-block walls still have to be plastered, and the floor still needs tiles, but for Yaya this is much better than sharing a house with her father-in-law.

'So,' she explains, 'we now have three plots altogether, all of them from Jarwo's father'. They cultivate 0.24 ha, but receive only the harvest from the 1,000 m² plot (which they do not sell but keep for their own use), half of the money from the sale of the harvest from the share-tenanted 700 m², and nothing from the third plot of 700 m². Yaya clearly does not find this arrangement fair: 'We do all the work and pay all the costs, but when we join the harvest, we only get a one-sixth share of what we harvest, like the other harvest workers, that's only 3 or 4 kilograms of rice. But what can I do, I can't protest.'

Yaya says that she is the 'main' farmer in almost all farming operations. Being the farm manager involves, first, making decisions about the timing of the activities, choice of seeds and other inputs, and the wages to be given to those who help with planting and weeding, and second, being the one who does most of the work.

> I decide almost everything, and do almost all the work, choosing the seed variety, making the seed bed, germinating the seeds, levelling the field, making the lines for the planting, recruiting and paying the planters, weeding, fertilizing, spraying, and checking the crop every day. I manage all this, Jarwo just helps, in everything except hoeing – in hoeing, he is the main one and I help him.

They have agreed on this division of work and responsibility, she says, because Jarwo has to do other work that brings in money more regularly than farming. About a year ago, Jarwo went to work for a small-scale coconut oil enterprise in the neighbouring hamlet, where he works from 7 a.m. to 3 p.m. for a daily wage of IDR 60,000 (about USD 4); and twice a year, in the rice-planting season, he is busy working as a hand-tractor operator on a daily basis for about a month. For this, he gets paid after all the tractor work is finished: 'In one season he can earn up to IDR 2.0 m (about USD 130).'

So far, they plant only rice on all three fields, which Yaya says has both advantages and disadvantages. On the plus side, they never have to buy rice, and it is a relatively low-cost crop with few risks. She compared this with horticulture crops like chillies and watermelon, two high-value crops that are popular among other young farmers in the village. 'I haven't yet dared to plant chillies; the cost and the risks are too high.' The downside of rice is that it is a low-value crop and provides little cash income; this is why both Yaya and Jarwo are also engaged in other farm and non-farm work to earn cash.

Yaya and her husband are busy earning wages in a range of activities. Jarwo works as a tractor operator and in the coconut oil enterprise while Yaya earns wages both as a farm labourer (planting, weeding, and harvesting) and in handicrafts, making woven laundry baskets for export on a putting-out basis (working at home for a buyer who provides the raw materials and pays per completed basket). Her farm labour brings in about IDR 1 m (USD 71) each season (2–4 weeks). Yaya is part of a basket-weaving group of about 26 women, both old and young, who are also share tenants and farm workers. The buyer gives the group a production target, and Yaya works long hours to produce about 120 baskets each month, which brings in about IDR 600,000–700,000 (USD 43–50) per month. Besides this work, Yaya and Jarwo have also organized a group of four *tebasan* harvesters, working with another young couple for an intermediary in the next village, and using a small portable thresher that Jarwo designed himself. Yaya's group can harvest up to a tonne of rice paddy each day, and each couple takes home about 50 kilograms. The sale of these in-kind harvest wages can bring in up to IDR 2.5 m (USD 179) for about 15 days' work.

When asked (in 2017) whether she thinks that she will still be a farmer 10 years from now, Yaya answers: 'Yes, I will still be a farmer, but maybe only a tenant farmer. Actually I really want to buy some land, even only a small plot. But rice land is very expensive now, it costs tens of millions for only a couple of hundred square metres. But I will keep trying, maybe I can save little by little.' She has few expectations from the 700 m² plot that her father-in-law owns. It will have to be divided between Jarwo and his two younger siblings: 'How much will be left for us when 700 m² is split three ways?'

Yaya's access to land, as we have seen, depended mostly on her father-in-law's position as hamlet head. In 2019, Yaya's father-in-law passed away. She and Jarwo were lucky to retain the temporary use of an additional 2,500 m² of his former *pelungguh* land which had previously been sharecropped out to three neighbours. 'But I can only have the land for one season, after that there will be a new neighbourhood head.' Following the new village regulations, she and Jarwo will have the right to one-fifth (1,200 m²) of Widyanto's former *pelungguh,* as *pengarem-arem* (pension), but only for the next eight years. This precarity in land access is matched by the uncertainty of her non-farm income, requiring her to adapt quickly to changing conditions. Around the time of the onset of the Covid-19 pandemic in early 2021, basket-weaving orders began to decline and by mid-2022 had stopped completely. But Yaya had already, in October 2021, used a loan from Jarwo's employer to invest in a small egg-laying chicken initiative, with around 200 birds and bringing in about IDR 700,000 (USD 50) each month. And in 2022, besides the extra work of caring for the chickens, Yaya began a new business making *slondok* (the fried cassava snack that she had learned to make as a young girl – see above), which she packages and sells both to local buyers and – online via Facebook and Instagram – more distant ones.

Partini, like Yaya, became a farmer only after marriage, but has a different history involving an extended period of migration prior to farming, a different type of access to land, and she plants different crops. These differences also influence their respective choice of non-farm work. Partini is 36 years old. As soon as she finished secondary school in 1997 at age 16, she moved to Riau island to work for a year on an oil-palm plantation. She then moved to West Java to work in a shoe factory, and a year later when her contract expired, she moved to Batam island to work in a CD-ROM factory. After a further three years, her contract expired and she returned to West Java to work in a toy factory, but was only given a six-month contract. In 2001, she decided to move back to the village to live with her parents. She helped with housework and in her mother's small store, and a year later, now aged 21, she married Sarwidi. 'I started farming when I got married, before that I had never worked in the rice fields. Actually, I had never thought that I might become a farmer,' she says.

For many years, Partini and Sarwidi had no land of their own. She learned farm work when one of her husband's relatives invited her to join in planting rice for wages on nearby farms, and taught her how to do the work. For nine years, she only worked for wages as well as on her parents' and mother-in-law's land, which she and Sarwidi cultivated as share tenants. To make ends meet, Sarwidi worked in construction while Partini worked for wages planting and harvesting, and they have continued working for wages to the present.

Partini now farms 1,800 m² of land in three different plots: 1,200 m² is two rent-free plots (owned by Partini's father and mother-in-law respectively), while she sharecrops the third plot of 600 m², which belongs to Partini's mother and aunt. Unlike Yaya, Partini plants both rice and vegetables: rice on the sharecropped land, and chillies, cucumber, and some other vegetables on most of the two rent-free plots. This combination, she says, guarantees the supply of both rice and cash.

Only when their first child was born in 2011 did Sarwidi's parents give them 600 m² of rice land for Partini to cultivate rent-free. 'My mother-in-law said that it was to help provide the extra income that we needed. I planted both rice and chillies on it.' Then in 2013, she got access as a share tenant to another very small plot of 300 m² owned by her mother, providing all of the labour and other inputs. Two years later in 2015, when her father became too old to farm, he gave Partini a plot of 600 m² to cultivate rent-free; this whole plot is planted with chillies, and Partini and Sarwidi usually give her father a small amount of money when the crop is sold, in gratitude. They plant about 800 chillies on this land; input costs are about IDR 1.5 m (USD 100), but there are no labour costs as they do all of the work themselves. A year later, Partini got another share tenancy on a small plot of 300 m² belonging to her aunt. She grows rice on this land, and usually uses the crop for their own consumption. Partini considers rice to be their main crop: it's easy to cultivate and doesn't need a lot of working capital. Chillies, in contrast, need a lot of capital and intensive care.

Partini is involved in almost all of the stages of rice cultivation, but says that men can do more than women: 'Although we both go to the fields, there's still a difference. Men can do all the tasks, while women can't do the hoeing.' This view is quite strange, considering that Partini is involved in almost all of the different activities and is the decision maker in most of them, including choice of seed variety and fertilizers, deciding when to plant, weed, apply fertilizer, and harvest. She is the one who understands the timing and the work needed as the rice grows and ripens. When it's time to apply fertilizer, she tells Sarwidi to buy some. During the last planting season, when she decided to try fertilizer in tablet form, '[Sarwidi] just went along with it, leaving it to me as I am the one who applies the fertilizer'.

Our field observations suggest that the choice of crop has some influence on women's autonomy as farmers. Women feel more confident and autonomous in managing knowledge, production costs, the labour process, and the output when the crop is rice. In horticulture crops like chillies, they still consider men to be the main farmers, although women are involved in all stages of the production cycle, besides hoeing: 'growing chillies is like raising a small child, it has to be watered and cared for every day,' says Partini. But as it can provide a good income – they can get up to IDR 4 m (USD 286) net each harvest – Partini and Sarwidi continue to plant chillies on part of the land. This is perhaps one reason why Partini, unlike Yaya, has no significant non-farm activities, as she is busy every day looking after the chillies, while Sarwidi works in construction and looks after their goats. Partini estimates that their non-farm income provides about 60 per cent of total income, and farming 40 per cent. The non-farm income, being more regular, is used for day-to-day expenses.

Partini has a somewhat brighter picture of a farming future 10 years from now. She will have, at least, the 1,200 m^2 inherited from her father and father-in-law; although this land is not yet registered in their names, she is confident that it will become their property. 'My siblings are all living far away, and what's more we have been the ones cultivating the land from the beginning.' But later, she added, when she becomes old, maybe someone else will farm the land as neither of her two children are interested in farming futures: 'I agree with their wish not to become farmers. Farming is difficult, there's no money in it.'

Yaya and Partini's experiences clearly show that they are both real farmers – not just 'farm helpers' – with knowledge and direct involvement in farm management. But, like other women farmers, there is no farmer organization or group that recognizes them as farmers. Neither Yaya nor Partini are registered as members of the local farmers' group; nearly all registered members of this state-sponsored farmer group are men. We have come across only one registered woman member, an interesting case because of her different position in the village class structure; she provides our final illustration.

Menik, now aged 39, considers herself a farmer although she manages her farm in a quite different way from Yaya and Partini, using wage workers. She is the only woman farmer that we have met who is a registered member of the farmers' group. Menik comes from a wealthy family, members of the village elite. Her grandfather was village head and a large landowner, with both rice fields and garden land. Her father was a teacher and civil servant, while her mother was a homemaker. Menik herself is a graduate (in agriculture) of Muhammadiyah University in the nearby city of Yogyakarta. She has only a brief experience of out-migration for work; immediately after graduation, she worked for a year in customer service in Samarinda (Kalimantan), but was then offered a job back home in the 'village finance institute' (LKM, now known as the Bumdes or Village Enterprise Board). In 2009, Menik was appointed as an assistant village official in the office of Development and Empowerment.

In this position, she received 1 ha of *pelungguh* land. She parcelled out 0.7 ha of this land to various share tenants, but decided to manage 0.3 ha herself, using wage workers. She also inherited 0.15 ha from her late father, which she has given to her mother to be parcelled out to share tenants; her two elder sisters received the same amount, while her elder brother received a double portion of 0.3 ha. Neither her brothers or sisters farm their land themselves; Menik is the first and only member of her family who actually manages part of her land as a commercial farmer. Talking of her friends among the young village elite, she says: 'Most of my friends are civil servants, teachers, or entrepreneurs. If they own land, they don't farm it themselves but use paid workers or share tenants.'

Her biggest farm profits come from chillies. Each harvest she can earn IDR 30 m (USD 2,143), sometimes even more than this, after deducting all of the costs including hired labour. To this she can add half of the proceeds of the rice harvest of her 0.7 ha of share-tenanted land; she always sells the standing crop to a *penebas,* so the income is in cash. She has invested part of the surplus earned from agriculture in various non-farm enterprises: a laundry business, a poultry and livestock feed store, and a catering and wedding service that her husband runs. She has also established a commercial poultry farm, managed by a neighbour on a profit-sharing basis. In turn, she has invested part of the proceeds of this non-farm income back into land, buying 0.25 ha of residential/garden land. Unlike Yaya and Partini, Menik is an active member of the local farmers' group, attending meetings and voicing her opinions. Owning land in her own right as well as her *pelungguh,* she has no concerns about her continued existence as a farmer, and through the combination of farm and non-farm profits has set herself on a path of accumulation.

Langkap and Nigara, West Manggarai, Flores
Grace, a young woman farmer in Langkap village

Grace is 33 years old, married, and a mother of a four-year old daughter. Compared to other farmers in her village, she comes from a relatively elite background; her father is a *Tua Golo,* a neighbourhood head who has the traditional authority to allocate use-rights to the community's customary land (*lingko*). Grace is the oldest child, and has two younger brothers aged 29 and 23. One of her brothers is married and lives in the coastal town of Labuan Bajo (the district capital of West Manggarai, about 22 kilometres from the village) where he is a civil servant. The youngest brother is not yet married and is currently working away from Flores on the island of Bali. Grace herself completed lower secondary school in Labuan Bajo, where she was a boarder and returned home every Sunday.

Grace began helping in the rice fields when she was almost 10 years old and still in primary school. She remembers: 'When I came home from school, I helped Mama, usually planting rice. I didn't need any training; you just have to watch others and do as they do.' Learning to farm was not difficult for her: 'It was easy because my parents taught me.'

After completing lower secondary school at age 16, she took a job for two years in Labuan Bajo as a waitress in a café owned by a local non-governmental organization (NGO). This was her only experience of migration for work. When both of her brothers moved away from home, she decided to return to the village to live with her parents. Besides helping with various kinds of farm work, she also worked for wages on other farms.

Grace's husband, Mahon, also a lower secondary school graduate, is two years younger. He comes from Ruteng in the neighbouring district of Manggarai Raya. According to local custom in West Manggarai, women should move to their husband's village after marriage (*kawin keluar* or 'marrying outside'). In contrast to Java and many other regions of Indonesia, according to customary law, women in West Manggarai do not have inheritance rights to their parents' land or house, even though according to Indonesian national law, all Indonesian women have rights to inherit land.

In certain instances, women can get access to the family's land. For example, if the father asks a daughter to remain in his village after marriage (so the husband then moves to her village) or if she agrees to marry a cousin (in order to preserve the lineage). But women can only access land in these two ways if the father and all of her male relatives (siblings and uncles) agree. This is how Grace received access to land. She agreed to her father's request to remain in the village after marriage, and her two brothers agreed that their father could give her use-right to a part of their land (1,875 m² of rice fields), which belongs to her youngest brother Roni. The youngest brother was willing to re-lease the land because he was living far away in Bali. 'I was given the land to farm, but not as owner; I was given it because I was not given permission to leave the village.'

She cultivates the land on a sharecrop basis and the harvest is shared three ways: between her parents, Roni, and herself. Her father provides part of the cultivation costs, while she provides the other costs and all of the labour up to harvest. Her brother Roni, who owns the land, makes no contribution. Grace uses her share of the harvest for her own household's consumption.

Grace does almost all of the work of rice cultivation, including making the nursery, sowing and transplanting, applying fertilizer, and harvesting. She hires (male) workers for the land preparation, crop spraying, and cutting the grass around the fields, as she considers these tasks too heavy for her. The rice variety that she plants is Ciherang, which is used by many farmers in Java. The seeds come from the Department of Agriculture and are only available via the local farmers' group (Gapoktan); the one registered as member of the Gapoktan is her husband. To cut costs, Grace also joins a *julu* (exchange labour) group whose members contribute one day of labour to each other's farm work during planting, weeding, or harvesting. Most of the members of these exchange labour groups are women, while men are usually hired for IDR 30,000–40,000 (USD 2–3) per day. In addition, Grace also manages both *pekarangan* (residential land) and a 0.5 ha *kebun* (mixed garden) planted with candlenut and coffee, given by her father. The *kebun* doesn't require much work, as the candlenut trees are decades old and only require work at harvest time, and the coffee trees are also old and unproductive.

Besides the work in her rice fields and garden, Grace does day labour for other farmers during the planting and harvest seasons. Recruitment for this casual day labour is very uncertain. She also earns some money as a member of a village dance group called 'Compang Toe'. Many tourists, both domestic and foreign, come to the village to see traditional dance performances, mainly in the holiday season, which runs from July to September. Grace earns IDR 50,000 (USD 4) for each performance and on very busy days, there may be as many as three performances. She also raises pigs and dogs for the market. Feeding the pigs every day is normally considered women's work. Meanwhile, her husband is often employed as a construction worker, and only occasionally helps in the garden or the rice fields. 'Women are more diligent in farming; the husbands go to the rice fields or the *kebun* only occasionally. They're like teenagers, they love to sit around doing nothing.'

Besides acquiring farming skills from her parents, Grace also learned about horticulture when working on a small fruit and vegetable farm established by a foreign restaurant owner who rented land from one of the customary leaders. She learned how to plant fruits and vegetables, to weed, and to apply fertilizer; she was paid IDR 1.2 m (USD 85) per month. But the farm collapsed after only one year, as the harvests were very poor.

It is not easy to grow vegetables or fruit in this part of the village. The soil is mostly limestone and rocky, and the water supply is very limited. There is just enough water for the villagers' needs for drinking, bathing, and laundry. Another problem is the neighbours' chickens, which wander around freely. 'I tried to grow vegetables, they grew well but were destroyed by the neighbours' chickens; only cassava can grow, because their leaves are high above the ground. And I can't grow vegetables in the *kebun*, as the tall trees block out the sunlight.'

Grace has no expectation of buying land, either for farming or to build a house, because land prices have risen very fast in the past 10 years. Tens of hectares of land in the village, both privately owned and customary land, have been sold to absentee owners. The location has spectacular views to the sea. 'Land used to be cheap here, but now it's become expensive, especially after a *bule*[8] built a resort. Now many *bule* are buying land here, for billions of rupiah!'

She is also aware that local custom allows her brothers or uncles to reclaim the land that has been given to her, once her father has passed away. This is what has made her try to secure her gift of land from her father, a part of which Grace and Mahon have used to build their house. She has prepared an official letter, confirming the gift (*hibah*) of land by her father, to be signed by herself, her father, her husband, her two brothers as witnesses, and the village head. Three of the signatures are on *meterai* (duty stamps) to make the document legal. The document's signing can only be completed when her husband returns from his construction work in town, and this must be accompanied by a traditional ceremony as a gesture of thanks to her father and also as a means of preventing possible future conflict. Her brothers will likely be willing to sign, when the ceremony is organized. According to Grace, such a certificate of *hibah* is something new in the village; when it's complete, she will copy and laminate it and deposit one copy in the village office.

So far she has only made the certificate for the gift of residential land, and does not yet have a plan to make another certificate for the *kebun*; she gave priority to securing the residential land, being worried that her brother might change his mind and throw her out of the house. 'Land is important for us women, as most of us here are farmers and it's not possible to farm on others' land. There was a woman farmer who cultivated another man's rice field, but when she got good yields, the landowner claimed the land back.'

Noya (Nigara village)

Noya is 31 years old, married, and has two daughters aged 13 and 9 as well as a three-year-old son. Unlike Grace, she does not come from a local elite background. She left lower secondary school after three years without graduating. She has three siblings and only one attended university, without graduating.

Her husband, Abas, also 31, comes from another village where he has 1,250 m² of inherited rain-fed rice fields, yielding about 300 kilograms of milled rice once per year. At present, her father-in-law cultivates the land but Noya always is given a part of the harvest. Noya's husband, she says, has no talent for farming so he chose to become a construction worker in town. He comes home once a week and provides about IDR 1 m (USD 71) each month for the family.

After originally living in the husband's village, Noya and the family have been living in her village for the past three years. Noya's elder brother asked her to return to the village, as her mother was sick. At first, they lived with her younger brother in their parents' house, but Noya decided to rent her own house because the brother, who has some mental health issues, did not like to see her and the children in the house.

So long as they are in the village Noya's elder brother, who lives and works in the town of Labuan Bajo, lets her farm his inherited rice fields of 0.5 ha. Noya divides her harvest between her own family, her parents, and her elder brother; she sometimes also sells a part if there is a need for cash. If the harvest fails, she does not give any to her parents or brother. 'I just make sure they have enough to eat, because they gave the land to me, but it's not a sharecropping arrangement – however much or little I give them it's not a problem.' If in the future her brother claims the land back, Noya will move back to her husband's village. 'Here, daughters may not be given land, except their husband's land.' In her husband's village, she cannot afford to buy land but will try to build a house.

Noya says she likes farming, with all its challenges. She first learned to farm while still in lower secondary school, transplanting rice while watching how her more experienced girlfriends did it. She liked farm work, unlike her elder sister who had no farming talent and was always asking her parents for money to buy makeup. Before marrying at age 17, Noya was often invited to join her neighbour as a daily farm worker in nearby villages. She used to feel jealous watching her parents going to their own rice fields. And that, she says, is why she didn't want to migrate with her husband to Labuan Bajo, but to stay in the village and farm.

She does almost all of the work herself, from making the seedbed to ploughing, planting, weeding, fertilizing, spraying, and harvesting. She usually buys the seed from neighbouring farmers. The best seed, she says, comes from Bapak Bela, a neighbouring farmer who buys them from a farm store, not from the government. Noya regularly changes the seed, choosing varieties like IR, Balak, or Ciherang, so the yields will stay high and also to reduce damage from insect pests like the 'white pest' (*hama putih*)[9] or the 'brown pest' (*hama cokelat*).[10] She often asks her elder brother to purchase fertilizer on her behalf. For pest control, she has learned how to apply the correct dosages from other farmers so that she does not need to hire someone to apply the pesticides.

Although it is unusual for women in this region, Noya's mother taught her to plough using water buffalo and she regularly ploughs the land herself, to reduce the costs. A hired ploughman costs IDR 100,000 (USD 7) per day, while if she works for wages, she only earns IDR 30,000–40,000 (USD 2–3) per day. If her two older children are in school, she quite often takes the three-year-old to the rice fields with her, as there's no one to look after him. If the work on her own field is done, she earns extra money by working for other farmers, and sometimes asks the farmer's family to look after her son while she's working for them. This situation – working on the land while taking care of their children – is quite common among female farmers.

Childhood today, she feels, is different from her own childhood. She has never told her daughters to help in the fields, as they should be focused on their schoolwork. One of her daughters often has breathing problems if she does heavy work, so she only occasionally helps with lighter work like cooking, laundry, and looking after her brother. Noya doesn't want her children to be farmers and hopes that they will all get a good education.

Noya thinks that the most important issue for young farmers is the availability and ease of access to chemical fertilizer and pesticides. At times she has had difficulty finding fertilizer due to depleted stock in the local shop. She has never received government-subsidized fertilizer because her husband is an in-migrant in this village and priority is given to local-born farmers. The formal household head is the one who becomes a member of the *Poktan* farmers' group. Only once has she received subsidized fertilizer from the head of the Lembor Farmers' Alliance, because she helped in the shallot-planting programme. Once she was invited to a meeting at his house to discuss a plan for sorghum and shallot planting, but she only helped in the kitchen preparing food. She felt ignorant and shy to join the group of farmers, because they were all men – even though, she says, it's the women who planted and cared for the sorghum and the shallots.

Reflections

Tasniah, Jamini, Yaya, Partini, Menik, Grace, and Noya are all skilled and knowledgeable farmers. Their experiences give some idea of the main problems, both practical and cultural, that (would-be) young women farmers often encounter either while making a start or once established as farmers. We have also seen how they navigate these problems. In contexts like this, what would it mean to mainstream both generational issues and gender issues in rural development policy discourse and practice and to develop a youth- and gender-inclusive agricultural and rural development agenda?

The two most important areas for attention, clearly, relate first to access to land for young women (would-be) farmers, and second to the needs of young women (would-be) farmers for visibility, recognition, and support as farmers in their own right, in both formal and informal institutions, and in society as well as in agricultural statistics.

Indonesia was an early signatory (1980) and ratifier (1984) of the United Nations' 1979 Convention on the Elimination of all Forms of Discrimination Against Women (CEDAW). CEDAW establishes that both spouses must have 'the same rights ... in respect of the ownership, acquisition, management, administration, enjoyment and disposition of property' (Article 16 [h]) and specifically for rural women, their right 'to have access to agricultural credit and loans, marketing facilities, appropriate technology and equal treatment in land and agrarian reform as well as in land resettlement schemes' (Article 14 [g]). More than three decades later, these rights are far from achieved, and indeed routinely violated. In addition, Indonesian state law No. 5/1960 regarding the Basic Rules of Agrarian Principles (President of Indonesia 1960) explicitly recognizes the same rights and opportunities between men and women to obtain land rights and to receive benefits for both themselves and their families (Clause 9, Article 2).

The two intersecting issues of young people and access to land, and gender equality in access to land, need to be taken seriously. Both the secondary data presented in Chapter 8, and our case studies in this chapter, have shown how women face discrimination in land ownership rights. While men and women formally have equal rights to own land in Indonesia, there are many customary and practical gender distinctions and barriers to young women's access to land and farming opportunities. As we have seen, there are regions in Indonesia (like our case study region of West Manggarai, Flores) where customary law prevents women from inheriting land. State interference with local custom is a sensitive issue. Nonetheless, even without rocking the boat of customary land law, there is much that can be done to promote secure tenure for women. For example, the initiative of Grace in securing her male kin's formal written agreement to the gift of land from her father – to protect her against the possibility of male kin reclaiming the land – is an option that could be more widely used and that local government and peasant movements could formally promote. Furthermore, the practice of allocating a part of community land to widows in Langkap offers a precedent for a more general policy of reserving part of community land for women farmers.

Given the large number of rural youth, both men and women, who have either no prospect of inheriting land (those whose parents are landless or tenant farmers) or the prospect of a long wait before parental land becomes available (those whose parents are smallholders), there is a need to promote the transfer of land between generations (not necessarily between parents and their children), and also to provide young would-be farmers with access to unused or public land at low cost. In several countries, programmes of this kind exist, including some which have given special attention to young women farmers (see for example, FAO-CTA-IFAD 2014, Chapter 2 'Access to Land').

We have seen that many young women farmers, besides bearing the greater burden of farm work, are also the main decision makers and managers of the farm, but not recognized as such by formal agricultural support institutions (such as farmers' groups and the extension service), by the National Bureau of Statistics, or in local discourse and practice. Women need recognition as farmers in their own right, and access – without a husband's or male relative's intermediation – to the institutions and groups supporting smallholder farmers. In some cases, as in the case of our village official respondent Menik, who does go to farmers' group meetings and is a vocal participant, class status can overcome constraints of gender or generation.

The large number of young women farmers who have a history of migration before turning to farming underlines the importance of a *life-course perspective* in the study of young women's aspirations and their move out of, and perhaps later back into, farming. The various government and NGO programmes that aim to 'prevent the out-migration of rural youth' are perhaps, in this respect, misguided. The experience of migration can provide returning young women not only with savings for acquiring agricultural resources (animals, purchase or rental of a land plot) but also with the confidence and self-assurance to become active local citizens and vocal champions of gender equality and youth rights in farming and in the rural economy and society generally.

The male bias of formal government institutions and peasant organizations is deeply entrenched. The Ministry of Agriculture's *Guideline on the development of the young generation in agriculture* (Government of Indonesia 2013) does not once mention young women farmers.[11] And the Secretary-General of Indonesia's only nationwide, state-supported farmers' organization, the Indonesian Farmers' Harmony Association (HKTI), told one of the authors at a meeting in Jakarta: 'Today's youth are no longer interested in farming, they prefer to become motorcycle taxi (*Gojek*)[12] drivers. There are only two options [for agriculture], large-scale agriculture or contract farming for private corporations.' This suggests not only that he is only thinking of young men, but also that he has given up both on young farmers and on family/smallholder farming altogether. This does not bode well for Indonesian official commitment to the goals of the recently launched UN Decade of Family Farming, and its Pillars 2 ('support youth and ensure the generational stability of family farming') and 3 ('promote gender equality in farming and the leadership role of rural women') (FAO-IFAD 2019: 28–41).

It is unlikely that gender- and generation-biased policies, institutions, attitudes, and practices will change without the emergence of strong and dedicated organizations and movements of young women farmers. The two alternatives (young women organizing themselves or joining existing youth and women's organizations) are not mutually exclusive and it may be suggested that both are necessary; as we have learned from gender-based movements, young people should not be channelled (only) into youth-based organizations, which may result in marginalization, but they and their interests need also to be mainstreamed in adult organizations and social/political movements, from the local to the national levels.

The 1950s and 1960s saw the emergence of strong mass movements of women, peasants, and youth with branches active at the local level. The largest of these were Gerwani (Indonesian Women's Movement), the Barisan Tani Indonesia (BTI – Indonesian Peasant Front), and Pemuda Rakyat (People's Youth Organization), all movements of the left respectively, but other political parties had similar organizations that were strong in various regions. In the early 1970s, the 'New Order' regime of President Soeharto demonized all leftist organizations and dissolved not only them but all mass organizations, replacing them with corporatist, monolithic government-controlled organizations such as KOWANI (Indonesian Women's Congress), KNPI (Indonesian National Youth Committee), and for peasants, the HKTI that we have already mentioned. Two decades after the fall of the New Order regime and the return of democracy under successive *reformasi* governments, Indonesia still lacks any large-scale, independent women's, peasants', or youth organizations that could become a force in national and regional politics.

Finally, we have seen that most of our young women farmer respondents are engaged in pluriactive livelihoods, a feature that holds for smallholder farming more generally. Both farm and non-farm opportunities and incomes, however, are precarious. Young rural men and women, as shown in many surveys of rural youth aspirations in different parts of the world, consider farming a possible option if it is combined with other sources of income (White 2020: 112–22). This is understandable in light of the seasonality and uncertainty of farming incomes, a feature of smallholder farming that is certain to become more pronounced as climatic conditions become more extreme and unpredictable (for example, see the case of Jamini). In retrospect, we regret that we did not make more effort to explore our respondents' perceptions, experiences, and concerns about climate change and its implications for their farming activities and livelihoods in the coming decades. In this connection it is useful to note a recent survey on perceptions of the problems of Indonesia's climate crisis among 4,020 young respondents (aged 17–35, male and female, rural and urban). Ninety-six per cent of respondents expressed some degree of concern about environmental degradation, which came narrowly behind corruption as their top level of concern for the future. Seventy-nine per cent of the young rural respondents expressed 'extreme or moderate' concern about 'environmental breakdown', and 69 per cent about 'climate change'; concern was higher among younger respondents (17–26) than among those aged 27–35, and slightly higher among young women than young men (Indikator 2021). This is an important area for future research.

Notes

1. Names of all locations and persons in this chapter have been changed.
2. USD 1.00 was approximately IDR 14,000 at the time of our research.
3. Sidosari has village-owned land, a part of which is distributed by lottery in the form of temporary use-right with reasonable rents.
4. *Bawon* harvest wages are paid in-kind (in threshed but unhusked rice, immediately after the harvest) with a certain proportion of the amount harvested. For example, in a 1/6 (or 1:5) *bawon* wage, the labourer will get 1 kilogram for every 6 kilograms harvested.
5. People tend to talk about their land areas in square metres rather than hectares, at least when the area is below 0.5 ha. The couple's first land acquisition of 420 m² is 0.04 hectares, about half the area of a standard tennis court.
6. Kaliloro has 26 *dusun*, or neighbourhoods, the smallest administrative unit, each with around 100 households.
7. *Pelungguh* is village-owned land that is allocated as compensation in lieu of salary for village government staff and the village's 26 neighbourhood (*dusun*) heads for the duration of their office. They also receive a smaller portion as pension (*pengarem-arem*) for some years after retirement. They may manage the land themselves, rent in or out for cash, or – by far the most common practice – parcel it out to share tenants.
8. *Bule* (lit. albino) is the popular term used for Western foreigners.
9. *Cnaphalocrocis medinalis* (rice leaf folder moth).
10. *Nilaparvata lugens* (brown planthopper).
11. This guideline details numerous top-down strategies for organizing rural youth in groups and instilling their interest in entrepreneurial farming, but it focuses on symptoms (their apparent lack of interest in farming futures) and ignores causes (the many constraints in access to resources, etc.), which make independent farming an impossible option for most rural young men and women.

12. *Gojek* is an Indonesian Uber-like application for transportation services, ordering food, payments, and other daily necessities. Becoming a *Gojek* driver is a popular job for (mostly young) men in urban areas.

References

Ambarwati, A., Chazali, C., Sadoko, I., and White, B. (2025) 'Young women and farming in Indonesia'. In S. Srinivasan, A. Ambarwati and Pan Lu (eds.), *Young and Female: International perspectives on the future of farming*. Rugby, UK: Practical Action Publishing. http://doi.org/10.3362/9781788534369

FAO-CTA-IFAD (2014) *Youth and agriculture: Key challenges and concrete solutions*. Rome: Food and Agriculture Organization of the United Nations, Technical Centre for Agricultural and Rural Cooperation, and the International Fund for Agricultural Development. http://www.fao.org/3/a-i3947e.pdf

FAO-IFAD (2019) *UN Decade of Family Farming 2019–2028: Global action plan*. Rome: Food and Agriculture Organization of the United Nations and International Fund for Agricultural Development. http://www.fao.org/3/ca4672en/ca4672en.pdf

Government of Indonesia, Ministry of Agriculture (2013) *Peraturan Menteri Pertanian No. 7/2013 Tentang Pedoman Pengembangan Generasi Muda Pertanian [Regulation No. 7/2013 Guidelines on agricultural youth generation development]*. Accessed 4 November 2024. https://peraturanpedia.com/peraturan-menteri-pertanian-nomor-7-permentan-ot-140-1-2013/

Indikator (2021) *Survei Nasional Persepsi Pemilih Pertama dan Muda (Gen-Z dan Millennial) Atas Permasalahan Krisis Iklim di Indonesia. [National survey on the perceptions of young and first-time voters (Gen.-Z and Millennials) on the problems of climate crisis in Indonesia]*. Jakarta: Indikator. https://www.cerah.or.id/id/publications/report/detail/persepsi-pemilih-muda-dan-pemula-terhadap-krisis-iklim accessed 7 February 2024

President of Indonesia (1960) *Undang-Undang Pokok Agraria Np. 5/1960 [Basic Agrarian Law No. 5/1960]*. Accessed October 2019. https://spi.or.id/wp-content/uploads/2014/11/UNDANG-UNDANG-No-5-Tahun-1960-1.pdf

UN General Assembly (1979) *The Convention on the Elimination of All Forms of Discrimination against Women*. UN Women. Accessed 9 October 2019. https://www.un.org/womenwatch/daw/cedaw/text/econvention.htm

White, B. (2020) *Agriculture and the generation problem*. Rugby: Practical Action Publishing. https://practicalactionpublishing.com/book/45/agriculture-and-the-generation-problem (Open Access).

CHAPTER 10

Forward-looking and forward-pushing: A commentary on why young women farmers should be at the centre of rural transformation

Clara Mi Young Park

Young women farmers are a neglected category, as the editors of this book rightly highlight. While attracting and fruitfully engaging young people in agriculture has become a priority for many countries, young women, though occasionally mentioned, are rarely the focus of specific policy intention and action. Youth are automatically thought of as young men; when young women are recognized, their particular challenges and needs may not be addressed. As the editors also point out, young women farmers' invisibility is exacerbated by the lack of sex- and age-disaggregated data, particularly by location, and the corresponding research knowledge gap that this book seeks to fill.[1] Despite progress in promoting intersectional analyses that help to understand how different social identities interact to produce specific forms of discrimination and marginalization, policy commitment to looking closely at the challenges, needs, and aspirations of young women remains low. Often, policy documents and programmes lump or address 'women and youth' together, making it even more difficult to recognize the differences and to design appropriate policies and programmes. The *Voluntary guidelines on gender equality and women's and girls' empowerment in the context of national food and nutrition security* (henceforth the CFS Gender Guidelines), recently endorsed by the Committee of World Food Security, make the importance of a focus on girls very clear. However, the issues specific to young women are not systematically mentioned and reflected in the policy recommendations, which tend to refer generically to 'women' and sometimes to 'women and girls' or 'women and young women' (CFS 2023).

Agriculture is perceived to be inherently masculine – despite the data that tells us otherwise! – and a world that young women have no visible place in, may not find attractive, or would not choose if given the option. In most rural contexts, girls transition directly into womanhood without the freedom of choice and the right to voice their opinions and concerns as girls and young adults. My interviews with young women in Taninthary, Myanmar, revealed that, while they often perceived marriage as a liberation from family expectations, restrictive gender norms, and marginalization (as boys enjoyed much more freedom and were prioritized for education), as young wives, they soon found themselves trapped by additional normative, material, and emotional burdens that limited their mobility, access to information, and participation in community politics (Park 2021). The view of agriculture as predominantly male, where adult women are seen as helpers rather than farmers, only perpetuates the idea that young women are not a group worthy of study and policy attention, and reproduces gender inequalities that affect young women throughout their lives and across generations. This in itself highlights the important contribution that this book makes by filling this analytical and empirical gap. By zooming in on the voices and experiences of young women as they enter, navigate, and grow in agriculture, the various chapters reveal the specific challenges they face and their effects, which so often go unrecognized and thus unaddressed.

The 2023 FAO report *The status of women in agrifood systems* (SWAFS) is the latest effort to assess the current standing of women and gender equality in agrifood systems (FAO 2023). It is one of the most comprehensive efforts of its kind since 2011, when FAO published *The state of food and agriculture: women in agriculture – closing the gender gap for development* (FAO 2011), data from which have been widely cited for years. The message of the report is clear: we are not making enough meaningful progress and gender gaps remain significant in several areas critical to women's likelihood of success as farmers, workers, processors, and entrepreneurs, and to the realization of women's rights more broadly. With its focus on gender equality in agrifood systems, the report goes beyond looking only at gender gaps to consider the multiple and diverse ways in which gender inequalities affect women's and men's participation as farmers as well as small business owners, wage workers, processors, and traders. This is an aspect that resonates well with the stories in this book, which portray women in a variety of roles and capacities. However, the SWAFS lacks comprehensive data and evidence focusing on young women. This is an important and alarming finding considering the extensive review of the literature and data that were analysed for the report.

Even so, several insights from the SWAFS are relevant to this book. Agrifood systems,[2] beyond just primary agriculture, continue to be an important source of livelihood for women and men across the world, employing 38 per cent and 36 per cent, respectively, of working women and men. This is more the case for women, especially in countries of the Global South. In South Asia, for example, the share of women employed in agrifood systems is 71 per cent of the total number of working women, compared with 47 per cent of men. Agrifood systems are also important employers of young people. In a sample of 11 countries in sub-Saharan Africa, for example, agrifood systems were found to employ more than

50 per cent of workers under the age of 25 (FAO 2023). Young women are more likely than young men to enter and stay in the sector, while young men are more likely than women to leave agrifood systems between the ages of 25 and 35 and come back after 35, levelling the gender gap until it closes by the age of 65 (*Ibid.* p. 29). Overall, in countries of the Global South, agrifood systems continue to be an important source of employment for young women between the ages of 15 and 24 (Ibid. p. 29).[3]

The above data, although limited to a few countries, strongly suggest that a focus on young women in research, policy, and programming is an investment that would have long-term benefits for the development and growth of the sector, as well as benefits for women across generations. This would add to the evidence that women's empowerment has multiple additional trickle-down benefits, from increased household income and food security to dietary diversity and resilience (FAO 2023). To date, however, such a focus on young women is largely missing.

In addition to the lack of specific services and programmes benefiting them, the lives of young women are also influenced by family expectations and obligations, patterns of inheritance and marriage, and gender roles and relations, remarkably across geographies, economies, and cultures, as seen in the chapters of this book. This underscores the role of formal and informal social institutions and norms in shaping women's experiences as farmers and entrepreneurs, as they enter and make a living from agriculture, and transition from being only daughters to being wives, mothers, and daughters-in-law. While it is important to look at the impacts of social norms and gender inequalities at specific points in the lifetime of a woman, it is also analytically important to see how they are enacted across and affect generations.

Recognizing the diverse landscapes and experiences of young women who venture into agriculture – whether through marriage, constrained options, familial duties, or personal choice – the evidence and stories collected in this book reflect the broader range of social conditions, environments, and challenges faced by significant numbers of young women, and adult women who once identified as young around the world. As the editors point out, the protagonists of these chapters are not all chronologically young; some still are, while some others were young when they started farming. This highlights another valuable contribution of this book, namely, the importance of looking more closely at the intersection of age and gender. While chronological age may be important from a policy and targeting perspective, women's social age, which consists of the roles and meanings that society assigns to different stages of life (Clark-Kazak 2009), should also be considered an important factor in shaping women's agency with ascribed gender roles and norms.

This book shows that the experience of becoming a farmer as a girl and young woman is fundamentally different from that of becoming a farmer as a boy and young man, and urges the research and policy agenda to take this into account. In promoting such a forward-looking agenda, a few areas of attention and action could be considered as possible drivers of transformative change.

Access to land

As also noted by the editors of this volume, women's secure tenure rights are widely recognized as critical to their empowerment in the household and the broader public sphere (Doss et al. 2015; Grabe 2015; Mishra and Sam 2016; Pradhan et al. 2019). Yet, progress in their realization has been painfully slow. Across various contexts and cultures, the young women featured in this book commonly faced barriers to securing farmland, often due to gender-biased inheritance practices, limited resources, and alternative mechanisms for acquiring land. Despite current global policy discussions highlighting the importance of women's land tenure security, evidence shows that women still face more challenges than men in accessing and controlling land (Doss et al. 2015; Kieran et al. 2015; FAO 2023).

Poor access to secure land for rural youth has also been repeatedly identified as a major obstacle to their productive engagement in agriculture, as young people inherit smaller plots of land later in life and have little or no financial means to access land markets (White 2012; Kidido et al. 2017; IFAD 2019; Moreda 2023). Young rural women face additional barriers. According to IFAD (2019), they are half as likely to be sole landowners, in addition to being twice as likely to be out of work and out of school, and much more likely to be married and fully engaged in care work, child-rearing, and family work.

Importantly, gender- and age-disaggregated data on land tenure remain scarce. Sex-disaggregated data on Sustainable Development Goal (SDG) 5.a.1[4] are available for only about 49 countries, while 77 countries have reported on SDG indicator 5.a.2[5] (FAO 2023; Slavchevska et al. forthcoming). It could be argued that the limited uptake by countries signals a general lack of commitment to the issue, and weak efforts to place the land question at the heart of rural transformation processes, in conflicting efforts of governments to restrict and support agriculture and farmers (Hall et al. 2011). In addition, much of the land in the Global South is still unregistered, and there are technical and political challenges to promoting systematic registration, particularly through technocratic solutions that do not capture the socio-cultural complexity of tenure systems in pluricultural and legal contexts (Abubakari et al. 2020).

The women whose life stories are told in this book share similar experiences and constraints, albeit with variations across countries and contexts: limited educational opportunities, lack of choice, early migration experience, marriage into farming households, burdened with care and unpaid work, including for their in-laws, and few direct means of access to land. Their access to land is often mediated and affected by family ties, obligations, and social norms. For example, Shanti (India) agrees to sell the land her father gave her to her stepbrothers to avoid conflict. As Suman (India) says, 'Women do have a claim to their father's land legally, but most choose to give up their share for their brothers. Women who insist on their share are generally ostracized from the family.' Kamla (India) works on her father-in-law's land but has no say in any decisions because the land belongs to him; at the same time, she has no hope of getting a share of her parents' land. Jamini (Indonesia) and her husband access and manage the land of her father-in-law on a share-cropping basis. The intersection of gender with age, class, and caste creates additional forms of discrimination. Suman and Kamla's trajectories are influenced by their land-poor family background and indigenous heritage (Kamla), as they had no access to education and no prospects of inheriting land.

As the introduction points out, traditional and customary norms, particularly those influencing inheritance and virilocal residence patterns, obstruct women's access to land, despite existing legal protections. It is noteworthy that equal inheritance rights for all children, regardless of their sex, is mandated in 60 per cent of the countries that have reported on SDG 5.a.2 (FAO 2023; Slavchevska et al. forthcoming). Where formal or informal mechanisms to access land exist, they have the potential to be a game changer, allowing women and their families to invest in infrastructure, access extension, and lease more land for example. This was clear in the examples from China and Canada.

Enforcing existing laws, revising laws where they do not adequately protect women's rights, and formulating and implementing policies and programmes that promote women's and girls' access to land clearly need more attention. This has also been prioritized in the CFS Gender Guidelines, the first negotiated policy document of its kind, which provide important guidance on what needs to be done, and urge governments to (CFS 2023: 20–21):

(i) Design, strengthen, and implement legislation or introduce new legislation, as appropriate, to promote equal access to and control over natural resources for all women. Ensure respect of women's land tenure rights and property rights, ownership, use and transfer – including through inheritance and divorce, taking into consideration national legal frameworks and priorities ...

(ii) Promote that all women and girls, including from Indigenous Peoples, and local communities, have equal, secure and transparent legitimate tenure rights, as applicable, and safe access to and control over and use of land, water, fisheries and forests, as applicable, independent of their civil and marital status. When tenure rights are formalized, women and girls should be granted equal tenure rights as men and boys – for instance through the provision of title deeds or land tenure certificates in accordance with national laws. All women and girls, including widows and orphan girls, should be treated equally with regards to access to and control over and use of their land under all governance structures, including in existing regimes as applicable ...

Similarly, reprioritizing agrarian and land reform with concrete mechanisms that address young women's challenges, including those rooted in discriminatory social norms, and facilitate their increased access to land, including through inheritance, distributive reforms, leases, joint titling, and communal and group-based access, should be a priority for governments committed to women's empowerment in agrifood systems.

Unpaid care work

Debates about the importance of care work have moved out of the feminist ghetto and made it into the mainstream. Recently (re)accelerated by the Covid-19 pandemic, which highlighted the crisis of care and the role of women in social reproduction, the issue of unpaid care work has been widely discussed in United Nations (UN) and multilateral fora and documents,[6] including in a UN System policy paper (United Nations 2024) and the G20 Working Group on Women's Empowerment, as one of two pillars of the equality theme.[7]

As early as 1995, at the landmark Fourth World Conference on Women in Beijing, the UN adopted a resolution calling for the development of 'suitable statistical means to recognize and make visible the full extent of the work of women and all their contributions to the national economy, including their contribution in the unremunerated and domestic sectors, and examine the relationship of women's unremunerated work to the incidence of and their vulnerability to poverty.'[8] Decades later, SDG 5, 'Achieve gender equality and empower all women and girls', commits the global community to 'recognize and value unpaid care and domestic work through the provision of public services, infrastructure and social protection policies and the promotion of shared responsibility within the household and the family as nationally appropriate' (Target 5.4).

Yet progress has been slow, not only in recognizing women's roles in unpaid care work, but also in identifying solutions. In rural areas, where women's work burden also involves tasks such as water and fuelwood collection, the gender gap in unpaid domestic and care work tends to be higher than in urban areas, with women spending 7.0 hours on care and domestic work compared to 1.4 hours for men[9] (FAO 2023).

The stories in this book clearly show that the burden of care and domestic work and the social expectations associated with it affect young women in many ways, limiting their personal and work-related choices, constraining their incomes, restricting their mobility, making their working days longer and harder, and affecting their physical and mental health. In many cases, caring for children is combined with caring for ageing parents and in-laws as a matter of filial piety, custom, and in exchange for access to land. This is the case for Kamla (India), who takes care of her elderly parents and their land, while her brothers, unlike her, have been able to continue their education and have settled in a nearby town. Gender roles and social expectations shape women's lives from an early age. Yao (China) recalls that from the age of seven, she was responsible for 'cooking, herding sheep, and harvesting wheat,' as well as caring for her young brother after school.

This is also true in countries in the Global North, for example in Canada, as Kaitlyn highlights, complaining about the lack of free time she has compared to her boyfriend, although positive shifts towards a better distribution of care work are also noticed by women in Manitoba.

Policymakers' concern with care work stems from its role in creating inequalities in labour market participation and outcomes (Ferrant et al. 2014). Labour-saving technologies and infrastructure, compliance with labour standards, and promotion of care-responsive work settings, and social policies that, for example, support the provision of childcare options are all key (Sida 2009; FAO 2023; UNDP n.d.). But there is a much deeper argument that speaks to the realization of human rights for all, social justice, and the need to fundamentally change norms, attitudes, and behaviours towards a better distribution of roles and parental and family responsibilities, the promotion of positive masculinities, and the deconstruction of the feminization of care. Initiatives in this direction can have a profound impact on the likelihood that young women farmers will improve the quality and level of their productivity, their mental and physical health and well-being, and promote positive models of better and more equitable gender roles and relations for future generations.

Social and gender norms

The common thread in the experiences and struggles described by the women in this book and beyond is the influence of social and gender norms, which are often rooted in patriarchal structures and orders and underpinned by unequal power relations. Gender norms directly affect individuals' choices, freedoms, and capabilities by reinforcing and creating expectations for women and men's appropriate and socially acceptable behaviour. In so doing, gender norms keep the unequal gender system alive and functioning (Cislaghi and Heise 2020).

Gender norms are pervasive in agrifood systems. A recent assessment finds that men are seen as the breadwinners, holders of assets, and decision makers, whereas women are by default in charge of household management, childcare, and subsistence agriculture. In community settings, men are those who speak out, which sidelines women from influencing decisions that affect their lives (Rietveld et al. 2023).

There are many such examples in the book too. For example, Tasniah (Indonesia) says she gave up the possibility of a factory job in Jakarta she was interested in because her parents wanted her to return home to help in the village, as was expected of her as the eldest daughter. Wu (China) notes that very few women participate in decision-making and technical aspects of agricultural production due to lack of opportunities and dismissal by husbands, despite their abilities. Shanti (India), although recognized as a farmer and the main breadwinner of her household since her husband is disabled, says that when she goes to the market, a male-dominated space, men sometimes try to take sexual advantage of her if she accepts their help.

Those women who can break out of patriarchal structures and oppressive gender norms can benefit from increased agency and decision-making power or can benefit from supportive social institutions, such as Yan Yugiong (China), who can use her uxorilocal marriage to enhance her status and decision-making power. These gender norms are also clearly shaped by the interaction with other social norms related to age, class, and ethnicity, to name a few. Although she comes from a farming family, Kaitlyn (Canada) faced discrimination and disregard because she is a woman and young, therefore not expected to be a farmer, similar to the experience of women in Manitoba. In contrast, Naomi, also from Canada, does not feel discriminated against but initially felt the burden of her young age when managing workers much older than herself, even though her father was very supportive.

The need to address discriminatory social and gender norms has been increasingly recognized in development practice and policy fora. This is reflected in the promotion and increasing use of interventions based on behavioural science (see, for example, United Nations n.d.) and gender transformative approaches (GTA); that is, approaches that identify the root causes of gender inequalities in discriminatory social institutions and seek to address them in order to promote transformative change, including in agriculture.[10] However, it is also recognized that there is limited evidence that documents the effectiveness of GTAs on women's empowerment and in changing social norms (Singh and Puskur 2023). The FAO's *Status of women in agrifood systems* (2023) highlights GTAs as promising for changing discriminatory norms in a wide range of areas and as cost-effective, but suggests that more work is needed to implement gender transformative approaches at scale.

Changing dominant social norms takes time and requires a deliberate, whole-of-society approach that involves civil society, academia, development organizations, and women and men as norm holders, champions, and agents of change. Research can provide the needed evidence on the impacts of GTAs and support efforts to bring them to scale. Development organizations and governments can promote awareness and behaviour change strategies and initiatives. Social movements, including agrarian and environmental movements, have an important role to play. However, they have not always stepped up their game, especially in confronting patriarchal structures and power hierarchies, which have remained the purview of women's movements, as documented in the relevant literature (Deere 2003; Resurrección 2006; Agarwal 2015; Park et al. 2015; Park 2019, 2021). More recently, global peasant movements, such as La Via Campesina, have called out patriarchy and promoted internal reflections to promote gender equality and respect for diversity (LVC 2023). In the political space, amid the backlash against women's rights, tentative signals are also visible. For example, at the third edition of the African Union 'Men's Conference on Positive Masculinity', the heads of state adopted a Declaration in which they pledged 'to take the lead to dismantle patriarchal systems that create inequalities, and to foster positive masculinity to rebuild the African social fabric through processes that heal and rehumanize individuals, institutions, leadership, and societies to embody the values of human dignity, equality, freedom, and self-determination' (African Union 2023). While these are positive signs, much more remains to be done.

Forging the way forward

The propositions outlined above are far from comprehensive. Many helpful suggestions are also made by the authors of the country chapters, such as the call to address male bias in government institutions and peasant organizations in Indonesia (Ambarwati et al. 2025, this volume), the need to create formal mechanisms to access land for young people wishing to enter farming (Canada), and the need for appropriate gender-responsive training and extension services (Indonesia).

From the outset, this book highlights another critical issue: the lack of data and evidence documenting the constraints and needs of young women farmers, which consequently are rarely addressed in policy debates at all levels and in the advocacy and mobilization efforts of civil society organizations and peasant movements, as previously discussed. The lack of sex- and age-disaggregated data, and gender and intersectional data and evidence, makes it difficult to identify the unique challenges and forms of discrimination that arise at the intersections of gender with age, class, race, and caste, among others. Feminist approaches to data collection and research are crucial for uncovering forms of marginalization and silencing that occur at the intersection of different forms of discrimination and questioning dominant epistemologies. They are also critical for complementing quantitative data and methods with situated qualitative insights that can provide a nuanced understanding of realities on the ground. At the same time, efforts are needed to strengthen the capacity of national statistical offices and policymakers to collect, analyse, and use gender- and age-disaggregated data. This should be done in collaboration with grassroots civil society, feminist, women's, and youth organizations to spearhead complementary citizen-led data collection and advocacy efforts. Better integration of gendered research findings on young farmers into policymaking is also needed to provide evidence on critical issues where it is most needed, and thus to make policy decisions in processes of rural transformation more effective and inclusive.

As emphasized above, placing the issue of social reproduction and care work at the centre of the future of agriculture and agrifood systems is a must for promoting women's economic empowerment, autonomy, and well-being (Park et al. 2021). This is especially true when we consider young women farmers as critical actors in rural transformation and the future of agriculture, and it calls for more evidence and analysis that integrates gender, intersectional, and generational perspectives into research, policies, and programmes.

Equally important is transforming unequal gender relations and power dynamics and addressing the underlying social structures, power relations, policies, and norms that perpetuate gender inequalities, in order to enhance the role and status of young women and women in agriculture, and to promote more equitable gender relations in farming households, communities, and society at large. These efforts should be accompanied by policy reforms that focus on social and gender justice, such as distributive land reforms with special provisions for young women's secure access to land, social protection and social policies that support them in their productive and caregiving roles, and campaigns and initiatives that promote positive and caring masculinities and the elimination of all forms of gender-based violence. Governments have a special role to play and the CFS Gender Guidelines can provide useful policy guidance and international benchmarks.

As I have emphasized in previous work (Park 2019), it is also necessary to build the leadership skills and capacities of women and women's groups, as well as of young women and men, and to help link horizontally with other local groups and vertically with national and transnational groups. Women's organizing is central to efforts 'to question, destabilize and, eventually transform the gender order of patriarchal domination', as Sardenberg highlights (2016). Finally, development organizations and governments could strengthen their commitment to gender equality by redirecting domestic and international finance to gender equality initiatives in the agricultural sector, earmarking gender budgets, strengthening gender capacity and human resources, improving their use of intersectionality analysis and frameworks, and promoting greater exchange and cross-fertilization with feminist scholars and groups.

Incremental change is no longer enough. In the current context of women's and human rights backlashes and polycrises, we must all work together to push a more transformative agenda forward and invest in young women farmers to promote inclusive and sustainable rural transformation.

Notes

1. For example, while the UNICEF Adolescent Data Portal compiles a wide range of indicators focused on adolescent girls, it does not include data disaggregated by urban versus rural location (https://data.unicef.org/adp/).
2. Agrifood systems encompass the full range of actors and their interlinked activities that create value in food and non-food agricultural production and related off-farm activities such as food storage, aggregation, post-harvest handling, transportation, processing, distribution, marketing, disposal, and consumption (FAO 2023: 5).
3. Young women were found to enter the sector at higher rates than men in six countries of the sample, and men to exit at higher rates than women between the ages of 25 and 35. For more information, refer to FAO (2023).
4. Under SDG5 Target A on women's equal rights to economic resources and access to ownership and control over land and other forms of property, indicator 5.a.1 measures the percentage of people with ownership or secure rights over agricultural land (out of total agricultural population), by sex; and the share of women among owners or rights-bearers of agricultural land, by type of tenure.

5. Indicator 5.a.2 measures the proportion of countries where the legal framework (including customary law) guarantees women's equal rights to land ownership and/or control.
6. See for example, Women's economic empowerment in the changing world of work, Report of the Secretary-General, E/CN.6/2017/3, December 2016; UN Women, 2018, Promoting women's economic empowerment: Recognizing and investing in the care economy; UN Women, 2021, World Survey on the role of women in development: Report of the Secretary General (2019): Why addressing women's income and time poverty matters for sustainable development.
7. For more information, see https://www.g20.org/en/tracks/sherpa-track/womens_empowerment
8. Beijing Declaration and Platform for Action, Art. 68(b), available at https://www.un.org/womenwatch/daw/beijing/platform/index.html
9. These figures include time spent on care as a secondary activity (FAO 2023).
10. See for example: https://www.fao.org/joint-programme-gender-transfor-mative-approaches/en

References

Abubakari, Z., Richter, C., and Zevenbergen, J. (2020) 'Evaluating some major assumptions in land registration: Insights from Ghana's context of land tenure and registration'. *Land* 9(9): 281. https://doi.org/10.3390/land9090281

African Union (2023) 'African leaders push to dismantle patriarchal systems that perpetuate inequalities: AU men's conference' [press release]. African Union, 30 November 2023. https://au.int/en/pressreleases/20231130/african-leaders-push-dismantle-patriarchal-systems-perpetuate-inequalities-au

Agarwal, B. (2015) 'The power of numbers in gender dynamics: Illustrations from community forestry groups'. *Journal of Peasant Studies* 42(1): 1–20. https://doi.org/10.1080/03066150.2014.936007

Ambarwati, A., Chazali, C., Huijsmans, R., Wijaya, H., and White, B. (2025) 'At the intersection of class, generation, and gender: Young women farmers in Java and Flores, Indonesia'. In S. Srinivasan, A. Ambarwati and Pan Lu (eds.), *Young and Female: International perspectives on the future of farming*. Rugby, UK: Practical Action Publishing. http://doi.org/10.3362/9781788534369

Cislaghi, B. and Heise, L. (2020) 'Gender norms and social norms: Differences, similarities and why they matter in prevention science'. *Sociology of Health & Illness* 42(2): 407–22. https://doi.org/10.1111/1467-9566.13008

Clark-Kazak, C.R. (2009) 'Towards a working definition and application of social age in international development studies'. *Journal of Development Studies* 45(8): 1307–24. https://doi.org/10.1080/00220380902862952

Committee on World Food Security (CFS) (2023) *Voluntary guidelines on gender equality and women's and girls' empowerment in the context of food security and nutrition*. Rome, Italy: CFS.

Deere, C.D. (2003) 'Women's land rights and rural social movements in the Brazilian agrarian reform'. *Journal of Agrarian Change* 3(1–2): 257–88. https://doi.org/10.1111/1471-0366.00056

Doss, C., Kovarik, C., Peterman, A., Quisumbing, A., and van den Bold, M. (2015) 'Gender inequalities in ownership and control of land in Africa: Myth and reality.' *Agricultural Economics* 46(3): 403–34. https://doi.org/10.1111/agec.12171

Food and Agriculture Organization of the United Nations (FAO) (2023) *The status of women in agrifood systems*. Rome, Italy: FAO. https://doi.org/10.4060/cc5343en

Ferrant, G., Pesando, L.M., and Nowacka, K. (2014) 'Unpaid care work: The missing link in the analysis of gender gaps in labour outcomes'. Paris: OECD Development Centre.

Grabe, S. (2015) 'Participation: Structural and relational power and Maasai women's political subjectivity in Tanzania.' *Feminism & Psychology* 25(4): 528–48. https://doi.org/10.1177/0959353515591369

Hall, D., Hirsch, P., and Li, T.M. (2011) *Powers of exclusion: Land dilemmas in Southeast Asia*. Honolulu, HI: University of Hawai'i Press.

IFAD (2019) *2019 Rural development report*. Rome, Italy. https://www.ifad.org/en/web/knowledge/-/publication/2019-rural-development-report

Kidido, J.K., Bugri, J.T., and Kasanga, R.K. (2017) 'Dynamics of youth access to agricultural land under the customary tenure regime in the Techiman Traditional Area of Ghana'. *Land Use Policy* 60 (January): 254–66. https://doi.org/10.1016/j.landusepol.2016.10.040

Kieran, C., Sproule, K., Doss, C., Quisumbing, A., and Kim, S.M. (2015) 'Examining gender inequalities in land rights indicators in Asia'. *Agricultural Economics* 46(S1): 119–38. https://doi.org/10.1111/agec.12202

La Via Campesina (LVC) (2023) 'La Via Campesina reaffirms its stand against patriarchy' [online], 2 December 2023. https://viacampesina.org/en/la-via-campesina-takes-a-definitive-stand-against-patriarchy/

Mishra, K., and Sam, A.G. (2016) 'Does women's land ownership promote their empowerment? Empirical evidence from Nepal'. *World Development* 78 (February): 360–71. https://doi.org/10.1016/j.worlddev.2015.10.003

Moreda, T. (2023) 'The social dynamics of access to land, livelihoods and the rural youth in an era of rapid rural change: Evidence from Ethiopia'. *Land Use Policy* 128 (May): 106616. https://doi.org/10.1016/j.landusepol.2023.106616

Park, C.M.Y. (2019) *Gender, generation and agrarian change: Cases from Myanmar and Cambodia*. Rotterdam: Erasmus University Rotterdam.

Park, C.M.Y. (2021) 'Gender and generation in rural politics in Myanmar: A missed space for (re)negotiation?' *Journal of Peasant Studies* 48(3): 560–85. https://doi.org/10.1080/03066150.2020.1837778

Park, C.M.Y., White, B., and White, J. (2015) 'We are not all the same: Taking gender seriously in food sovereignty discourse'. *Third World Quarterly* 36(3): 584–99. https://doi.org/10.1080/01436597.2015.1002988

Park, C.M.Y., Picchioni, F., and Franchi, V. (2021) 'Feminist approaches to transforming food systems: A roadmap towards a socially just transition'. *Agriculture for Development* 42: 17–19.

Pradhan, R., Meinzen-Dick, R., and Theis, S. (2019) 'Property rights, intersectionality, and women's empowerment in Nepal'. *Journal of Rural Studies* 70 (August): 26–35. https://doi.org/10.1016/j.jrurstud.2019.05.003

Resurrección, B.P. (2006) 'Gender, identity and agency in Philippine upland development'. *Development and Change* 37(2): 375–400. https://doi.org/10.1111/j.0012-155X.2006.00482.x

Rietveld, A.M., Farnworth, C.R., Shijagurumayum, M., Meentzen, A., Voss, R.C., Morahan, G., and López, D.E. (2023) *An evidence synthesis of gender norms in agrifood systems: Pathways towards improved women's economic resilience to climate change.* Rome, Italy: Bioversity International. https://hdl.handle.net/10568/136053

Sardenberg, C.M.B. (2016) 'Liberal vs. liberating empowerment: A Latin American feminist perspective on conceptualising women's empowerment'. *IDS Bulletin* 47(1A): 18–27. https://doi.org/10.19088/1968-2016.115

Singh, S., and Puskur, R. (2023) *Implementing and evaluating gender-transformative approaches in agrifood systems: What does the evidence say?* CGIAR GENDER Impact Platform. https://gender.cgiar.org/news/implementing-and-evaluating-gender-transformative-approaches-agrifood-systems-what-does

Slavchevska, V., Veldman, M., Boero, V., Gurbuzer, Y., Giaquinto, A., and Park, C.M.Y. (forthcoming) 'From law to practice: A cross-country assessment of gender inequalities in rights to land'. *Global Food Security.*

Swedish International Development Cooperation Agency (Sida) (2009) *Quick guide to what and how: Unpaid care work.* Sida. https://cdn.sida.se/publications/files/sida61314en-quick-guide-to-what-and-how-unpaid-care-work.pdf

United Nations (no date) *Secretary-General's guidance note on behavioural science.* United Nations. https://www.un.org/en/content/behaviouralscience/

United Nations (2016) *Women's economic empowerment in the changing world of work*: *Report of the Secretary-General.* E/CN.6/2017/3. United Nations. https://digitallibrary.un.org/record/856760?ln=en&v=pdf

United Nations (2024) *Transforming care systems in the context of the Sustainable Development Goals and Our Common Agenda.* UN System Policy Paper. https://unsdg.un.org/sites/default/files/2024-07/FINAL_UN%20System%20Care%20Policy%20Paper_24June2024.pdf

United Nations Development Programme (UNDP) (no date) *Policy brief: Unpaid care work.* UNDP. Accessed 10 April 2024. https://www.undp.org/publications/policy-brief-unpaid-care-work

United Nations Entity for Gender Equality and the Empowerment of Women (UN Women) (2018) *Promoting women's economic empowerment: Recognizing and investing in the care economy.* United Nations. https://www.unwomen.org/en/digital-library/publications/2018/5/issue-paper-recognizing-and-investing-in-the-care-economy

United Nations Entity for Gender Equality and the Empowerment of Women (UN Women) (2021) *World Survey on the role of women in development 2019: Why addressing women's income and time poverty matters for sustainable development.* United Nations. https://www.unwomen.org/sites/default/files/Headquarters/Attachments/Sections/Library/Publications/2019/World-survey-on-the-role-of-women-in-development-2019.pdf

White, B. (2012) 'Indonesian rural youth transitions: Employment, mobility and the future of agriculture,' in A. Booth, C. Manning, K.W. Thee, and J.M. Hardjono (eds), *Land, livelihood, the economy, and the environment in Indonesia: Essays in honour of Joan Hardjono*, 1st edn, pp. 243–63. Jakarta: Yayasan Pustaka Obor Indonesia.

Index

www.ingramcontent.com/pod-product-compliance
Lightning Source LLC
Chambersburg PA
CBHW051257020426
42333CB00026B/3240